THE

SLOW COOKER COOKBOOK

365 DAYS OF RECIPES

THE

HEALTH PROJECT

The Slow Cooker Cookbook

365 Days of Recipes

By

The Health Project

Copyright ©2017

Table of Contents

Introduction

According to research, healthy nutrition and eating are all centered towards having more vitality plus energy, feeling great, alongside stabilizing your moods and hence keeping your body as healthy as one can be. All this can be accomplished by getting to learn some fundamental nutritional basics and utilizing them in a way that fits you best.

This eBook will be convenient for use by everybody who is searching for a healthier life, with respect to the outstanding conditions slow cooking has to offer, like the amplified cooking period that gives room for better circulation of flavors in various recipes. Hardy meats, for example, steak, stew beef, and chunk roasts are mollified through the long cooking method.

The eBook is subdivided into four parts or seasons: Spring, fall, summer, winter. Each part is made up of 13 weeks of daily recipes from Sunday to Saturday. Make sure to go through all the recipes before going to the grocery market.

We all know that restrictive eating regimens don't work over the extended period and except for two or three lost pounds, they don't do much with respect to improving your general health and wellbeing. This is the reason you ought not to concentrate on eating less but instead focus more on practicing a healthy lifestyle that will enable you to take control over your body weight and also lets you enjoy tasty meals without stressing over your wellbeing and weight.

The accumulation of recipes has widened quickly, and we will take a look at some recipes for slow cooking that you ought to try out. They are tried and genuinely authentic, healthy and flavorful. So, in case you appreciate saucy, tasty, rich dishes that makes one salivate, then this book is undeniably what you should go for.

Do not feel tied down from investigating and trying diverse approaches to use different ingredients in a way that works for you and to adjust to the taste accordingly to suit your specific desires. However, stick to the proposed time periods and amount of ingredients. Cooking food using the slow cooker calls for patience, yet the reward is certainly justified regardless of the time and the exertion.

A slow cooker can ordinarily be left unattended for the all through the day for most recipes, so you can just put your recipe ingredients in it, before going to work and return to devour on your ready cooked hot meal.

One of the primary reasons that make slow cookers a kitchen must have is that they will help you in getting the chance to learn to make meals appropriately. You won't have to be worried about purchasing any additional meals out nor will you have to stress over whether the food will be ready when you return home from work.

Slow cookers are not only viable in the preparation of large volumes of food but are versatile enough to accommodate lesser quantities; just load your slow cooker with some ingredients you want to use and let the cooking begin.

How to use a slow cooker

Each slow cooker comes along with a manual, which you ought to always read before utilizing. When you are familiar with your machine, utilizing it is relatively straightforward.

1. Preparation: Slow cookers require less preparation. You just have to chop your meat and vegetables (smaller lumps work best) and pre-heat the cooker. A few ingredients oblige you to braise the meat beforehand to give the meat a more pleasant color, although this is not an essential part of the cooking procedure.

2. Loading: Root vegetables will take longer to cook therefore they should be placed at the bottom of your cooker (things at the bottom usually cook faster). The meat ought to be put on top, and then followed by the liquid. You ought to make beyond any doubt that the slow cooker is at least 33% of the way full to avoid overcooking. Dairy items, seafood & brisk cook vegetables are usually added for the last hour as they tend to break down & separate.

3. Cooking: Once all ingredients are placed in the cooker, you just set the temperature (low for a more extended cooking period, high for shorter) and the clock (you can purchase cookers with an implicit clock.) Timings are not as strict with the slow cookers as you can decrease the heat & leave the nourishment to stew until you are ready for eating. This is good if you are giving food to the children before your partner as you can be able to leave your portion stewing until the kids are asleep.

4. Cleaning: Among the best things about one-pot cooking is the fact that there is less washing up. Pick a slow cooker that has a removable pot & when you are done, expel it & then load with hot soapy water. Leave to soak and dry the pot totally before storing. Never put cool water straight into a slow cooker as it may crack.

Advantages of slow cooking

Getting back home from a tedious day's work or other stressful duties or elands to find a hot ready cooked meal is most people's, if not everyone's dream. And that is where the slow cooker comes into play.

With slow cookers, you never miss effectiveness and efficiency. Put the ingredients in the slow cooker in the morning, let them cook for the whole day and come home late at night to find a hot, delicious, mouthwatering meal. Slow cooking makes food fit for dieting. Extremely high temperatures have two adverse effects on food: breakdown their supplements and hence produce unhealthy chemicals that have been associated with diseases like, diabetes, renal problems, and Alzheimer's sickness. Cooking on low heat gives the food a chance to keep their supplements and prevent the production of hazardous chemicals. Slow cooking as well spares the pleasant flavors plus the freshness of the ingredients since slow cooking prevents your food from overcooking. Eventually, you get to save cash in three dimensions:

1) Ingredients used in the preparation of most slow cooker meals are mostly cheap.

2) The amount is plenty enough so you can heat and re-heat for more than one day.

3) You save much on gas, power and furthermore water since you are utilizing only one pot.

Other advantages include:

Easy and quick: Slow cookers make cooking healthy meals very easy. You just put the ingredients into the cooker and set it to cook; it then slowly cooks the meal - either on a low heat (which can take up to 8 hours) or high (which is generally 3-4 hours.) The delight of utilizing a slow cooker is the ease, you can prepare the meal in the morning (or at whatever point you have a spare moment) and slowly cook it for the duration of the day without stressing over overcooking your nourishment and serve at whatever point you wish, which gives you additional time away from the kitchen to go through with your family.

Cheap: The sorts of sustenance that work best in a slow cooker are the cheaper ones. Cheap cuts of meat like casserole meat or shanks are the best kind to use as well as cheap lentils and heartbeats. Also, the slow cooker uses less power than your average cooker - which is useful for your energy charges.

Healthy: Slow cookers typically create healthier meals. This is because they rarely require oils or fats in the cooking procedure. The sustenance is left to stew in its juices, which protects a considerable measure of the vitamins and minerals lost amid conventional cooking. Slow cooker recipes are also usually packed loaded with vegetables and heartbeats, which is a great way of getting the family eating all the more healthily without drastically changing their eating regimen.

Flavor: With less effort, slow cookers create a substantially more full flavor than traditional cooking. As the nourishment is left to stew for quite a long time, the meat turns out to be tenderer & sauces wealthier as their full flavor is released. And because the nourishment is sealed in, none of the flavors is lost through evaporation.

What you have to know to cook in your slow cooker.

What is less demanding than putting your ingredients in a slow cooker early in the morning then returning to a hot ready to consume meal? Before you begin enjoying the merits that come with the slow cooker, here are a couple of things you ought to know.

Slow cookers are viable to prepare practically almost any dish that you can envision including the accompanying side dishes, desserts, and pieces of bread. You don't have to stress over the food during the cooking period; there's no requirement for continuous checks or mixing. To be precise, unless the recipe states otherwise, you ought not to lift the cover while cooking because the heat that will escape calls for an additional 30 minutes to the cooking time.

As you will learn, slow cookers are very efficient for making soup, and they're equally valuable for meals that need for harder, tough cuts of meat. You can likewise utilize them to prepare desserts and side dishes on the off chance that your oven is being used to set up another meal or dish. With all aspects considered your slow cooker can be utilized as a substitute oven or stove.

To make cleaning less tedious, spray your container with nonstick spray before introducing the food substances.

Remember that cooking times or periods in every one of the recipes are close estimations. A couple of components like the amount of food and humidity can vary cooking period. Additionally, don't let your cooked dish stay longer than it should else it could overcook your food and hence destroy its nourishment. Another thing is never to use your slow cooker for warming; the cooker is made to slowly achieve cooking temperature, which gives micro-organisms the chance to grow.

When it comes to quantity of water involved in the cooking, mostly half the water prescribed in the recipe will do unless it contains rice or pasta. When it comes to spices and herbs, their flavors tend to considerably increase in the slow cookers, so it is wise to first apply half the recommended amount then you can later adjust accordingly to suit your taste.

Tips for slow cooking of different foods

Dairy products: Full-fat dairy products are more steady and don't go bad as easily as fat milk items. In this eBook, dairy products are added towards the end of the cooking time and solidified with corn starch. Canned cream soups are astoundingly steady and may be included in the slow cooker at the beginning of the cooking time.

Dried lentils and split peas: Do not require drenching and can be added to the recipe toward at the start of cooking time.

Vegetables: Vegetables with high moisture like the zucchini and the yellow winter squash cook more quickly than root vegetables, so you need to cut them into larger pieces or bring them on towards the last 30 minutes of cooking.

Dried Beans: Dried beans will cook well in soups and stews with adequate water in 7 to 8 hours. They don't need to be pre-soaked. Ingredients like tomatoes and vinegar can be added toward the last few minutes of cooking time to keep the beans from getting overly tender.

Meats: Less sensitive cuts of meat, for instance, pork, chunk roast, beef rump are perfect for long slow cooking. Ground meat should be cooked and separated with a fork before adding to the slow cooker; else they will cook into a "bundle" in the slow cooker.

Fish: Depending on the amount or number of fish and thickness of the fish, you can place them in the cooker in the last 10 to 15 minutes of cooking time.

Rice: Only converted long-grain rice can be cooked effectively in the slow cooker; make sure to add enough water to the cooker and introduce the uncooked rice at least in the last 1 1/2 to 2 hours of cooking time. Different sorts of rice, for example, jasmine, brown or basmati rice ought to be cooked first then added into the slow cooker close to the end of the cooking time.

Herbs: introduce fresh herbs into the slow cooker towards the end for perfect shade and flavor. Incorporate ground and dried herbs toward the beginning of the meal preparation. Add more to taste, at the end, if essential.

Some mistakes to avoid

1. Do not add crude meat to the slow cooker

Slow cookers are brilliantly advantageous and can change a touch of meat. To get the most delectable flavor out of your supper, it's best not to incorporate rough meat straightforwardly in the bowl of your slow cooker.

You should first brown meat on your stovetop just before adding it to your slow cooker. It incorporates a great caramelized season you can't get from the slow cooker.

2. Do not use the wrong kind of meat

There aren't good and bad cuts of meat to make in the slow cooker. In any case, there are certain slices that work course better than others. It's best to avoid grade and exorbitant slices, like chicken chest, and spare them for barbecuing, stovetop, or oven cooking. At the moment that grade meat is cooked for a long time, it can get super outrageous.

Slow cookers are ideal for harder, fattier, and economical cuts of meat, like stew meat and shoulder cuts. The more drawn out cook time separate the extreme connective tissue and you end up with delicate, succulent meat.

3. Do not open the top amid cooking

It's tempting to lift the cover to see what's happening inside, or even to take a taste, yet attempt to avoid this. Slow cookers work by catching warmth and cooking sustenance over a drawn out extent of time. Each time you oust the top, the slow cooker loses warmth, and it takes a while to warm again.

Unless you genuinely have to, there's no convincing reason to oust the cover. What's more, if you do open the cover, keep it brief.

4. Do not include a lot of wine or alcohol

Wine and alcohol don't descend and decrease in a slow cooker. So rather than unnoticeable wine insights, you may end up with the unforgiving sort of "unrefined" alcohol, which is far from enticing.

Use wine or alcohol to deglaze the dish in the wake of searing the meat, and then place it in the slow cooker. The high warmth will cook off the alcohol. You can in like manner skirt the alcohol altogether.

5. Do not include dairy products too early

Adding dairy products like a drain, cheddar, acrid cream, or yogurt — too early will make them sour. You should instead hold back until the very end of preparing to add any dairy products to the slow cooker.

Benefits beyond nutrients

The benefits of slow cooking widen past extending the bioaccessibility of supplements in plant nourishment. If you cook meat in a liquid at low high temperature, you can help reduce the number of cell-harming chemical products known as cutting edge glycation end products (AGES) that are produced in the meat by 50%, while boiling and roasting. That is the reason slow cooking is seemingly a standout amongst the safest ways to prepare meat as glycation end products regularly found in Roasted and charred meat have been associated with diseases such as diabetes, cancer, heart disease and inflammations.

SPRING

Week 1

This week's menu

Sunday: Orchard Ham

Monday: Split Pea Soup

Tuesday: Ham 'n' Apple Cheese Pie

Wednesday: Baked Lamb Shanks

Thursday: Lamb Rice

Friday: Easy Creamy Chicken

Saturday: Comforting chicken and stuffing

Recommended Side Dish: Green Bean Casserole

Special Dessert: Hot fudge cake

Orchard Ham

Ingredients:

- 1 cup brown sugar
- 1 1/4 cups golden seedless raisins
- 5-6 lb. bone-in ham
- Two tsp. Dry mustard
- One tsp. Ground cloves
- 4 cups cider or apple juice

Instructions:

1. Place ham in slow cooker. Pour cider over meat.

2. *Cover. Cook on low for 8-10 hours.*

3. While the ham is cooking, make a paste by mixing the brown sugar, cloves, dry mustard and a few tablespoons of the hot cider from the cooker in a bowl. Set it aside.

4. As your cooking time nears the end, remove ham from cider and place in a nine by thirteen-inch baking pan, or one that is big enough to hold the ham.

5. Brush the paste over ham. Later, pour a cup of juice from the slow cooker into your baking pan. (Don't pour it over the ham: you do not want to wash off the paste.) Stir raisins into the cider in the baking pan.

6. Bake at 375° for about 20-30 minutes, or until the paste has turned into a glaze.

7. Let the ham stand for about 10-15 minutes, & then slice and serve. Top the slices with the cider-raisin mixture.

8. Split pea soup

Split Pea Soup

Ingredients:

- 1 cup chopped celery
- Three qts. Water
- 1 cup diced/thinly sliced carrots
- 3 cups dried split peas
- One tsp. Salt

- ½ tsp. Dried oregano
- ¼-1/2 tsp. Pepper
- Leftover meaty hambone
- ½ tsp. Garlic powder

Instructions:

1. Place the ingredients in the slow cooker, except the hambone and then stir well.
2. Settle hambone into the mixture.
3. Cover. Cook for about 4-8 hours on low, or until ham is tender and the peas are very soft.
4. Use a slotted spoon to lift the ham bone out of the soup. Allow it to cool until you can handle it without burning yourself.
5. Cut the ham into bite-sized pieces. Stir it back into the soup.
6. Heat the soup for 10 minutes, & then serve.

Ham 'n' Apple Cheese Pie

Ingredients:

- Leftover ham slices
- 2-3 tart apples, pared, cored and sliced
- 2 tbsp. (1/4 stick) butter, melted
- 1/3 cup flour
- ½ cup brown sugar
- 6-8 slices mild cheese of your choice
- 1 cup sour cream

Instructions:

1. Grease interior of slow-cooker crock.
2. Arrange ham slices over bottom of the crock. If you would like to create a second layer, then stagger pieces, so they don't directly overlap each other.
3. Arrange apple slices over each piece of ham, including those that might be covered partly.
4. In a bowl, mix melted butter, flour, and brown sugar.
5. Crumble over apples, again making sure that ham pieces on bottom layer get crumbs, too.
6. Top each ham piece with a slice of cheese.
7. Cover. Cook on low 3 hours, or until ham is heated through but not dry.
8. Ten minutes before the end of cooking time, spoon a dollop of sour cream on each piece of ham.
9. Continue cooking uncovered.

Baked lamb shanks

Ingredients:

- One medium onion, thinly sliced
- Two small carrots cut into thin strips
- One rib celery, chopped
- Five lamb shanks, cracked
- Four cloves garlic, split
- Two tsp. salt
- ½ tsp. pepper
- One tsp. Dried oregano
- One tsp. Dried thyme
- Two bay leaves, crumbled
- ½ cup dry white wine

- 8-oz. can tomato sauce

Instructions:

1. Place the onion, carrots, and celery in your slow cooker
2. Rub lamb with garlic and season with salt and pepper. Add to slow cooker.
3. Mix remaining ingredients together in the separate bowl and add to meat and vegetables.
4. Cover. Cook on low 810 hours, or on high 46 hours

Lamb Rice

Ingredients:

- Leftover lamb meat, chopped
- 1 cup pine nuts
- 2 cups long-grain basmati rice, uncooked
- 4 cups chicken stock
- One tsp. Crushed allspice
- One tsp. salt
- One tsp. pepper

Instructions:

1. Put all ingredients into a slow cooker. Mix well.
2. Cover. Cook 6-8 hours on low, or until rice is cooked.

Easy cream chicken

Ingredients:

- Ten boneless, skinless chicken thighs
- Two envelopes dry onion soup mix
- 1 cup reduced fat sour cream
- 10 ¾ 0z. can cream of chicken soup

Instructions:

1. Grease interior of slow cooker crock
2. Place thighs in the crock.
3. In a bowl combine dry soup mix, sour cream, and chicken soup until well mixed
4. Pour over chicken, making sure to cover pieces on the bottom with sauce too.
5. Cover. Cook on low 4 hours.
6. Serve with rice or noodles.

Comforting chicken and stuffing

Ingredients:

- 2 ½ cups chicken broth
- Two sticks butter, melted
- ½ cup chopped onion
- ½ cup chopped celery
- ¼ cup dried parsley flakes
- 1 ½ tsp. rubbed sage
- One tsp. Poultry seasoning
- One tsp. salt
- 1 1/3 tsp. coarsely ground black pepper
- 2 eggs
- 10 ¾ oz. can cream of chicken soup

- 12 cups day-old bread cubes
- Leftover chicken, chopped

Instructions:

1. Grease interior of slow-cooker crock.
2. In a bowl, combine chicken broth, butter, chopped onion & celery, parsley flakes, sage, poultry seasoning, salt & pepper.
3. In another bowl combine eggs and soup and stir until smooth
4. Put bread cubes in a large bowl. Pour broth soup mixture over bread. Toss well until all bread cubes become damp.
5. Layer 1/3 of bread mixture into crock
6. Cover with half of remaining bread mixture.
7. Top with remaining chicken.
8. Cover with remaining bread mixture
9. Cover. Cook on low3-4 hours.

Week 2

This week's menu

Sunday: Leg of Lamb with Rosemary and Garlic

Monday: Herbed Lamp Stew

Tuesday: White Bean Fennel Soup

Wednesday: Glazed Holiday Ham

Thursday: Creamy Ham and Red Beans over Rice

Friday: Tasty Ranch Chicken

Saturday: Ranch chicken avocado wraps

Recommended Side Dish: Scalloped Potatoes

Special Dessert: Bread Pudding

Leg of Lamb with Rosemary and Garlic

Ingredients:

- One tsp. Olive oil
- 4-5 lb. leg of lamb
- Six cloves garlic, crushed
- 3 tbsp. Dijon mustard
- 1 tbsp. fresh chopped rosemary
- One tsp. Black pepper
- ½ cup white wine

Instructions:

1. Coat the bottom of your crock with olive oil
2. Pat the leg of lamb dry with a paper towel
3. Mix the garlic, Dijon mustard, rosemary, salt & pepper.
4. Rub this mixture all over the leg of lamb in the slow cooker.
5. Pour the wine into the crock around the leg of lamb.
6. Cover and cook on low 7-8 hours.

Herbed Lamb stew

Ingredients:

- Leftover lamb, chopped
- Two medium onions, chopped
- 4 cups beef broth
- 3-4 medium potatoes, peeled and thinly sliced
- ½-1 tsp. Salt
- ¼ tsp. Pepper
- ¼ tsp. Celery seed
- ¼ tsp. Marjoram
- ¼ tsp. thyme
- 10 oz. Pkg. Frozen peas
- 6 tbsp. flour
- ½ cup cold water

Instructions:

1. Add all ingredients to slow cooker except the peas, flour & water

2. Cover. Cook on low 6 hours, or until potatoes are tender

3. Stir in peas

4. Dissolve flour in the water in a small bowl. When smooth, stir into pot

5. Cover. Turn cooker to high and cook an additional 15-20 minutes.

White bean fennel soup

Ingredients:

- 1 tbsp. olive or canola oil
- One large chopped onion
- One small fennel bulb
- 5 cups fat-free chicken broth
- 15 oz. can white kidney or cannellini
- Beans, rinsed and drained
- 14 ½ oz. can diced tomatoes, un-drained
- One tsp. Dried thyme
- ¼ tsp. black pepper
- One bay leaf
- 3 cups chopped fresh spinach

Instructions:

1. Sauté onion and fennel in oil in skillet until brown

2. Combine onion, fennel, broth, beans, tomatoes, thyme, pepper, and bay leaf.

3. Cook on low 2-3 hours, or on high 1 hour, until fennel and onions are tender

4. Remove bay leaf

5.   Add spinach about 10 minutes before serving

Glazed holiday ham

- 4-5 lb. bone-in, cured ham
- ½ cup apple juice
- ½ cup orange juice
- ½ cup brown sugar
- ½ cup honey

Instructions:

1.   Grease interior of slow-cooker crock
2.   Place ham in crock
3.   In a bowl, mix remaining ingredients until combined
4.   Pour over ham
5.   Cover. Cook on low 4-5 hours
6.   If you are home and available, baste ham with glaze every hour or so
7.   Using two sturdy metal spatulas lift cooked ham onto cutting board and cover it for 15 minutes
8.   Cut into slices or chunks
9.   Pass additional glaze in a bowl to dinners to add more to their individual servings

Creamy Ham and red beans over rice

Ingredients:

- 1 lb. dried red skinned kidney beans
- 2 tbsp. oil
- 2 cups diced onions

- 1 1/2 -2 cups diced celery
- 1 cup diced green bell pepper
- Four large cloves garlic, minced
- 1 tbsp. creole seasoning
- Four bay leaves
- One tsp. Dried thyme
- Two qts. Water
- Leftover meaty ham bone
- Salt and pepper
- 6 cups cooked rice

Instructions:

1. Place dried beans in a stockpot. Cover with water by 3 inches
2. Bring it to a boil & then cook for 2 minutes
3. Cover. Remove from heat and let stand 1 hour. Drain
4. Grease interior of slow cooker
5. Pour beans into slow cooker
6. Stir in oil and then add water
7. Submerge ham bone in mixture
8. Cover. Cook for nine to eleven hours on low or five to seven hours on high
9. Using tongs or a slotted spoon remove ham bone from the cooker. Fish out the bay leaves too.
10. Allow meat to cool enough to pull or cut into bite sized pieces.
11. Stir meat chunks back into bean mixture. Heat for 15 minutes.
12. Place 1 cup cooked rice into each serving bowl. Top with creamy ham and beans.

Tasty ranch chicken

Ingredients:

- ½ cup ranch salad dressing
- 1 tbsp. flour
- Eight boneless, skinless chicken thighs
- ½ cup shredded cheddar cheese
- 1/3 cup grated parmesan cheese

Instructions:

1. Grease interior of slow cooker crock
2. Mix salad dressing and flour in a shallow bowl
3. Coat each thigh with dressing/flour mixture. Place in slow cooker.
4. Mix cheeses together in a small bowl
5. Cover. Cook on low for 4 hours

Ranch chicken avocado wraps

Ingredients:

- Leftover chicken, sliced
- 4-6 sandwich wraps
- One avocado, sliced
- Avocado ranch aioli:
- One large, pit removed, sliced
- ½ cup plain Greek yogurt
- ¼ cup milk
- One tsp. Apple cider vinegar
- Two cloves garlic, minced

- Two tsp. Fresh minced parsley
- 1 tbsp. lime juice
- ¼ tsp. salt

Instructions:

1. These are good with either warm or cold chicken; warm it when you make the aioli
2. In a food processor, place all the avocado ranch aioli ingredients. Blend until smoothly mixed.
3. On each sandwich wrap, lay out the chicken and a couple of slices of avocado. Drizzle the garlic ranch aioli over each sandwich.

Week 3

This week's menu

Sunday: Favorite Ribs

Monday: Classic Beef Chili

Tuesday: Barbecued chicken

Wednesday: Baked potatoes with chili

Thursday: BBQ Pork Rib Soup

Friday: Barbecued Chicken Pizza

Saturday: Herby Fish on a bed of vegetables

Recommended Side Dish: Garden Vegetables

Special Dessert: Chocolate Soufflé

Favorite ribs

Ingredients:

- 4 tbsp. oil
- 1 cup brown sugar
- 28 oz. cans crushed pineapple, un-drained
- ½ cup chopped onion
- 4 tbsp. ketchup
- 4lbs. pork spareribs
- ½ cup chopped green bell pepper
- ¾ cups water

- 1 ½ cups vinegar of one's choice
- 4 tbsp. soy sauce
- Two tsp. Worcestershire sauce
- 4 tbsp. cornstarch
- Four cloves garlic, thinly sliced.

Instructions:

1. Brown spareribs in oil in large skillet. Remove meat and place in slow cooker.
2. Pour off all but 2 tbsp. drippings from the skillet.
3. Add the onion & green pepper then cook until tender.
4. Stir in pineapple, vinegar, ½ cup water, Worcestershire, garlic, brown sugar, sauce, and ketchup. Bring to boil.
5. Pour hot sauce over spareribs in slow cooker
6. Cover and cook on low for 3-4 hours, until ribs start falling off the bone tender
7. Whisk together the remaining ¼ cup water with cornstarch. Cover and cook on low for an additional 10-20 minutes, until thickened.

Classic beef chili

Ingredients:

- One medium onion, chopped
- One tsp. Ground cumin
- 1 ½ lb. extra lean ground beef
- 2 tbsp. chili powder
- 15 oz. can red kidney beans

- 4 oz. can diced green chilies, undrained
- 28 oz. can crushed tomatoes
- Two cloves garlic, finely chopped
- 2 tbsp. tomato paste fresh oregano sprigs

Instructions:

1. Brown beef & garlic over medium heat in a large nonstick skillet
2. Stir to break up the meat, add chili powder & cumin. Stir to combine
3. Mix tomatoes, onions, tomato paste, beans and chilies in the slow cooker. Add beef mixture & mix thoroughly
4. Cook on high 2-3 hours
5. Garnish with oregano to serve

Barbecued chicken

Ingredients:

- ½ cup of water
- 1 cup ketchup
- ½ cup brown sugar
- One tsp. Chili powder
- 1/3 cup Worcestershire sauce
- Six chicken breast halves

Instructions:

1. Place chicken in slow cooker
2. Whisk remaining ingredients in a large bowl

3.   Pour sauce mixture over the chicken

4.   Cover and then cook on low for about 6-8 hours

Baked potatoes with chili

Ingredients:

- Olive oil
- Chopped chives
- Leftover chili
- 4-6 russet potatoes
- Sea salt
- Sour cream
- Pepper
- Cooked and crumbled bacon
- Shredded cheese

Instructions:

1.   Lay out a piece of foil for every potato & place the potato on each. Prick each potato several times with a fork or knife

2.   Drizzle olive oil over each potato then rub it in

3.   Sprinkle sea salt & pepper over each potato and wrap up the foil on each potato

4.   Place the potatoes into the slow cooker

5.   Cook on low for 8 hours

6.   Warm up leftover chili

7.   To serve, cut each potato in half and top with chili plus any other toppings of your choice

BBQ pork rib soup

Ingredients:

- Leftover meat
- Four cloves garlic
- 15 oz. can great northern beans
- One medium onion
- 15 oz. can cannellini beans
- One rib celery

Instructions:

- Place all ingredients into the slow cooker.
- Cook on low for 6-8 hours.

Barbecued chicken pizza

Ingredients:

- 1 cup barbecue sauce
- 8 or 12 oz. prepare pizza dough
- Chopped leftover chicken
- ½ cup green bell pepper

Instructions:

1. If your dough is refrigerated then let it stand at room temperature for 2 hours
2. Grease interior of the slow cooker crock
3. Stretch the dough into large circles so that it fits into the crock
4. Bake crust, uncovered, on high, 1 hour
5. Spread barbecue sauce over hot crust

6.   Drop chopped chicken evenly over sauce

7.   Sprinkle evenly with cheese

8.   Cover. Cook on high for about 2 hours

9.   Uncover but make sure that the condensation on the lid does not fall on the pizza

10.   Let stand for 10 minutes

11.   Cut into wedges & serve

Herby fish on a bed of vegetables

Ingredients:

- Two tsp. Dried drill
- 2-3 leeks
- Pepper
- 8-12 little new potatoes
- Salt
- ¼-1/2 cup diced red/white onion
- 15 ½ oz. can diced tomatoes
- 8-12 plum tomatoes
- 4 tbsp. olive oil
- 4-6 oz. white fish fillets
- Two tsp. Dried basil

Instructions:

1.   Grease the interior of the crock

2.   Wash the potatoes well and thinly slice them

3.   Layer the slices into the slow cooker. Drizzle each layer with oil using about 2 tbsp. Salt and pepper

4. Cut the dark green tops off each leek. Split each leak from top to bottom into quarters and wash them in running water

5. Chop leeks into ½ inch wide slices

6. Layer into the slow cooker on top of the potatoes. Salt & pepper these layers too.

Week 4

Sunday: Slurping good sausages

Monday: Creamy Ziti in the crock

Tuesday: Savory Turkey and mushrooms

Wednesday: Sweet pepper and sausage Burritos

Thursday: Magical Turkey pie

Friday: California Tacos

Saturday: Hamburger Lentil soup

Recommended Side Dish: Risi Bisi (peas and rice)

Special Dessert: Apple peanut crumble

Slurping good sausages

Ingredients:

- 1 tbsp. grated parmesan cheese
- 1 cup of water
- 4 lbs. sweet Italian sausage
- One pepper, chopped
- One thinly sliced onion
- 6 oz. can tomato paste
- One large green, yellow or red bell pepper
- 2 tbsp. chopped fresh parsley
- 24 oz. jar of paste sauce

Instructions:

1. Place sausage pieces in skillet and add water to cover. Simmer for 10 minutes and drain
2. Combine pasta sauce, water, tomato paste, sliced onion, green pepper & 1 tbsp. Grated cheese in slow cooker. Stir in sausage pieces
3. Cover. Cook on low for 6 hours
4. Just before serving, stir in parsley

Creamy Ziti in the crock

Ingredients:

- 4 cups uncooked ziti pasta
- 1/8 tsp. pepper
- 5 cups spaghetti or marinara sauce
- 8 oz. pkg. cream cheese, cubed at room temperature
- 1 cup mozzarella cheese
- One tsp. Dried basil
- 14 ½ oz. can diced tomatoes
- ¾ cup chopped leftover sausage
- 1/3 cup parmesan cheese

Instructions:

1. Grease interior of slow cooker crock
2. Heat around 2 cups spaghetti sauce in saucepan and add cheese cubes then stir till melted
3. Mix spaghetti sauce, diced tomatoes, basil, warmed creamy sauce, pepper, and leftover sausage
4. Put 1/3 tomato sauce mixture in bottom of the crock

5. Add 2 cups ziti, topped with ½ cup mozzarella
6. Add half of the remaining tomato mixture
7. Layer in final 2 cups of ziti and ½ cup mozzarella
8. Spoon on remaining tomato mixture. Sprinkle with parmesan
9. Cover. Cook on high for 2-3 hours

Savory Turkey and mushrooms

- One medium, chopped onion
- 3 lbs. boneless Turkey thighs
- 1 cup beef broth
- 4 tbsp. cornstarch
- Salt and pepper
- ½ stick butter
- 2 tbsp. soy sauce
- 3 cups fresh sliced mushrooms

Instructions:

1. Sauté chopped onion in butter in a saucepan
2. Stir in mushrooms and cornstarch
3. Stir in beef broth and soy sauce. Bring it to a boil, stirring to make it thicken but also ensure that it does not stick
4. Grease interior of slow cooker crock
5. Place cut up Turkey evenly over bottom of crock and pour sauce over meat
6. Cover. Cook on low for 4 to 4 ½ hours
7. Taste the broth and then season with salt & pepper if you wish
8. Serve over cooked rice or noodles

Sweet pepper and sausage Burritos

Ingredients:

- One medium chopped onion
- Leftover sliced sausage
- ½ tsp. black pepper
- Two tsp. Ground cumin
- 3/4 cup raw brown rice
- 1 ½ cups shredded cheddar cheese
- 3 oz. Pkg. Cream cheese
- Five medium red, yellow or green bell peppers
- 1 ¼ cups of water
- Six whole wheat tortillas

Instructions:

1. Grease interior of slow cooker crock
2. Place raw brown rice, onion, water, cumin, leftover sausage slices and black pepper in a crock and stir till thoroughly mixed
3. Cover. Cook on high for 1 ¾ hours
4. Stir in peppers at the end of cooking time, along with cheddar and cream cheeses.
5. Cover. Continue cooking on high 30 more minutes or until rice and peppers are as tender as you like
6. Spoon 2/3 cup rice-pepper-cheese mixture onto lower half of each tortilla. Fold in the sides. Then bring up the bottom and roll
7. Place each burrito, seam side down in greased nine by thirteen-inch baking pan

8.   Cover. Bake at 425 degrees Fahrenheit for 10-15 minutes

9.   Let stand for 4 minutes and then serve with salsa if you wish

Magical Turkey pie

Ingredients:

- ½ lb. frozen or fresh green beans
- ¼ tsp. salt
- 1 cup sliced potatoes
- 10 ¾ oz. can cream of celery soup
- Leftover chicken, chopped
- 1 cup sliced carrots
- 1 cup frozen or fresh corn
- 19-inch pie crust
- ¼ soup can water

Instructions:

1.   Grease interior of slow cooker crock

2.   Put green beans, potatoes, carrots, corns, onions and chicken cubes in the crock following that order

3.   In a bowl, blend salt, water, and soup and after mixing pour other ingredients in the crock

4.   Cover. Cook on low for 4-5 hours

5.   Serve. For a special touch, stir all ingredients well and transfer to a greased baking dish

6.   Top "pie" with baked pie crust made ahead and serve

7.   To make hearts, use recipe for one 9 inch pie crust, rolled out and cut into heart shapes

8.   Put hearts on baking sheet and prick each with a fork

9.   Bake at 400 degrees Fahrenheit for 10-12 minutes. Store in a tightly covered container until ready to use

California Tacos

Ingredients:

- 1 ½ lb. ground beef
- Taco shells
- Salt and pepper
- One medium onion
- 2 cups salsa
- 15 ½ oz. can pinto beans, rinsed & drained
- One green bell pepper
- One envelope, or 4 tbsp., dry taco seasoning

Instructions:

1.   Grease interior of slow cooker crock

2.   Brown beef in the skillet if there is time. Drain off drippings and place meat in crock

3.   If there is no time crumble beef over bottom of crock

4.   Stir in onion and bell pepper, taco seasoning, salsa and pinto beans

5.   Cover. Cook on low for 3 hours

6.   Serve in taco shells

Hamburger Lentil soup

Ingredients:

- Leftover beef

- 1 ½ tsp. salt
- ½ cup chopped onions
- 1 cup dry lentils, washed, with stones removed
- Two diced carrots
- 1 ½ celery, diced
- ½ qt. tomato juice
- One garlic clove, minced
- 1 ½ tsp. brown sugar
- 6 cups water
- ¼ tsp. dried marjoram

Instructions:

1. Combine all ingredients in a slow cooker
2. Cover. Cook it for about 8-10 hours on low or high for 4-6 hours

Week 5

Sunday: Pita Burgers

Monday: Pork Chops Pierre

Tuesday: Ohio Chili

Wednesday: Slow- cooked pork stew

Thursday: Israeli couscous with vegetables

Friday: Kona chicken

Saturday: Szechwan-style chicken and broccoli

Recommended Side Dish: Baked Lima Beans

Special Dessert: Fruit- Filled cake

Pita Burgers

Ingredients:

- 2 lbs. lean ground chuck
- 1 egg
- 1 tbsp. soy sauce
- 1 tbsp. Worcestershire sauce
- 1 cup dry oatmeal
- ½ tsp. salt
- 12 slice pkg. pita bread
- 2 tbsp. apple cider vinegar
- 2 tbsp. brown sugar

- 15 oz. can tomato sauce
- One medium finely chopped onion

Instructions:

1. Combine the ground chuck, dry oatmeal, chopped onion, and egg in a mixing bowl.
2. In a medium-sized bowl, combine the tomato sauce, vinegar, Worcestershire sauce, brown sugar, soy sauce and salt
3. Dip each burger in the sauce, and then stack them into your slow cooker. Pour any remaining sauce over the burgers in the cooker
4. Cover. Cook on low for 4-6 hours
5. Invite everyone who is eating to lift a burger out of the cooker with tongs and put it into a pita pocket with some dribbles of sauce.

Pork chops Pierre

Ingredients:

- Two ribs celery, chopped
- ½ cup ketchup
- 1/8 tsp. pepper
- Two chopped medium onions
- ½ tsp. salt
- 6-8 bone-in, lean pork chops, each ½ inch thick
- 14 oz. can no-salt-added stewed tomatoes
- One large green bell sliced pepper
- 2 tbsp. water
- 2 tbsp. cornstarch

- 2 tbsp. apple cider vinegar
- 2 tbsp. Worcestershire
- 1 tbsp. lemon juice
- 2 tbsp. brown sugar
- One beef bouillon cube

Ingredients:

1. Place chops in slow cooker. Sprinkle with salt & pepper
2. Spoon onions, celery, tomatoes and green pepper over chops
3. In a small bowl, combine ketchup, sugar, lemon juice, bouillon cube and apple cider vinegar. Pour over vegetables
4. Cover. Cook for 4-6 hours on low until chops are tender yet not dry
5. Remove chops to a platter & keep warm
6. In a small bowl, mix cornstarch &water until smooth. Stir liquid into slow cooker.
7. Cover. Cook on high 30 minutes or until sauce thickens. Serve over chops

Ohio chili

Ingredients:

- Two large onions, chopped
- 2 15 oz. cans diced tomatoes, un- drained
- Two bay leaves
- 15 oz. can green chilies, chopped
- One tsp. ground cinnamon

- Three cloves garlic smashed and chopped
- Two ribs celery, chopped
- Two large green bell peppers, chopped
- 15 oz. can pinto beans, rinsed & drained
- Two 15 oz. cans (dark red) kidney beans
- 15 oz. can tomato sauce
- 1 tbsp. unsweetened cocoa powder
- Four leftover burgers, bite-sized

Instructions:

1. Place all ingredients in slow cooker
2. Cover & cook for about eight hours on low

Slow cooked pork stew

Ingredients:

- One tsp. ground black pepper as per your preferences
- Two cloves garlic, minced
- Leftover pork chops, chopped
- One parsnip cut in 1-inch cubes
- ¼ lb. baby carrots
- One medium onion cut into wedges or chopped coarsely
- 1 ½ large potatoes cut into 1-inch cubes
- ½ tsp. dried thyme
- Two tsp. quick cooking tapioca
- 3 cups low-sodium canned vegetable juice
- ½ tsp. salt
- 1 ½ tsp. prepared mustard
- 1 tbsp. brown sugar

Instructions:

1. Place pork, carrots, potatoes, parsnips, onion, garlic, thyme, pepper, tapioca, and mustard. Pour over meat and vegetables
2. Cover. Cook for around six hours on low, or three hours on high

Israeli couscous with vegetables

Ingredients:

- Five mushrooms, thinly sliced
- 2 tbsp. butter
- 1 ½ cups vegetable stock
- ½ cup coarsely shredded carrots
- One clove garlic, minced
- 1 cup uncooked Israeli couscous
- One tsp. dried dill weed
- 1/3 cup chopped scallions, including tops
- Red pepper flakes

Instructions:

1. In a medium saucepan, combine stock & red pepper. Bring to boil & add couscous
2. Turn off heat. Cover. Let stand for 30 minutes
3. In a large skillet melt butter & add dill, scallions, mushrooms, garlic and carrots. Sauté 5 to 6 minutes or until soft
4. Add couscous to vegetable mixture. Stir gently and serve immediately

Kona Chicken

Ingredients:

- 3 tbsp. corn starch
- Eight good sized boneless and skinless thighs
- One minced clove garlic
- 20 oz. can pineapple chunks
- 1 tbsp. soy sauce
- 3 tbsp. cold water
- One medium green bell pepper, chopped
- 2 tbsp. olive oil
- 1 tbsp. grated fresh ginger
- ½ cup white wine
- One minced clove garlic
- 2 tbsp. packed dark brown sugar
- 14 ½ oz. can, or 1 ¾ cups homemade, chicken broth

Instructions:

1. Grease interior of slow-cooker crock
2. Brown chicken briefly in a large skillet in olive oil. Do it in batches over high heat so the pieces brown
3. Deglaze pan with wine
4. Combine broth, brown sugar, green pepper, fresh ginger, soy sauce, pineapple chunks and garlic in a bowl. Pour over chicken
5. Cover. Cook on low 4 hours
6. Lift cooked thighs onto platter, cover and keep warm.
7. In a small bowl, stir together cornstarch & water until smooth

8. Stir into sauce in crock until smooth
9. Cover. Cook for 10 minutes on high, or until thickened
10. Serve chicken, on deep platter, covered with sauce

Szechwan-style chicken and broccoli

Ingredients:

- Leftover chicken, chopped
- One medium, chopped onion
- 2 cups broccoli florets
- ½ cup Picante sauce
- 2 tbsp. soy sauce
- ½ tsp. ground ginger
- ½ tbsp. quick cooking tapioca
- Two cloves garlic, minced
- ½ tsp. sugar
- Cooked rice
- One medium red bell pepper, cut into pieces

Instructions:

1. Place all ingredients except rice in the slow cooker and stir
2. Cover. Cook on high 1- 1 ½ hours or low for 2-3 hours
3. Serve over cooked rice

Week 6

This week's menu

Sunday: Melt-in-your-mouth sausage

Monday: Chicken Ginger

Tuesday: Zuppa Toscana

Wednesday: Dad's Spicy chicken curry

Thursday: Machacha Beef

Friday: Creamy spirals with beef

Saturday: Tuna salad casserole

Recommended Side Dish: creamy red potatoes

Special Dessert: Creamy orange cheesecake

Melt- in- your- mouth sausage

Ingredients:

- One large onion that should be thinly sliced
- 48 oz. jar spaghetti sauce
- 1 tbsp. grated parmesan cheese
- 6 oz. can tomato paste
- 3 lbs. sweet Italian sausage that are cut in 5-inch length
- One tsp. dried parsley, or 1 tbsp.
- Chopped fresh parsley
- 1 cup water

Instructions:

1. Place sausage in skillet. Cover with water. Simmer 10 minutes. Drain
2. Combine remaining ingredient in a slow cooker. Add sausage
3. Cover. Cook on low 6 hours

Chicken ginger

Ingredients:

- ¾ tsp. salt
- ¼ cup rice vinegar
- 1 cup diced carrots
- ¼ cup sesame seeds
- ½ cup minced onion
- 1 tbsp. ground ginger, or ¼ cup grated fresh ginger
- ½ cup low-sodium soy sauce
- One tsp. Sesame oil
- 2 cups broccoli florets
- 1 cup cauliflower florets

Instructions:

1. Combine the ingredients apart from broccoli & cauliflower in the slow cooker
2. Cover. Cook on low 3-5 hours. Stir in broccoli & cauliflower and cook an additional hour
3. Serve over brown rice

Zuppa Toscana

Ingredients:

- 4-6 potatoes, chopped
- Salt & pepper
- 2 tbsp. flour
- 1 cup chopped kale or Swiss chard
- 3-4 cloves minced garlic
- 1 cup heavy whipping cream, room temperature
- Leftover sliced Italian sausage
- 32 oz. carton chicken broth
- One large chopped onion

Instructions:

1. Add potatoes, onions, broth, and garlic to cooker. Add enough water to cover the vegetables
2. Cover and cook on high 3-4 hours or low 5-6 hours, until potatoes are tender. Add in the leftover sausage the last hour of cooking
3. Separately, whisk together flour and cream until smooth
4. Thirty minutes before serving, add cream or flour mixture to cooker. Stir. Add kale
5. Cook on high for 30 minutes till broth thickens slightly
6. Taste for salt & pepper and adjust as needed

Dad's spicy chicken curry

Ingredients:

- ½ tsp. ground cumin

- Chopped leftover chicken
- Water
- Two diced red potatoes
- One medium diced onion
- ½ tsp. ground ginger
- ½ tsp. ground coriander
- ½ tsp. ground cloves
- 1 ½ tsp. turmeric
- 5 oz. pkg. frozen chopped spinach, squeezed and thawed
- ½ tsp. ground cinnamon
- ½ tsp. salt
- ½ cup plain low-fat yogurt
- ½ tsp. ground cloves
- ½ tsp. pepper
- ½ tsp. red pepper flakes
- ¼ tsp. chili powder
- ½ tsp. garlic powder

Instructions:

1. Place the ingredients into your slow cooker except for the leftover chicken
2. Cover. Cook on low for 4-6 hours, or until potatoes are tender. Stir in the leftover chicken the last hour of cooking

Machacha beef

Ingredients:

- 2 lb. beef roast

- 1 cup salsa
- Two beef bouillon cubes
- 1 ½ tsp. dry mustard
- ½ tsp. pepper
- 4 oz. can chopped green chilies
- 1 ½ tsp. garlic powder
- One large sliced onion
- One tsp. seasoning salt

Instructions:

1. Combine the ingredients except for the salsa in the slow cooker. Just add enough water in order to cover
2. Cover the cooker & cook on low for ten to twelve hours, or until beef is tender. Drain and reserve liquid
3. Shred the beef using two forks in order to pull it apart
4. Combine beef, salsa and enough of the reserved liquid to make desired consistency
5. Use this filling for burritos, quesadillas, chalupas or tacos

Creamy spirals with beef

Ingredients:

- 2-4 cups shredded cheddar cheese as per your preferences
- 1 lb. uncooked spiral pasta
- 2 cups half-and-half
- 1 ½ cups leftover shredded beef
- ¾ stick butter
- 10 ¾ oz. can cheddar cheese soup

Instructions:

1. Cook pasta as per the package directions, however, be careful not to overcook it. Drain
2. Return pasta to saucepan. Stir in butter until it melts
3. Combine half-and-half and soup in slow cooker, blending well
4. Stir pasta, leftover shredded beef, and shredded cheese into mixture in cooker
5. Cover and cook on low 2-2 ½ hours

Tuna Salad Casserole

Ingredients:

1. 1 ½ cups crushed potato chips, divided
2. 27 oz. cans tuna
3. Three hard-boiled eggs, chopped
4. ½ cup mayonnaise
5. ½ - 1 ½ cups diced celery
6. ¼ tsp. ground pepper
7. ½ cups diced onions
8. 10 ¾ oz. can cream of celery soup

Instructions:

1. Combine all ingredients except ¼ cup potato chips in slow cooker. Top with remaining chips
2. Cover. Cook on low for 5-8 hours

Week 7

This week's menu

Sunday: Turkey loaf

Monday: Turkey burgers

Tuesday: Glazed ham in a bag

Wednesday: Cheddar and ham soup

Thursday: Creamy Lasagna

Friday: Sweet potato chowder

Saturday: Easy stuffed shells

Recommended Side Dish: Country French Vegetables

Special Dessert: Apple Coconut Pudding

Turkey loaf

Ingredients:

- 1-2 tbsp. sesame seeds
- ¼ tbsp. black pepper
- 2 lbs. ground turkey
- Two eggs, beaten
- 2 tbsp. Worcestershire sauce
- Four green onions, finely chopped
- ¾ cup dry bread crumbs
- 2 tbsp. ketchup

- ½ tsp. salt
- 2/3 cup finely chopped celery

Instructions:

1. Grease interior of slow cooker crock
2. Make a tinfoil for your slow cooker so you can lift the cooked turkey loaf easily. Begin by folding a strip of tinfoil accordion-fashion so that it's about 1 1/2 -2 inches wide and long enough to fit from the top edge of the crock, down inside & up the other side plus an additional 2-inch overhang on each side of your cooker. Make a second strip exactly like the first
3. Place the one strip in the crock, running from end to end. Place the second piece in the crock, so that it runs from side to side. The two strips should form a cross in the bottom of the crock
4. Combine all ingredients except ketchup and sesame seeds in a bowl, mixing gently but well. Once well mixed, set aside half of the mixture and refrigerate for turkey burgers later on this week
5. From the remaining turkey mixture into a 6 inch long and place in crock, centering loaf where foil strip cross
6. Spread ketchup over top of the loaf. Sprinkle with sesame seeds
7. Cover. Cook on low for 3-4 hours,
8. Using foil handles, lift the loaf out of the crock and onto the cutting board. Cover and keep warm for 10 minutes. Then slice and serve

Turkey burgers

Ingredients:

- Extra turkey meatloaf mixture from earlier this week
- Hamburger buns
- Optional toppings:
- Onions sliced in rings
- Ketchup
- Relish
- Pickles
- Cheese slices
- Mayonnaise
- Prepared mustard

Instructions:

1. In the bottom of your crock, crumble up some foil. This will prop the burgers off the bottom of the crock, so they do not stick to one another
2. Form the meatloaf mixture into 6-8 hamburger patties
3. Place them into the crock. You may have to make two layers, depending on the shape or size of your crock. If so, make some foil strips and place them across the other burgers, then put the remaining patties on top of those.
4. Cover. Cook on low for 3-4 hours

Glazed ham in a bag

Ingredients:

- 5 lb. cooked bone-in ham

- 1 tbsp. Dijon mustard
- 3 tbsp. orange juice

Instructions:

1. Rinse meat. Place in cooking bag
2. Combine orange juice and mustard. Spread over ham
3. Seal bag with twist tie. Poke about 4 holes in the top of the bag. Place in slow cooker
4. Cover. Cook on low for 6-8 hours
5. To serve, you will require removing the ham from the bag, reserving juices. Slice ham and spoon juices over. Serve additional juice in a small bowl

Cheddar and ham soup

Ingredients:

- 2 cups milk
- ½ cup chopped carrots
- 2 cups water
- ¼ cup flour
- 2 cups shredded cheese
- 1 cup frozen peas
- 2 cups peeled and diced potatoes
- ½ tsp. Salt
- ½ stick butter
- ½ cup chopped onion
- ¼ tsp. pepper
- 1 ½ cups leftover ham, diced

Instructions:

1. Place the pepper, onions, potatoes, carrots, salt and water in the crock
2. Cover. Cook on low for 6 hours
3. Melt the butter in a saucepan & stir in the flour until it is smooth. Gradually add the milk and bring to a boil so it can thicken. Add this mixture to the crock
4. Add the shredded cheese, leftover ham and peas to the slow cooker and cook for one additional hour

Creamy Lasagna

Ingredients:

- 3-4 un –cooked lasagna noodles
- ¼ tsp. pepper
- 2 eggs
- 8 oz. sour cream
- 1 16 oz. can evaporated milk
- 1 cup cubed leftover ham
- 1 ½ cups cottage cheese
- ½ tsp. salt

Ingredients:

1. Crack eggs into large mixing bowl
2. Using a safety can opener, open the can of evaporated milk. Add the evaporated milk to the eggs in the mixing bowl
3. Add the cottage cheese, sour cream, salt, cubed cooked ham and pepper to your mixing bowl. Stir well using a large wooden spoon

4.   Place 1/3 of creamy ham mixture into the bottom of your slow cooker

5.   Layer half the uncooked noodles on top of the ham mixture. Break them if you require them to fit

6.   Repeat again step 4, using half of the creamy mixture that remained

7.   Repeat process 5, with all the remaining noodles.

8.   Cover the noodles with the remaining creamy ham sauce. Ensure the noodles aren't sticking out of the sauce. Push them down in so they are fully covered

9.   Cover your slow cooker. Cook on low for 5-6 hours

Sweet potato powder

Ingredients:

- 1 cup cubed leftover ham
- One cup water
- One rib celery, chopped
- One medium sweet potato peeled and cubed
- 1 14 ½ oz. can chicken broth
- 1 tbsp. melted butter
- One tsp. Melted butter
- Two medium red potatoes peeled and cubed
- One tsp. Chicken bouillon granules
- 1 cup milk
- ¼ chopped onion
- ¼ tsp. parsley flakes
- 1/8 cup flour
- ½ tsp. garlic powder or 1 minced clove garlic
- 1/8 crushed red pepper flakes

- ¼ tsp. seasoning salt
- ¼ tsp. dried oregano

Instructions:

1. Mix all ingredients except flour and milk in slow cooker
2. Cover. Cook 8 hours on low
3. One hour before the cooking time ends, combine milk and flour in a small bowl, or place in the covered jar and shake until smooth. Stir in hot soup

Easy stuffed shells

Ingredients:

- 20 oz. bag frozen stuffed shells
- 15 oz. can green beans, drained
- 15 oz. can marinara or spaghetti sauce

Instructions:

1. Place shells around inside edge of greased slow cooker
2. Cover with marinara sauce
3. Pour green beans in center
4. Cover. Cook for eight hours on low, or on high for 3 hours

Week 8

Sunday: Tempting Tortilla Casserole

Monday: Hamburger Vegetable Soup

Tuesday: Old-fashioned stewed chicken

Wednesday: Chicken Gumbo

Thursday: Chicken pasta

Friday: Cedric's Casserole

Saturday: Pizza in a bowl

Recommended Side Dish: Maple-Nut cornbread with country bacon

Special Dessert: Blueberry Crisp

Tempting tortilla casserole

Ingredients:

- 16 oz. can fat-free refried beans
- 2 ¾ ground beef
- Bag of tortilla chips
- One envelope dry taco seasoning

- 1 ½ cups grated cheese of your choice, divided

Instructions:

1. Brown the ground beef. Reserve 1 ¾ lb. of it for later this week in your fridge
2. Add the remaining brown ground beef and the taco seasoning to your slow cooker and mix well
3. Sprinkle a cup of cheese over the top of the meat
4. Use a rubber spatula to scrape the refried beans on top of the cheese. Spread your beans out in an even layer. Be careful not to disturb the grated cheese while you do it
5. Sprinkle the remaining cheese over the beans
6. Cover your slow cooker. Cook on low for 3-4 hours
7. Top the casserole with tortilla chips just before serving

Hamburger Vegetable Soup

Ingredients:

- ¼ cup ketchup
- Salt & pepper
- One tsp. seasoned salt
- ¾ lb. leftover browned ground beef
- One bay leaf
- ½ cup chopped carrots
- ¼ cup barley
- ½ cup chopped onion
- Two tsp. beef bouillon granules
- 16 oz. can diced tomatoes

- 3 cups water
- ½ cup chopped celery

Instructions:

1.   Place all ingredients into your slow cooker
2.   Cover and then cook on high for 4 hours or six to eight hours on low

Old fashioned stewed chicken

Instructions:

- 1/3 cup flour
- Three tsp. salt
- 6 lb. chicken, cut up
- 1 tbsp. chopped fresh rosemary, or 1 tsp. dried rosemary
- One rib sliced celery
- ¼ tsp. pepper
- One small onion, cut into wedges
- 3-4 cups hot water
- One sliced carrot
- 1 tbsp. chopped fresh thyme, or 1 tsp. dried thyme
- 1 tbsp. chopped fresh parsley, or 1 tsp. dried parsley

Instructions:

1.   Place chicken in slow cooker. Scatter vegetables, herbs, and seasonings around it and over the top. Pour water down along interior wall of the cooker so as not to disturb the other ingredients
2.   Cover. Cook on low for 8 hours

3. Remove chicken from cooker. When cool enough to handle, debone. Set aside and keep warm
4. In a small bowl, stir one/ cup flour into 1 cup chicken broth from slow cooker
5. When smooth, stir back into slow cooker. Continue cooking on low till soup thickens occasionally stirring to prevent lumps from forming. When gravy is bubbly and thickened it is ready
6. Spoon sauce over the chicken when serving

Chicken Gumbo

Ingredients:

- 2 cups chopped leftover chicken
- One medium onion, chopped
- 3 cups chicken broth
- 3-4 cloves minced garlic
- One tsp. old bay seasoning
- 1 cup diced tomatoes
- ½ green diced bell pepper
- 1 cup sliced okra

Instructions:

1. Combine all ingredients in slow cooker, except the leftover chicken
2. Cover. Cook on low 3-4 hours. The last hour of cooking, add the leftover chicken and stir
3. Serve over rice

Chicken pasta

Ingredients:

- 4 cups cooked macaroni
- Remaining leftover chicken, diced
- 8 oz. Gouda cheese, grated
- One large chopped tomato
- One large zucchini, diced
- 2 tbsp. water
- One envelope chicken gravy mix
- 2 tbsp. evaporated milk or cream

Instructions:

1. Place the chicken, gravy mix, chicken and water in the slow cooker and stir together
2. Cover. Cook on low for 4 hours
3. Add milk and tomato. Cook an additional 20 minutes
4. Stir in pasta. Top with cheese and serve immediately

Cedric's Casserole

Ingredients:

- 10 ¾ can tomato soup
- 3 tbsp. butter
- 3 cups shredded divided cabbage
- One medium chopped onion
- ¼ tsp. pepper
- The remaining one lb. browned ground beef
- ½-3/4 tsp. salt

Instructions:

1. Sauté onion in skillet in butter
2. Add ground beef and onions
3. Season the meat and onions with salt and pepper
4. Layer half of cabbage in slow cooker, followed by half of meat mixture
5. Repeat layers again
6. Pour soup over top
7. Cover. Cook on low 3-4 hours

Pizza in a bowl

Ingredients:

- 1 ½ cups fresh mushrooms, sliced
- 14 ½ can low-sodium diced tomatoes
- 1 cup uncooked macaroni
- 26 oz. jar fat-free, low-sodium marinara sauce
- 1 tbsp. Italian seasoning
- 4 oz. sliced pepperoni
- 1 cup water
- 1 cup chopped bell peppers
- 1 cup chopped onions
- 1 ½ cups shredded mozzarella cheese

Instructions:

1. Pour the tomatoes, marinara sauce, water, onions, mushrooms, pepperoni, chopped peppers, dry macaroni and Italian seasoning into your slow cooker
2. Cover the slow cooker. Cook your pasta mixture for five to six hours on low

3.   After the pasta has cooked, use a potholder to take the lid off your slow cooker

4.   Carefully spoon the hot pasta mixture among six bowls

5.   Sprinkle each with mozzarella cheese

Week 9

This week's menu

Sunday: Spiced pot roast

Monday: Applesauce Meatballs

Tuesday: Losta tomatoes beef stew

Wednesday: Homemade spaghetti sauce

Thursday: Chicken delicious

Friday: Downright flavorful Macaroni and cheese

Saturday: Wild rice with chicken

Recommended Side Dish: Red bliss potato salad

Special Dessert: Rustic Apples Squares

Spiced pot roast

Ingredients:

- 2 lb. boneless beef top round roast
- 2-3 tbsp. ground cinnamon
- 1 tbsp. olive oil
- 1 tbsp. Salt
- ¾ tsp. Ground ginger, or 1 tbsp. Fresh and minced ginger
- Two small onions, chopped
- 2 cups apple juice
- 1 cup water

- 16 oz. can tomato sauce
- ¼ cup cornstarch
- 3 tbsp. white vinegar

Instructions:

1. Brown roast in the olive oil on all sides in a skillet. Then place in slow cooker
2. Combine juice, vinegar, ginger, onions, cinnamon, and tomato sauce. Pour over roast
3. Cook on high for 2-3 hours
4. Mix cornstarch and water until smooth. Remove roast from the cooker & keep warm on a platter. Stir cornstarch water into juices in cooker
5. Return roast to cooker and continue cooking 1 hour on high, or until meat is done and gravy thickens

Applesauce Meatballs

Ingredients:

- ¼ cup water
- 1 lb. Ground beef
- ¾ tsp. salt
- Oil of your choice
- One egg
- ¼ tsp. pepper
- 1 cup soft bread crumbs
- ¼ cup ketchup
- ¾ unsweetened applesauce
- ¾ tsp. Salt

- ¾ lb. Ground pork

Instructions:

1. Combine beef, pork, pepper, applesauce, bread crumbs and salt in a bowl. Form into 1 ½ inch balls.
2. Brown in oil in batches in skillet. Stir up browned drippings and mix well. Spoon over meatballs, making sure that you cover all of them
3. Cover. Cook on low 4-6 hours

Losta tomatoes beef stew

Ingredients:

- 5-6 carrots cut into 1-inch pieces
- Leftover chopped beef
- Two bay leaves
- ½ cup quick-cooking tapioca
- Six medium tomatoes, cut up and gently mashed
- Three ribs celery, sliced
- 3-4 potatoes
- One whole clove, or ¼- 1/2 tsp. ground cloves
- One tsp. dried basil
- Two tsp. salt
- ½ tsp. black pepper

Instructions:

1. Place the ingredients in slow cooker except for the beef. Mix well

2.   Cover. Cook on low 4-6 hours. The last hour of cooking, add the beef and continue cooking until it warms through

Homemade spaghetti sauce

Ingredients:

- Hot cooked spaghetti
- Four qts. Cherry tomatoes
- Leftover meatballs
- ½ tsp. pepper
- One medium onion, minced
- 1 tbsp. oil of your choice
- Two tsp. Italian herb seasoning
- Two cloves garlic, minced
- One tsp. dried thyme
- One tsp. dried rosemary
- Three tsp. sugar
- One tsp. salt

Instructions:

1.   Stem tomatoes, leaving the skins on. Blend until smooth in blender
2.   In a skillet, sauté onions and garlic in oil
3.   Add sautéed onions to your slow cooker. Add tomatoes, sugar, pepper, Italian seasoning, thyme, and rosemary
4.   Add in the leftover meatballs

5.   Simmer on low in slow cooker until thickened, about 4-5 hours. Remove the lid for the final 30-60 minutes of cooking time if you would like a thicker sauce

6.   Serve over spaghetti

Chicken delicious

Ingredients:

- Eight boneless, skinless chicken breast halves
- ¼ cup grated parmesan cheese
- Salt & pepper
- 1/3 cup sherry or wine
- One tsp. fresh lemon juice
- 2 10 ¾ oz. cans cream of celery soup

Instructions:

1.   Rinse the chicken breasts & pat dry. Put your chicken in a slow cooker in layers. Season each layer with sprinkling of lemon juice, pepper, and salt

2.   Mix soups in a medium bowl with sherry or wine if you wish. Pour the mixture over chicken. Sprinkle with parmesan cheese

3.   Cover and then cook on low for about eight to ten hours, or on high for about four to five hours

Downright flavorful Macaroni and cheese

Ingredients:

- 2 tbsp. dry minced onion
- 8 oz. elbow macaroni, uncooked

- ½ tsp. dry mustard
- ¼ tsp. black pepper
- 1 ½ cups milk
- One tsp. salt
- 3 cups shredded sharp cheddar or Swiss cheese
- 12 oz. can evaporated milk
- 2 eggs

Instructions:

1. Combine the ingredients, apart from the cup of cheese, in your greased slow cooker. Sprinkle the reserved cup of cheese on top
2. Cover & then cook on low for about three to four hours. Do not remove the lid or stir until the mixture has finished cooking
3. If you would like a bit of a crusty top, uncover the cooker and cook another 15 minutes

Wild rice with chicken

Ingredients:

- 1 tbsp. fresh parsley
- 1 cup wild rice, uncooked
- ¼ lb. fresh sliced mushrooms
- ½ tsp. dried sage
- ¼ tsp. garlic powder
- ¼ cup slivered almonds
- ¼ cup chopped onion
- Leftover chicken, chopped

- ¼ cup chopped celery
- 3 cups chicken stock
- 1/8 tsp. pepper
- ¼-1/2 tsp. salt

Instructions:

1. Wash and drain rice
2. Combine all ingredients except parsley, almonds, and mushrooms in greased slow cooker. Mix well
3. Cover. Cook on low 4-8 hours
4. 10 minutes earlier of cooking time, stir in the mushrooms. Cover and continue cooking
5. Just before serving, stir in the mushrooms. Cover and continue cooking
6. Just before serving, stir in slivered almonds. Garnish with fresh parsley

Week 10

This week's menu

Sunday: Middle Eastern sandwiches

Monday: Middle Eastern Beef lettuce boats

Tuesday: Sunny chicken

Wednesday: Apple chicken salad

Thursday: Garden vegetable bake

Friday: Shredded Taco Beef

Saturday: Tostadas

Recommended Side Dish: The best Broccoli salad

Special Dessert: Lemon Pudding Cake

Middle Eastern sandwiches

Ingredients:

- 4 lb. boneless beef chuck roast, cut into 1 ½ inch cubes
- ½ tsp. dried rosemary
- 4 tbsp. divided cooking oil
- One cup dry wine
- One tsp. dried oregano
- 2 cups chopped onions
- One tsp. dried basil
- Two cloves garlic, minced

- 6 oz. can tomato paste
- Two tsp. salt
- 10-16 pita breads
- Dash of pepper
- ¼ cup cornstarch
- Lettuce, tomato, plain yogurt and cucumber
- ¼ cup cold water

Instructions:

1. Brown meat, 1 lb. at a time, in skillet in 1 tbsp. oil. As each pound finishes browning, remove the meat with a slotted spoon and transfer it to the slow cooker. Add more oil as needed with each new pound of beef. Reserve drippings in the skillet.
2. Sauté the chopped onions and garlic in drippings until tender
3. Add wine, basil, pepper, tomato paste, rosemary, salt and oregano to the onions. Stir and then spoon over the meat in the cooker
4. Cover. Cook on low 8-10 hours, or on high 5-6 or until meat is falling apart tender but not dry
5. Turn cooker to high. Combine the cornstarch & the water in a small bowl until smooth. Stir into meat mixture. Cook until bubbly and thickened, 15-30 minutes, stirring occasionally
6. Open pita bread. Fill each with the meat mixture, yogurt, lettuce, cucumber, tomato and yogurt as desired

Middle Eastern beef lettuce boats

Ingredients:

- One head romaine, washed and dried
- Leftover beef and warmed
- Tzatziki sauce:
- ½ cup plain non-fat Greek yogurt
- 1 tbsp. fresh chopped dill
- 1 ½ tsp. lemon juice
- ½ cup diced English cucumber
- ½ tsp. lemon zest
- One clove garlic, minced
- 1/8 tsp. pepper
- ¼ tsp. salt

Instructions:

1. Wash and dry the lettuce
2. Warm the leftover beef
3. Mix up all of the ingredients for the Tzatziki sauce
4. To serve, spoon some of the beef into each boat and drizzle with Tzatziki sauce
5. Serve with garnish with chopped tomatoes

Sunny chicken

Ingredients:

- Salt and pepper
- One large onion, sliced into thin rings, divided
- Three lemons, thinly sliced and divided
- 6 lb. chicken

- Nine fresh rosemary sprigs, divided
- Three sweet, juicy each cut into thin slices and divided
- 2 tbsp. minced garlic and divided
- Three limes, thinly and divided

Instructions:

1. Layer 1/3 of the onions slices, one sliced lime, one sliced orange and one sliced lemon into your slow cooker. Top with three rosemary sprigs and 1/3 of the minced garlic

2. Stuff with half the remaining onion slices, one sliced orange, one sliced lime, one sliced lemon, half the remaining garlic and three rosemary sprigs. Place the stuffed chicken-upside down in your slow cooker. (that helps to keep the breast meat from drying out.)

3. Sprinkle with plenty of salt and pepper. Spread the rest of the onion, lemon, lime slices, orange, lemon, and the remaining garlic and rosemary sprigs around the chicken and on top of it

4. Cover. Cook on low 4-6 hours, or until meat is tender but not dry

5. Remove chicken from cooker and place right-side up on a rimmed baking sheet. Place under broiler until top is nicely browned, only a minute or so, watching carefully

6. Cover chicken with foil for 15 min. Then carve, put the pieces on a platter and spoon the citrus and onion slices over top before serving

Apple chicken

Ingredients:

- ½ cup mayonnaise or salad dressing
- One red apple, chopped
- 2-3 tbsp. lemon juice
- 1/3 cup dried cranberries
- 2 tbsp. apple cider vinegar
- ¼ cup diced onion
- 2-3 tbsp. Dijon mustard
- One green apple, chopped
- Two ribs celery, chopped
- 2 cups chopped leftover chicken
- Salt and pepper

Instructions:

1. Whisk together mayonnaise, apple cider vinegar, lemon juice and mustard. Set aside
2. Mix chicken, onion, pepper, apples, cranberries, and salt
3. Pour on dressing and toss to mix. Refrigerate until serving. Flavor develops with longer chilling
4. Tips:
5. Break up and soften a handful of rice sticks: drain and add to the finished salad. This salad is gluten free
6. If you are starting with raw chicken, chop into bite-sized pieces. In a saucepan, cover the chicken pieces with water or chicken broth. Cover & later cook on medium heat till the chicken pieces are white through 10-20 minutes. Drain. One can do this ahead of time

7.   You can substitute 12 ½ oz. can chicken, drained and broken up, for the leftover chicken in this salad

Garden vegetable bake

Ingredients:

- 1 cup cubed bread
- 1 cup green beans, trimmed and halved
- 2 tbsp. butter
- One zucchini, sliced
- ¾ cup grated sharp cheese
- Two tomatoes, sliced
- 2-3 ears corn, kernels cut off
- Salt and pepper
- One medium onion, sliced in rings
- One bell pepper, sliced in rings

Instructions:

1.   In lightly greased slow cooker, layer the vegetables in the order listed, starting with green beans and ending with tomatoes, adding a sprinkle of salt and pepper every other layer
2.   Sprinkle with cheese
3.   Cover and cook on high for 2-2 ½ hours until green beans are as tender as you like them
4.   In a skillet melt butter and add cubed bread. Stir occasionally until bread cubes are toasted
5.   Sprinkle toasted bread cubes on top bake, pressing down lightly. Continue cooking, uncovered, until dough warms but remains crisp

Shredded taco beef

Instructions:

- Flour
- ¼ cup hot pepper sauce
- Water
- 4 lb. boneless beef chuck roast
- ½ cup chipotle salsa
- 2 tbsp. oil
- One ¼ cups canned diced green chili peppers
- One tsp. chili powder
- One tsp. salt
- One tsp. garlic powder
- One tsp. pepper
- One medium chopped onion

Instructions:

1. Sear the roast on all the sides in oil in skillet until well browned. Place in slow cooker. Season on all the sides with salt & pepper
2. Mix the remaining ingredients except for water and flour in a bowl. Spoon over the meat
3. Pour water in along the side of the roast, so you do not wash off the topping until the bottom 1/3 of the roast is covered
4. Cover. Cook on high 5-6 hours. Reduce to low and cook 2-4 hours more, just until meat falls apart
5. If you want a thickened sauce, lift the meat onto a platter using a slotted spoon. Then remove 2 cups

broth from the cooker. Stir ¼ cup flour into the hot broth until smooth. Pour the broth back into the cooker, stirring until blended in. return the meat to the cooker and mix the chunks of meat and sauce together

Tostadas

Ingredients:

- Ten tostadas shells
- Leftover shredded beef
- One can refried beans
- 8 oz. can tomato sauce
- ½ cup water
- One envelope dry taco seasoning mix

Instructions:

1. Combine beef, tomato sauce, refried beans, taco seasoning mix and water in slow cooker
2. Cover. Cook on low 6 hours
3. Crisp tostada shells according to package directions
4. Divide the beef mixture evenly among the tostada shell

Week 11

This week's menu

Sunday: Frances's Roast chicken

Monday: Garlic and Tomato Italian sausage bites

Tuesday: Lentil Rice Salad Bowl

Wednesday: Mexican Egg Rolls

Thursday: Pasta Vanessa

Friday: Apricot-Glazed Pork Roast

Saturday: Pork, Apricot, and Almond Salad

Recommended Side Dish: Crunchy Romaine Toss

Special Dessert: Chocolate Éclair Dessert

France's roast chicken

Ingredients:

- ¼ tsp. dried basil
- 4-5 basil whole frying chicken
- ½ tsp. poultry seasoning
- ½ medium chopped onion
- Salt and pepper
- One rib chopped celery

Instructions:

1. Sprinkle chicken cavity with salt and pepper poultry seasoning. Put onion and celery inside the cavity. Place chicken in slow cooker. Sprinkle with basil
2. Cover. Cook for about eight to ten hours on low or on high for six to eight hours

Garlic and tomato Italian sausage bites

Ingredients:

- 2 tbsp. minced fresh basil
- 2 lbs. Italian sausage, cut into 1-inch pieces
- Cooked rice or quinoa
- One medium onion, cut into half and then sliced into strips
- 2 cups fresh diced tomatoes
- 1/3 cup balsamic vinegar
- Eight cloves minced garlic

Instructions:

1. Place the Italian sausage into the slow cooker. Top with the remaining ingredients except for rice or quinoa
2. Cover. Cook on low for 4-5 hours
3. Serve over cooked rice or quinoa

Lentil rice salad bowl

Ingredients:

- ½ tsp. ground cumin
- 1 cup brown lentils, rinsed

- ¼ tsp. freshly ground pepper
- One tsp. Salt, or less if you used salted stock
- 1 cup brown long-grain uncooked rice
- One bay leaf
- 3 ½ cups water, stock or combination
- One medium chopped onion

Salad Topping:

- ½ cup crumbled feta cheese
- ½ tsp. salt
- Three springs sliced onions
- 2 tbsp. fresh lemon juice
- 2 tbsp. olive oil
- 1/3 cup chopped fresh basil
- ½ tsp. grated lemon peel
- Two medium tomatoes, diced
- Two small diced cucumbers

Instructions:

1. Combine lentils, salt, cumin, onion, bay leaf, water/stock, rice and pepper in slow cooker
2. Cook for three to four hours on high, until lentils and rice are tender but not mushy
3. Remove bay leaf. Keep rice mixture in the slow cooker while you prepare the salad topping. The salad will wilt if it sits in its dressing too long
4. In a medium bowl, combine lemon juice, peel, salt and olive oil. Whisk well

5. Place the rest of the topping ingredients in the bowl and mix gently

6. To serve, place a scoop of the lentil rice mixture in a soup bowl. Top with a scoop of the salad. Enjoy outside with a tall iced tea.

Mexican egg rolls

Ingredients:

- Oil for deep fat frying
- 2 ½ cups leftover chicken, diced or shredded
- One tsp. Ground cumin
- One tsp. salt
- 16 oz. Pkg. Egg roll wrappers
- 1 ½ cups shredded Mexican blend cheese
- ¼ tsp. cayenne pepper
- Five green onions, chopped
- One tsp. Cayenne pepper
- 1 cup frozen corn, thawed
- ¼ cup minced fresh cilantro
- 1 cup of canned black beans that are rinsed and drained
- One tsp. Grated lime peel

Instructions:

1. In a large bowl combine corn, lime peel, pepper, green onions, cumin, cheese, beans, cilantro, and chicken

2. Place ¼ cup of mixture in center of one egg roll wrapper. Keep remaining wrappers covered with damp paper towel until ready to use

3. Fold bottom corner over filling. Moisten remaining corner with water. Roll up tightly to seal. Repeat with each wrapper

4. In an electrical skillet or deep-fat fryer, heat oil to 375 degrees. Fry egg rolls, a few at a time, for 2 minutes on each side or until golden brown

5. Drain on paper towels

Pasta Vanessa

Ingredients:

- 1 ½ tsp. Italian seasoning
- Two medium chopped onions
- Salt and pepper
- One yellow, chopped bell pepper
- 1 cup water
- 10 ¾ oz. can tomato puree
- One orange, chopped bell pepper
- 6 oz. can tomato paste
- 3 6 oz. cans tomato paste
- 2 tbsp. Chopped fresh parsley
- ¼ tsp. Fennel seeds
- 1 lb. whole wheat rotini pasta
- 2 tbsp. honey
- Three cloves garlic, chopped fine
- Leftover Italian sausage
- ¾ cup heavy whipping cream

Instructions:

1. In the slow cooker, place the onions, peppers, paste, water, tomato puree. Blend well.
2. Cook on low 4-6 hours
3. Season with pepper, garlic, salt, Italian seasoning, and fennel. Stir in honey. Add in the leftover Italian sausage
4. Cook on low for thirty to sixty additional minutes, or until the sausage becomes warm all through
5. Bring a pot of water in order to boil for the pasta
6. Separately, heat the heavy whipping cream in the microwave or a small saucepan until steaming hot. Just before serving, add whipping cream to tomato mixture. Now that the two are combined, turn off the slow cooker and do not allow the sauce to boil.
7. Serve sauce over cooked rotini. Sprinkle with fresh parsley

Apricot-glazed pork roast

Ingredients:

- 3 ½-4 lb. boneless pork loin
- 10 ½ oz. can condensed chicken broth
- 2 tbsp. Dijon mustard
- 8 oz. jar apricot preserves
- One large chopped onion

Instructions:

1. Mix broth, onion, preserves and mustard in a bowl

2.   Cut roast to fit if necessary and place in cooker. Pour glaze over meat

3.   Cover & then cook for four to six hours on low or on high for three hours, or until tender

Pork, Apricot and almond salad

Ingredients:

- ¼ cup shredded red cabbage
- Leftover pork
- 4 cups baby spinach
- 4 cups chopped lettuce

Dressing:

- Two tsp. Apricot marmalade or preserves
- ¼ cup balsamic vinegar
- ½ tsp. salt
- ¼ cup olive oil
- 1/8 tsp. pepper

Toppings:

- Slivered almonds
- Craisins
- Goat cheese
- Dried apricots

Instructions:

1.   Warm the leftover pork

2. Mix the lettuce, cabbage, and spinach. Divide the salad mixture up among plates or bowls. Place a serving of pork on each salad

3. Mix the dressing ingredients together

4. Add desired toppings to each salad

5. Drizzle dressing over each salad

Week 12

This week's menu

Sunday: Garlic lime chicken

Monday: Chicken pasta salad

Tuesday: Super beef barbecue

Wednesday: Sausage and sauerkraut supper

Thursday: Slow cooker pizza

Friday: Beef barbecue Street Tacos

Saturday: Cabbage Roll Casserole

Recommended Side Dish: Extra good mashed potatoes

Special Dessert: Slow cooker crème Brulee

Garlic lime chicken

Ingredients:

- 8-10 skinless chicken thighs
- ½ tsp. ground pepper
- ½ tsp. dry mustard
- ½ cup soy sauce
- 1 tbsp. Worcestershire sauce
- 1/4 -1/3 cup lime juice
- Two cloves, minced or 1 tsp. garlic powder

Instructions:

1. Grease interior of slow-cooker crock
2. Place chicken in slow cooker
3. Combine remaining ingredients in a bowl. Pour over chicken
4. Cover. Cook on low for 4 hours

Chicken pasta salad

Ingredients:

- 15 oz. can pineapple tidbits, drained
- Leftover chicken, diced
- 2 cups diced celery
- 2 cups cooked small pasta or 1 cup dry macaroni
- Four hard-boiled diced eggs
- 2 cups seedless grape halves

Dressing:

- ½ cup sour cream
- 1 cup mayonnaise
- ½ cup cashew pieces
- ½ cup frozen whipped topping, thawed
- ½ tsp. salt
- 1 tbsp. lemon juice
- 1 tbsp. sugar

Instructions:

1.   In a large bowl, combine macaroni, eggs, chicken, pineapple, celery and grapes
2.   Whisk dressing ingredients until smooth. Pour dressing over salad; toss to coat
3.   Chill at least one hour. Just before serving, fold in cashews

Super beef barbecue

Ingredients:

- Sandwich rolls
- 1 cup ketchup
- 3-4 lb. rump roast
- 16 oz. jar whole dill pickles, un-drained
- One clove garlic, minced or ¼ cup finely chopped onion
- 18 oz. bottle barbecue sauce

Instructions:

1.   Cut roast into quarters and place in slow cooker
2.   In a bowl stir together garlic, ketchup and barbecue sauce. Once it becomes blended well, fold in the pickles & their juice. You can later pour over the meat
3.   Cover & then cook for about eight to nine hours on low, or until the meat starts falling apart
4.   Remove the pickles & discard them
5.   Lift your meat out on a platter & shred by pulling it apart with two forks
6.   Return meat to sauce and heat thoroughly on low, about 1 hour
7.   Serve with sandwich rolls

Sausage and sauerkraut supper

Ingredients:

- Water
- 2 lb. pkg. smoked sausage links, cut into 2-inch pieces
- ½ medium chopped onion
- 32 oz. bag refrigerated or canned sauerkraut, drained
- One apple, cored & cut
- 2-3 tbsp. brown sugar

Instructions:

1. Combine all ingredients in slow cooker, with water covering half the contents
2. Cover and cook on low 6-10 hours, or until vegetables are as tender as you like them

Slow cooker pizza

Ingredients:

- 1/3 cup boiling water
- 1 tbsp. olive oil
- 1 ½ cups buttermilk baking mix
- 1 ½ cups pizza sauce, divided
- Your choice of pizza toppings like sliced mushrooms, chipped ham or cooked hamburger
- 1-2 cups shredded mozzarella cheese

Instructions:

1. Drizzle the olive oil at the bottom of your slow cooker. Using a paper towel wipe it around the sides too

2. Mix your baking mix & hot water together in a bowl until it forms a smooth ball

3. Using fingers or a rolling pin, stretch the ball until it's about four inches bigger around than the bottom of your cooker. Put the dough in your cooker, spreading it out in order to reach up the sides of your cooker by an inch or so whole way around

4. Pour a cup of sauce on top of the crust. Spread out the sauce in order to cover the crust evenly

5. Scatter pizza toppings evenly over the sauce

6. Spoon a new cup of sauce over the toppings

7. Sprinkle evenly with cheese

8. Cover. Cook on high for about 2 hours, or until the crust starts to brown around its edges

9. Uncover, but take care not to let the condensation on the cooker's lid drip onto the pizza. Let it stand for fifteen minutes. Cut into wedges and serve

Beef barbecue street tacos

Ingredients:

- Two limes, chopped into wedges
- Leftover beef
- ½ cup onions
- 20 white corn tortillas
- ½ cup quesco fresco
- ¾ shredded red cabbage
- ½ cup onions, diced

Instructions:

1. Warm the leftover beef
2. Warm tortillas in the skillet or on the griddle
3. To serve, spoon some of the beef into the warmed tortilla. Top with some red cabbage, onions, quesco fresco and fresh cilantro. Squeeze some fresh lime juice over the top

Cabbage roll casserole

Ingredients:

- 3-4 cups water
- One medium head cabbage chopped
- One tsp. pepper
- Leftover sausage cut into bite-sized pieces
- Two tsp. garlic powder
- One tsp. salt
- One onion, cut
- 1 ½ cups brown rice
- ¼ cup lemon juice, divided
- 1 cup fresh parsley, chopped
- 14 ½ oz. can diced garlic and onion tomatoes

Instructions:

1. Place the chopped cabbage in the crock. Pour ½ of the lemon juice over it
2. In a bowl, mix diced tomatoes rice, onion, garlic powder, remaining lemon juice, pepper, and parsley

3. Pour the rice or parsley mixture or tomato or onion over the top of the cabbage and spread evenly. Pour water over the top

4. Push the sausage pieces down into the rice mixture, spreading them around evenly as possible.

5. Cook on low for 4-6 hours

Week 13

This week's menu

Sunday: Easy ham steaks

Monday: Greek chicken pita filling

Tuesday: Hearty Brunch Casserole

Wednesday: Greek chicken pizza

Thursday: French dip

Friday: Beef stew

Saturday: Cherry Tomato spaghetti sauce

Recommended Side Dish: Baked corn

Special Dessert: Black and Blue Cobbler

Easy ham steaks

Ingredients:

- 3 tbsp. brown sugar
- 2 ½ lbs. ham steaks
- 2o oz. can pineapple ring slices
- 6 oz. jar maraschino cherries

Instructions:

1.   Place ham steaks into the slow cooker
2.   Lay out the pineapple slices over the steaks

3.   Pour the jar of maraschino cherries over the top, juice included

4.   Sprinkle the brown sugar over the top

5.   Cover. Cook on low for 5 hours

Greek chicken pita filling

Ingredients:

- Pita bread
- 1 medium chopped onion
- 2 tsp. lemon pepper
- 5-6 lbs. boneless, skinless chicken thighs
- ½ cup plain yogurt
- ½ tsp. dried oregano

Instructions:

1.   Combine lemon pepper, onion and chicken thighs in slow cooker. Cover and cook on low for 6-8 hours or until the chicken is tender

2.   Just prior to serving, remove chicken and shred with two forks

3.   Add shredded chicken back into slow cooker and stir in oregano and yogurt

4.   Serve as filling for pita bread

Hearty brunch casserole

Ingredients:

- 8 slices firm white bread, crusts removed
- 1 tbsp. dried parsley

- 1 ¾ cups whole milk
- 1 ½ cups shredded extra sharp cheddar cheese, divide
- ½ cup diced bell pepper, or broccoli florets, divided
- ½ cup freshly grated parmesan cheese, divided
- 1 cup leftover ham, divided
- 5 eggs
- ½ tsp. seasoning salt
- 2 spring onions, sliced and divided
- ¼ tsp. dry mustard
- ½ cup sliced mushrooms, divided

Toppings:

- 3 tbsp. butter, melted
- 1 ½ cups cornflakes

Instructions:

1. Grease the slow cooker crock. You are going to make layers. Cover bottom of the crock with 4 slices of bread, cutting to fit. Slight overlap is okay
2. Top with half the meat, half the veggies and, half the cheeses
3. Whisk together eggs, dry mustard, parsley, milk, and seasoning salt. Mix well and pour over layers
4. Cover & later refrigerate for about eight hours or overnight
5. Remove from refrigerator 30 minutes before baking
6. Place crock in cooker. Cook on low for 3 ½ hours
7. Combine the cornflakes & the butter and sprinkle over casserole. Drape several paper towels over the

crock and then put the lid back on. The paper towels will catch condensation and keep it off the cornflake topping. Cook an additional 30 minutes on low

Green chicken pizza

Ingredients:

- Leftover chicken, chopped
- 8 or 12 oz. pkg. prepared pizza dough, depending on how thick you like your pizza crust
- Dash pepper
- 1 tbsp. olive oil
- ¼ tsp. oregano
- 3 cloves garlic, minced
- ¼ tsp. salt
- 2 cups feta cheese
- ½ cup kalamata olives, chopped and pitted
- ¼ cup red onion, diced or sliced
- 10-12 slices of tomato

Instructions:

1. Take the prepared pizza dough out of the refrigerator and let it come up to room temperature
2. Once the dough is at room temperature, grease the inside of your crock and then stretch the dough out around the bottom of your crock, making sure it goes up about an inch on the sides
3. Bake the crust, uncovered on high for one hour
4. Prick the crust gently with a fork all around the bottom. Mix together the oregano, pepper, olive oil,

salt and, garlic. If you have a pastry brush, brush it all over the bottom of the crust. If not, wash your hand, drizzle the mixture around and spread it on the crust with your fingers

5. Drop the leftover chopped chicken evenly over the crust

6. Top it with the feta cheese

7. Cover and cook on high for about 2 hours, or until the crust begins to brown around the edges

8. Uncover, but take care not to let the condensation on the lid drip onto the pizza

9. Let stand for 10 minutes. Cut into wedges and serve

French dip

Ingredients:

- Cheese for rolls
- 1 can Progresso French Onion soup
- Butter and shredded mozzarella
- 1 bottle/ can beer
- 6 French rolls
- 1 can beef consommé
- 8 dashes Worcestershire sauce
- 3-4 lb. chuck roast
- 1 medium onion, chopped into rings
- 1 ½ tsp. garlic powder
- 1 ½ tsp. onion powder

Instructions:

1. Pour the French onion soup, Worcestershire sauce and, beef consommé beer in the crock
2. Add the onion, onion powder and garlic powder. Put the chuck roast on top
3. Cook on low 7-9 hours
4. Serve on French rolls, toasted with butter and melted mozzarella cheese if desired

Beef stew

Ingredients:

- Coarse salt and pepper
- 1 bay leaf
- 4 large beets, roasted in the oven at 425 degrees until tender then cooled, peeled and diced
- 2 ribs celery, diced
- 2 large onions, diced
- 4 cups beef broth
- 3 cloves garlic, diced
- Leftover beef, cut into pieces
- 15 ½ oz. can petite diced tomatoes, un-drained
- ¼ cup finely chopped fresh dill
- 2 large parsnips, peeled and diced
- 2 large carrots, peeled and diced

Instructions:

1. Grease interior of slow-cooker crock
2. If roasting beets yourself, halve them. Place face down in single layer in baking pan. Cover and bake at 425 degrees Fahrenheit until tender, about 20

minutes. Uncover and allow cooling until you can handle them. Peel. Dice

3. Place onion and garlic in crock. Stir in beets

4. Add rest of ingredients except dill, pepper and, salt to crock

5. Cover. Cook on low for 6 hours or until vegetables are tender

6. Stir in dill. Season to taste with salt and pepper

7. Fish out the bay leaf before serving

Cherry tomato spaghetti sauce

Ingredients:

- ½ tsp. coarsely ground black pepper
- 4 qts. Cherry tomatoes
- 1 tsp. dried basil
- 1 tsp. Dried rosemary
- 1 tsp. Dried thyme
- 3 tsp. sugar
- 1 tsp. Dried oregano
- 1 medium chopped onion
- 2 cloves minced garlic
- Cooked spaghetti

Instructions:

1. Grease interior of slow-cooker crock

2. Stem tomatoes and cut them in half. Place in slow cooker

3. Add chopped onions and garlic to cooker

4. Stir in sugar, seasonings and, herbs and mix well

5.   Cover. Cook on low for 4-5 hours or until the veggies are as tender as you like them

6.   For a thicker sauce, uncover the cooker for the last 30-60 minutes of cooking time

7.   Serve over just cooked spaghetti.

SUMMER

Week 1

This week's menu

Sunday: Stuffed Green Pepper

Monday: Marinated Asian Chicken Salad

Tuesday: Tamale Pie

Wednesday: Chicken Vegetable Soup

Thursday: Sausage and Apples

Friday: Asparagus Fettuccine

Saturday: Sausage Comfort Casserole

Recommended Side Dish: Festive apple salad

Special Dessert: Cherry delight

Stuffed Green Peppers

(To serve 6)

Preparation Time: 25 minutes

Cooking Time: 3-8 hours

Ideal slow-cooker size: 6-qt.

Ingredients:

- 6 Large green bell peppers
- 1¾ lbs. lean ground beef, browned and drained (set aside 1 lb. for Tamale Pie later this week)
- 2 Tbsp. Dried minced onion
- 1/8 tsp. salt
- 1/8 tsp. garlic powder
- 2 cups cooked long-grain rice
- 15-oz. can tomato sauce
- ½ cup reduced-fat shredded mozzarella cheese

Instructions:

1. Cut peppers in half and remove seeds.
2. Combine all remaining ingredients except cheese.
3. Stuff peppers with ground beef mixture. Place in the slow cooker.
4. Cover. Cook for around six to eight hours on low, or high for three to four hours. Sprinkle with cheese during last 30 minutes.

Marinated Asian Chicken Salad

(To serve 12)

Preparation Time: 40 minutes

Cooking Time: 3-8 hours

Ideal slow-cooker size: 5 or 6-qt.

Ingredients:

Marinade:

- Three cloves garlic, minced
- 1 Tbsp. Grated fresh ginger
- One tsp. Dried red pepper flakes
- 2 Tbsp. honey
- 3tbsp. low-sodium soy sauce
- Six boneless, skinless chicken breast halves

Dressing:

- ½ cup rice wine vinegar
- One clove garlic, minced
- One tsp. Grated fresh ginger
- 1 Tbsp. honey

Salad:

- One large head lettuce, shredded
- Two carrots, julienned
- ½ cup roasted peanuts, chopped
- ¼ cup fresh cilantro, chopped
- ½ pkg. maifun rice noodles, fried in hot oil

Instructions:

1. Mix the marinade fixings in a small bowl.
2. Place the chicken in the slow cooker & then pour marinade on top of the chicken, coating every piece well.
3. Cover. Cook it for around six to eight hours on low, or cook on high for three to four hours
4. Remove chicken from slow cooker and cool. Reserve juices. Shred chicken into bite-sized pieces.

5. In your small bowl, mix dressing ingredients with a ½ cup of juice from your slow cooker.
6. Toss together shredded chicken, lettuce, carrots, peanuts, cilantro, and noodles in a large serving bowl.
7. Just before serving, drizzle with the salad dressing. Toss well and serve.

Tamale Pie

(To serve 8)

Preparation Time: 20 minutes

Cooking Time: 4 hours

Ideal slow-cooker size: 4-qt

Ingredients:

- ¾ cup cornmeal
- 1½ cups fat-free milk
- One egg, beaten
- 1 lb. leftover browned ground beef
- 1¼-oz. envelope dry chili seasoning mix
- 16-oz. can diced tomatoes
- 16-oz. can corn, drained
- 1 cup grated fat-free cheddar cheese

Instructions:

1. Combine cornmeal, milk, and egg.
2. Stir in meat, chili seasoning mix, tomatoes, and corn until well blended. Pour into slow cooker.

3. Cover. Cook for one hour on high, then for three hours on low.

4. Sprinkle with cheese. Cook another 5 minutes until cheese is melted.

Chicken Vegetable Soup

(To serve 6)

Preparation Time: 15 minutes

Cooking Time: 3-4 hours

Ideal slow cooker size: 4-qt.

Ingredients:

- 28-oz. can low-sodium diced tomatoes, undrained
- 2 cups low-sodium, reduced fat chicken broth
- 1 cup frozen corn
- Two ribs celery, chopped
- ¼ cup dry lentils, rinsed
- 6-oz. can tomato paste
- 1 Tbsp. sugar
- 1 Tbsp. Worcestershire sauce
- Two tsp. Dried parsley flakes
- One tsp. Dried marjoram
- 2 cups cooked leftover chicken

Instructions:

1. Combine all your ingredients in the slow cooker except the chicken.

2.   Cover. Cook on low 3-4 hours. Stir in chicken in one hour before the end of cooking time.

Sausage and Apples

Preparation Time: 10 minutes

Cooking Time: 1-3 hours

Ideal slow-cooker size: 8-qt

Ingredients:

- 2 lb. spicy precooked sausage
- Two large apples, cored and sliced
- ¼ cup brown sugar
- ½ cup apple juice

Instructions:

1.   Cut sausage into 2-inch pieces.
2.   Place all fixings in the slow cooker & mix well.
3.   Cover and cook on low 1-3 hours, until heated through and until apples are as tender as you like them.

Asparagus Fettuccine

(To serve 2)

Preparation Time: 15 minutes

Cooking Time: 15-20 minutes

Ingredients:

- 4 oz. Uncooked fettuccine
- ½ lb. Fresh asparagus, cut into 1-inch pieces
- ¼ cup chopped onions
- One garlic clove, minced
- 1 Tbsp. butter
- 2 oz. cream cheese, cubed
- ¼ cup fat-free milk
- ¼ cup shredded parmesan cheese
- 1½ tsp. lemon juice
- 1¼ tsp. salt
- 1/8 tsp. pepper

Instructions:

1. Cook fettuccine according to package directions. Drain.
2. In large skillet, sauté asparagus, onions and garlic in butter until tender.
3. Add cream cheese, milk, parmesan cheese, lemon juice, salt, and pepper.
4. Cook & stir over medium heat for about five minutes or till the cheese is melted & sauce is blended.
5. Toss fettuccine with asparagus mixture.

Sausage Comfort Casserole

(To serve 4)

Preparation Time: 30 minutes

Cooking Time: 6 hours

Ideal slow-cooker size: 4- to 5-qt.

- 1 14-oz. can chicken broth, divided
- 1½ lbs. potatoes, sliced ¼ -inch thick, divided
- Salt and pepper, optional
- One large onion, thinly sliced, divided
- leftover sausage, cut into bite-sized pieces
- 3-oz. Sharp cheddar cheese, shredded, divided

Instructions:

1. Spray slow cooker with nonstick cooking spray.
2. Pour ½ cup chicken broth into slow cooker. Spread one-half of the potatoes on the bottom of the slow cooker. Sprinkle with salt and pepper if you wish.
3. Layer in half of the onions, half of the sausage, and half of the cheese.
4. Repeat the potato, salt, and pepper if you wish, onion, sausage, and cheese one more time.
5. Pour the remaining chicken broth on the top.
6. Cover and cook on low for six hours, or till the potatoes & onions are as per your wish.
7. Tip: Don't stir, however, check the potatoes to ensure that they are finished, but not overcooked.

Week 2

This week' menu

Sunday: Zesty Italian Beef

Monday: Slow-cooker Tex-Mex Chicken

Tuesday: Forgotten Minestrone

Wednesday: Chicken Tortilla Casserole

Thursday: Sloppy Beef Sandwiches

Friday: Quick 'n Easy Meat-Free Lasagna

Saturday: Beef Slow-Cooker Pizza

Recommended Side Dish: Macaroni salad

Special Dessert: Easy chocolate clusters

Zesty Italian Beef

(To Serve 8-10)

Preparation Time: 5 minutes

Cooking Time: 4-10 hours

Ideal slow-cooker size: 3½-qt.

Ingredients:

- One envelope of dry onion soup mix
- ½ tsp. Garlic powder

- One tsp. Dried basil
- ½ tsp. Dried oregano
- ¼ tsp. Paprika, optional
- ½ tsp. Red pepper, optional
- 2 cups water
- 3-4 lb. rump roast

Instructions:

1. Combine soup mix and seasoning with 2 cups water in slow cooker. Add roast.
2. Cook on High 4-6 hours, or on Low 8-10 hours, or until meat is tender but not dry.
3. Let the meat to stand for about ten minutes before slicing. Top the slices with cooking juices.

Slow Cooker Tex-Mex Chicken

(To serve 6)

Preparation Time: 15-20 minutes

Cooking Time: 2-6 hours

Ideal slow-cooker size: 3½-qt

Ingredients:

- 2 lbs. boneless, skinless chicken breasts, cut into ¾-inch-wide strips
- 2 Tbsp. Dry taco seasoning mix
- 2Tbsp. flour
- One green pepper, cut into strips

- One red bell pepper, cut into strips
- 1 cup frozen corn
- 1½ cup chunky salsa
- 1 cup shredded nonfat Mexican-style cheese

Instructions:

1.   Toss the chicken with the seasoning & flour in your slow cooker.
2.   Gently stir in vegetables and salsa.
3.   Cook for around four to six hours on low, or on high for two to three hours, till the chicken & vegetables are cooked through but are not dry or mushy.
4.   Stir before serving
5.   Serve topped with cheese.

Forgotten Minestrone

(To serve 8)

Preparation Time: 15 minutes

Cooking Time: 7 1/2 -9 ½ hours

Ideal slow-cooker size: 7-qt.

Ingredients:

- Leftover beef
- 6 cups water
- 28-oz. can diced tomatoes, undrained
- One beef bouillon cube
- One medium onion, chopped

- 2 Tbsp. Minced dried parsley
- 1 ½ tsp. salt
- 1 ½ tsp. Dried thyme
- ½ tsp. pepper
- One medium zucchini, thinly sliced
- 2 cups finely chopped cabbage
- 16-oz. can garbanzo beans, drained
- 1 cup uncooked small elbow, or shell' macaroni

Instructions:

1. Combine beef, water, tomatoes, bouillon, onion, parsley, salt, thyme and pepper in slow cooker.
2. Cover. Cook for around seven to nine hours on low, or until the meat is tender.
3. Stir in zucchini, cabbage, beans & macaroni. Cover & cook for thirty to forty-five minutes on high, or until the vegetables are tender.

Chicken Tortilla Casserole

(To serve 8-10)

Preparation Time: 30 minutes

Cooking Time: 3-6 hours

Ideal slow-cooker size: 5- or 6-qt

Ingredients:

- Leftover chicken cut in 1-inch pieces

- Ten 6-inch flour tortillas, cut in about 1/2*2-inch strips, divided
- Two medium onions, chopped
- One tsp. Canola oil
- 10 ¾ -oz. can fat-free chicken broth
- 10 ¾ -oz. can 98% fat-free cream of mushroom soup
- Two 4-oz. Cans mild green chilies, chopped
- 1 egg
- 1 cup grated low-fat cheddar cheese

Instructions:

1. Spray the crock with some cooking spray
2. Scatter half of the tortilla strips at the bottom of your slow cooker.
3. Mix the remaining ingredients together, except the second half of the tortilla strips and the cheese.
4. Layer half of the chicken mixture into your cooker, and then followed by the other half of the tortillas, and finally the rest of the chicken mix.
5. Cover. Cook on Low 4-6 hours or on High 3-5 hours.
6. Add the cheese to the dish during last 20-30 minutes of cooking.
7. Uncover and allow casserole to rest 15 minutes before serving.

Sloppy Beef Sandwiches

Preparation Time: 30 minutes

Cooking Tim: 2-3 hours

Ideal slow-cooker size: 3- or 4- qt.

Ingredients:

- 2 lbs. 95% lean ground beef
- One medium onion, chopped
- ½ cup water
- 16-oz. jar low-sodium salsa
- Whole wheat sandwich rolls
- 2 cups grated fat-free cheddar cheese
- ½ cup chopped lettuce

Instructions:

1. Cook beef and onion in a skillet with the ½ cup of water until meat is no longer pink. Stir with wooden spoon to break up clumps. Drain off drippings.
2. Place beef mixture into slow cooker. Add salsa. Mix well.
3. Cover. Cook on low 2-3 hours.
4. Divide sandwich meat among buns and sprinkle with cheese and lettuce.

Quick 'n Easy Meat-Free Lasagna

(To serve 6)

Preparation Time: 10 minutes

Cooking Time: 3-4 hours

Ideal slow-cooker size: 4-qt.

Ingredients:

- 28-oz. jar spaghetti sauce, your choice of flavor
- 6-7 uncooked lasagna noodles
- 2 cups shredded mozzarella cheese, divided
- 15-oz. ricotta cheese
- ¼ cup grated parmesan cheese

Instructions:

1. Spread one-fourth of sauce in bottom of slow cooker.
2. Lay 2 noodles, broken into 1-inch pieces, over sauce.
3. In a bowl, mix 1½ cups mozzarella cheese, the ricotta, and parmesan cheese.
4. Spoon half of the cheese mixture into the noodles and spread out to edges.
5. Spoon in 1/3 of the remaining sauce, and then two more broken noodles.
6. Spread remaining cheese mixture over the top then ½ the remaining sauce and all the remaining noodles.
7. Finish with remaining sauce.
8. Cover and then cook for 3-4 hours on low, or until noodles are tender and cheese is melted.
9. Add ½ cup mozzarella cheese and cook until noodles are tender and cheese is melted.
10. Add ½ cup mozzarella cheese and cook until cheese melts.

Beef Slow-Cooker Pizza

(To serve 8)

Preparation Time: 20-30 minutes

Cooking Time: 1-1½ hours

Ideal slow-cooker size: 6-qt

Ingredients:

- Leftover "sloppy beef."
- Two small onion, chopped
- 14-oz. can fat-free pizza sauce
- 14-oz. can low-fat, low-sodium
- Spaghetti sauce
- 1¼ tsp. black pepper
- One tsp. Dried oregano
- ¼ tsp. Rubbed sage
- 12-oz. dry kluski noodles

Instructions:

1. In a large bowl, mix leftover "sloppy beef," onions, pizza, sauce, spaghetti sauce, seasonings, and herbs.
2. Boil noodles according to directions on package until tender. Drain.
3. Layer half of beef sauce in bottom of cooker. Spoon in noodles. Top with remaining beef sauce.
4. Cook on low 1-1½ hours if ingredients are hot when placed in cooker. In case the sauce and noodles are at room temperature or have just been refrigerated, cook on high for 2- 2½ hours.

Week 3

This week's Menu

Sunday: Beef Brisket Barbecue

Monday: Chicken with Tropical Barbecue Sauce

Tuesday: BBQ Beef Enchiladas

Wednesday: Barbecue Chicken for Buns

Thursday: Easy Crock Taco Filling

Friday: Sweet and Sour Meatballs

Saturday: Pizza Rice Casserole

Recommended Side Dish: Cornbread from scratch

Special Dessert: Pineapple upside-down cake

Beef Brisket Barbecue

(To serve 8)

Preparation Time: 15 minutes

Cooking Time: 6¼-7¼ hours

Ideal slow-cooker size: 4- to 5-qt.

Ingredients:

- 2 cups barbecue sauce, divided
- One small onion, chopped

- 1/2 tsp. Beef bouillon granules, or otherwise two beef bouillon cubes
- Three to four lb. Boneless beef brisket
- Eight sandwich rolls

Instructions:

1. At the bottom of the slow cooker, blend one cup barbecue sauce, chopped onion, and bouillon.
2. Place beef brisket on top.
3. Cover & then cook for six to seven hours on low, or until the brisket shreds easily.
4. Remove brisket from the cooker. Using two forks shred your meat.
5. Tilt the cooker & spoon off fat from the cooking broth. Do away with the fat.
6. Pour the cooking broth in a bowl. Once again spoon off any remaining fat & do away with it.
7. Measure out one cup of cooking broth. Pour back into slow cooker, along with the remaining cup of barbecue sauce. Blend broth and sauce well.
8. Get back the shredded meat in the slow cooker. Stir into sauce thoroughly.
9. Cover and cook on high for 15 minutes, or until meat is hot.
10. Serve over a sandwich roll.

Chicken with Tropical Barbecue Sauce

(To serve 6)

Preparation Time: 5 minutes

Cooking Time: 3-9 hours

Ideal slow-cooker size: 4-qt.

Ingredients:

- ¼ cup molasses
- 2 Tbsp. Cider vinegar
- 2tsp. prepared mustard
- 1/8 – ¼ tsp. hot pepper sauce
- 2 Tbsp. Orange juice
- Three whole chicken breast, halved

Instructions:

1. Combine the molasses, mustard, hot pepper sauce, vinegar, Worcestershire sauce, and orange juice.
2. Place chicken in slow cooker. Splash sauce over the chicken.
3. Cover and then cook for around seven to nine hours on low, or on high for three to four hours.

BBQ Beef Enchiladas

(To serve 8)

Preparation Time: 10 Minutes

Cooking Time: 4-6 hours

Ideal slow-cooker size: 5-qt.

Ingredients:

- 15-oz. can enchilada sauce, green or red
- 15-oz. bottle sweet barbecue sauce
- 12-14 small flour tortillas leftover shredded beef
- One can black beans, drained, rinsed
- 1 cup chopped red onion
- 3 cups shredded cheese of your choice

Instructions:

1. Spray the slow cooker crock with nonstick spray.
2. Mix the enchilada sauce and barbecue sauce.
3. Line your slow cooker's bottom with the flour tortillas. One may require cutting some in half.
4. Spread 1/3 of the beef, 1/3 of the black beans, 1/3 of onions, 1/3 barbecue/enchilada sauce mixture, and ¼ of the shredded cheese over the bottom layer of tortillas. Repeat this procedure 2 more times, finishing with a little enchilada sauce for the top layer and spreading the remaining cheese on top.
5. Cook on low 4-6 hours.

Barbecue Chicken for Buns

(To serve 5)

Preparation Time: 25 minutes

Cooking Time: 3-4 hours

Ideal Slow-Cooker Size: 4-qt.

Ingredients:

- Leftover chicken, diced
- ½ cup chopped celery
- ¼ cup chopped onions
- ¼ cup chopped green bell peppers
- 1½ tsp. canola oil
- ¾ cup ketchup
- ¾ cups water
- 1½ tsp. brown sugar
- 1 Tbsp. Vinegar
- ¾ tsp. Dry mustard
- ¼ tsp. pepper
- 1/8 tsp. salt
- Steak rolls

Instructions:

1.   Combine all ingredients in your slow cooker.
2.   Cover. Cook on low 3-4 hours
3.   Pile into steak rolls and serve

Easy Crock Taco Filling

(To serve 6-8)

Preparation Time: 20 minutes

Cooking time: 6-8 hours

Ideal slow cooker size: 4-qt.

Ingredients:

- One large onion, chopped
- 1¾ lbs. ground beef
- 2 15-oz. cans chili beans
- 15-oz. can Santa Fe corn, Mexican, or fiesta corn
- ¾ cup water
- Optional Ingredients:
- ¼ tsp. Cayenne pepper
- ½ tsp. Garlic powder

Instructions:

1. Put the brown ground beef and chopped onion in a nonstick skillet. Drain.
2. Mix all ingredients well in the slow cooker, blending well.
3. Cover and cook on low for 6-8 hour

Sweet and Sour Meatballs

(To serve 8)

Preparation Time: 45 minutes

Cooking Time: 6 hours

Ideal slow-cooker size: 4-qt.

Ingredients:

Meatballs:

- 2 lbs. ground beef
- 1¼ cups bread crumbs

- ¼ tsp. salt
- One tsp. pepper
- 2-3 Tbsp. Worcestershire sauce
- One egg
- ½ tsp. Garlic salt
- ¼ cup finely chopped onions

Sauce:

- 20-oz. can pineapple chunks, juice reserved
- 3 Tbsp. Cornstarch
- ¼ cup cold water
- 1 cup ketchup
- 2 Tbsp. Worcestershire sauce
- ¼ tsp. Salt
- ¼ tsp. Pepper
- ¼ tsp. Garlic salt
- ½ cup chopped green bell pepper.

Instructions:

1. Combine all meatball ingredients. Shape into 60 meatballs. Brown in skillet, rolling so that all sides are browned. Place meatballs in the slow cooker.
2. Pour juice from pineapple into skillet. Stir into drippings.
3. Stir in ketchup and Worcestershire sauce. Season with salt, pepper and garlic salt. Add green peppers and pineapples. Pour over meatballs.
4. Cover and cook for around six hours on low.

Pizza Rice Casserole

(To serve 4-6)

Preparation Time: 20 minutes

Cooking Time: 6 Hours

Ideal slow-cooker size: 5-qt.

Ingredients:

- Leftover taco beef
- One small onion, chopped
- 2 cups uncooked long-grain rice
- 3 cups pizza sauce
- 2 cups shredded cheese, your favorite flavor
- ¾ cup cottage cheese, optional
- 3 cups water

Instructions:

1. Mix all ingredients in the slow-cooker.
2. Cover & cook for around six hours on high, or until the rice is tender.

Week 4

This week's menu

Sunday: Tracy's Barbequed Chicken Wings

Monday: Terrific Turkey Breast

Tuesday: Beef Pitas

Wednesday: Barbequed Turkey for Sandwiches

Thursday: Ham 'n Cola

Friday: Beef Marinara Casserole

Saturday: Barbequed Ham Sandwiches

Recommended Side Dish: Best baked beans

Special Dessert: Brownies with nuts

Tracy's Barbequed Chicken Wings

(To serve 4-6)

Preparation Time: 35 minutes

Cooking Time: 5-6 hours

Ideal slow-cooker size: 4-qt.

Ingredients:

- 3 lbs. chicken wings, skin removed
- Two large onions, chopped

- Two 6-oz. Cans tomato paste
- Two large cloves garlic, minced
- ¼ cup Worcestershire sauce
- ¼ cup cider vinegar
- 1 ¼ Tbsp. brown sugar
- 2 Tbsp. Sugar
- ½ cup sweet pickle relishes
- ½ cup red or white wine
- ¼ tsp. salt
- Two tsp. Dry mustard

Instructions:

1. Cut off wing tips. Cut the wings at joint. Place in slow cooker.
2. Combine remaining ingredients. Add to slow cooker. Stir.
3. Cover. Cook on Low 5-6 hours.

Terrific Turkey Breast

(Serve 10)

Preparation Time: 30 minutes

Cooking Time: 6 ¼ -8 ¼ hours

Ideal slow-cooker size: 5-qt

Ingredients:

- 2 ½ -lb. turkey breast
- 2 Tbsp. Canola oil

- 2 cups chopped onion
- Two cloves garlic, chopped
- One tsp. Black pepper
- One tsp. salt
- One tsp. Dried rosemary
- ½ tsp. Dried sage
- 2 cups fat-free, low-sodium chicken broth
- ¼ cup flour
- ½ cup white wine, optional

Instructions:

1. Brown turkey breast in oil in skillet. Remove from the skillet & place in the slow cooker.
2. Sauté onions & garlic in the reserved drippings. Stir in seasonings, broth, & wine and then mix well.
3. Pour seasoning broth over turkey in slow cooker.
4. Cover. Cook for around six to eight hours on Low or just until the turkey is tender.
5. Remove the turkey from your cooker & then allow it to rest for about ten minutes on a warm platter.
6. Evacuate a cup of broth from your cooker and then place in the bowl. Mix ¼ cup flour broth in a bowl until smooth. Stir it back into broth in your cooker until smooth. Cover and cook on High for 10 minutes, or until broth is thickened.
7. Meanwhile, slice turkey. Serve with gravy or au jus.

Beef Pitas

(To serve 8)

Preparation Time: 15 minutes

Cooking Time: 2-3 hours

Ideal slow-cooker size: 2-qt.

Ingredients:

- 2 lbs. ground beef
- One tsp. Dried oregano
- ¼ tsp. Black pepper
- 2 ½ cups chopped fresh tomatoes
- 2 Tbsp. Diced fresh green bell pepper
- 1 cup nonfat sour cream
- 1 Tbsp. Red wine vinegar
- 1 Tbsp. Vegetable oil
- Large pita breads, heated & also cut into half

Instructions:

1. Place meat in slow cooker. Sprinkle with oregano and black pepper.
2. Cook on Low 2-3 hours. Remove half of the beef and refrigerate for later this week.
3. In a separate bowl, combine tomatoes, green pepper, sour cream, vinegar, and oil.
4. Fill pitas with meat. Top with vegetable and sour cream.

Barbequed Turkey for Sandwiches

(To serve 4-5)

Preparation Time: 10 minutes

Cooking Time: 1 hour

Ideal slow-cooker size: 1 ½ - to 2- qt.

Ingredients:

- ½ cup ketchup
- ¼ cup brown sugar
- 1 Tbsp. Prepared mustard
- 1 Tbsp. Worcestershire sauce
- 2 cups leftover turkey, cut into bite-sized chunks
- One small onion, finely chopped, optional
- Buns

Instructions:

1. Mix ketchup, sugar, mustard and Worcestershire sauce together in the slow cooker. Add turkey, and onion, if you wish. Toss to coat well.
2. Cover and then cook on High 1 hour, or until heated through.
3. Serve on buns.

Ham 'n Cola

(To serve 8-10)

Preparation Time: 5 minutes

Cooking Time: 2-10 hours

Ideal slow-cooker size: 4- to 5-qt.

Ingredients:

- ½ cup brown sugar
- One tsp. Prepared horseradish
- One tsp. Dry mustard
- ¼ cup cola-flavored soda
- 3-4-lb. precooked ham

Instructions:

1. Combine mustard, brown sugar & the horseradish. Moisten this mixture with just enough cola in order to make a smooth paste. Reserve the remaining cola.
2. Rub entire ham with mixture. Place the ham into your slow cooker & then add the remaining cola.
3. Cover. Cook on Low 6-10 hours, or on High 2-3 hours.

Beef Marinara Casserole

(To serve 6-8)

Preparation Time: 20 minutes

Cooking Time: 6 hours

Ideal slow-cooker size: 5-qt.

Ingredients:

- One medium onion, chopped
- Leftover ground beef
- 3 cups uncooked long-grain rice

- One qt. Marinara sauce
- 3 cups shredded mozzarella or parmesan
- 4 cups water

Instructions:

1.   Place chopped onion in a nonstick skillet and brown.
2.   Mix all ingredients in slow cooker.
3.   Cover and cook on High for 6 hours, or until the rice is tender.

Barbequed Ham Sandwiches

(Makes 4-6 full-sized servings)

Preparation Time: 5-7 minutes

Cooking Time: 5 hours

Ideal slow-cooker size: 3-qt.

Ingredients:

- Leftover ham slices
- One small onion, finely chopped
- ½ ketchup
- 1 Tbsp. vinegar
- 3 Tbsp. Brown sugar
- Bread or buns

Instructions:

1.   Put half of the meat in a greased slow cooker.

2.   Combine other ingredients except for bread. Pour half of mixture over meat. Repeat layers.

3.   Cover. Cook on Low 5 hours.

4.   Serve with bread of your choice.

Week 5

This week's menu

Sunday: Shredded Beef for Tacos

Monday: Lemon Honey Chicken

Tuesday: Hearty Italian Sandwiches

Wednesday: Shredded Chicken Salad

Thursday: Pasta Sauce with Shredded Beef

Friday: Slow-Cooked Steak Fajitas

Saturday: Slow-Cooker Fajita Stew

Recommended Side Dish: Marinated Asparagus

Special Dessert: Sour Cherry Cobbler

Shredded Beef for Tacos

(To serve 10-12)

Preparation Time: 15 minutes

Cooking Time: 6-8 hours

Ideal slow-cooker size: 4-qt.

Ingredients:

- 6-lb. round roast, cut into large chunks
- 1½ cups onion, chopped

- 6 Tbsp. Oil of your choice
- 3 Serrano chilies, chopped
- Six cloves garlic, minced
- One tsp. salt
- 3 cup water
- Taco shells
- Optional toppings: diced tomatoes, chopped onions, chopped lettuce, shredded cheese of your choice

Instructions:

1. Brown meat and onion in oil. Transfer to slow cooker.
2. Add chilies, garlic, salt, and water.
3. Cover. Cook on high for around six to eight hours.
4. Pull meat apart with two forks until shredded.
5. Serve into taco shells with toppings of your choice.

Lemon Honey Chicken

(To serve 4-6)

Preparation Time: 5 minutes

Cooking Time: 8 hours

Ideal slow-cooker size: 4-qt

Ingredients:

- 1 lemon
- 5-6 lb. whole roasting chicken, rinsed
- ½ cup orange juice

- ½ cup honey

Instructions:

1. Pierce lemon with the fork. Place in chicken cavity. Place chicken in slow cooker.
2. Combine orange juice and honey. Pour over chicken.
3. Cover. Cook on low 8 hours. Remove lemon and squeeze over chicken.
4. Carve chicken and serve.

Hearty Italian Sandwiches

(To serve 4)

Preparation Time: 15 minutes

Cooking Time: 6 hours

Ideal slow cooker: 4-qt.

Ingredients:

- 2-3 cups leftover shredded beef
- ½ lb. bulk Italian sausage
- One large onion chopped
- One large green bell pepper, chopped
- One large red bell pepper, chopped
- ½ tsp. salt
- ½ tsp. pepper

Instructions:

1. In skillet, brown sausage. Drain. Mix in the leftover beef.
2. Place 1/3 onions & peppers in your slow cooker. Top with half of the meat mixture. Repeat layers. Sprinkle with salt and pepper
3. Cover. Cook on low 6 hours, or until vegetable is tender.

Shredded Chicken Salad

(To serve 4-6)

Preparation Time: 10 minutes

Ingredients:

- 6-8 cups chopped lettuce
- Leftover chicken

Toppings:

- 1 cup diced tomatoes
- 1 cup sugar snap peas
- ½ cup beans sprout

Dressing:

- ½ cup olive oil
- ¼ cup orange juice
- 1 Tbsp. honey
- One tsp. Lemon juice
- ½ tsp. salt
- ¼ tsp. pepper

Instructions:

1. To assemble salad, start with dividing the lettuce between plates or bowls and topping each with a portion of chicken
2. Add the toppings to each plate
3. Mix the dressing ingredients. Drizzle the dressing over each salad

Pasta Sauce with Shredded Beef

(To serve 4-5)

Preparation Time: 5 minutes

Cooking Time: 5 hours

Ideal slow-cooker size: 4-qt.

Ingredients:

- 1½ cups leftover shredded beef
- 15-oz. can tomato sauce
- 14½-oz. can stewed tomatoes
- 15-oz. can crushed tomatoes
- 2½ cups water
- 2 Tbsp. Garlic powder
- 1 Tbsp. Onion powder
- 1Tbsp. dried minced onion.
- ¼ tsp. pepper
- One tsp. Salt
- ½ tsp. Dried oregano

- ½ tsp. Dried basil
- 1 lb. pasta of your choice

Instructions:

1.   Place all ingredients except the pasta into the slow cooker and stir.
2.   Cook on low for 5 hours.
3.   Serve over your favorite type of pasta

Slow Cooked Steak Fajitas

(To serve 12)

Preparation Time: 25-30 minutes

Cooking Time: 1½-6½ hours

Ideal slow-cooker size: 4-qt.

Ingredients:

- 1½ lb. beef flank steak
- 15-oz. can low-sodium diced tomatoes with garlic and onion, undrained
- One jalapeno pepper, seeded and chopped
- Two cloves garlic, minced
- One tsp. Ground coriander
- One tsp. Ground cumin
- One tsp. Chili powder
- ½ tsp. salt
- Two medium onions, sliced
- Two medium green bell peppers, julienned

- Two medium sweet red bell peppers, julienned
- 1 Tbsp. Minced fresh parsley
- 2tsp. cornstarch
- 1 Tbsp. water
- 12 6-inch flour tortillas, warmed
- ¾ cup fat-free sour cream
- ¾ cup low sodium salsa

Instructions:

1. Slice steak thinly into strips across the grain. Place in the slow cooker.
2. Add tomatoes, coriander, cumin, jalapeno, garlic, chili powder, & salt.
3. Cover. Cook on low for 3-4 hours.
4. Add onions, peppers, and salt.
5. Cover. Cook on low 1-2 hours longer, or until the meat is tender.
6. Combine the cornstarch & water until smooth. Stir into slow cooker gradually.
7. Cover. Cook for thirty minutes on high, or until slightly thickened.
8. Using a slotted spoon, spoon about ½ cup of meat mixture down the center of each tortilla.
9. Add 1 Tbsp. Sour cream and 1 Tbsp. Salsa to each.
10. Fold the tortilla's bottom over the filling & then roll up.

Slow-Cooker Fajita Stew

(To serve 4)

Preparation Time: 20 minutes

Cooking Time: 2½ hours

Ideal slow-cooker: 3- or5-qt.

Ingredients:

- One small onion, chopped
- 1red bell pepper, cut into 1-inch pieces
- 1-oz. enveloped dry fajita seasoning mix (about 2 Tbsp.)
- 14-oz. can diced tomatoes; undrained
- Leftover steak
- ¼ cup flour
- ¼ cup water

Instructions:

1. Place the onion and the bell pepper into the slow cooker.
2. Mix fajita seasoning and un-drained tomatoes. Pour over the onions and peppers.
3. Cover. Cook on low 2 hours.
4. Add in the leftover steak.
5. Combine flour & the water in a small bowl. Stir well mix.
6. Cover. Cook on high 30 minutes until thickened, stirring occasionally and until steak is heated thoroughly.
7. Tip: It is delicious served over hot rice.

Week 6

This week's menu

Sunday: Lemony Turkey Breast

Monday: Turkey Enchiladas

Tuesday: 4-Bean Turkey Chili

Wednesday: Slow-Cooker Fresh Veggie Lasagna

Thursday: Super Easy Chicken

Friday: With Rice Soup

Saturday: Company Casserole

Recommended Side Dish: Whole Wheat Oatmeal Bread

Special Dessert: Slow-cooker Peach Crisp

Lemony Turkey Breast

(To serve 12)

Preparation Time: 15 minutes

Cooking Time: 7-8 hours

Ideal slow-cooker size: 6-qt.

Ingredients:

- 6 lb. bone-in turkey breast, it should be cut in half & the skin removed

- One medium lemon, halved
- One tsp. Lemon pepper
- One tsp. Garlic salt
- Four tsp. Cornstarch
- ½ cup, fat-free, reduced-sodium chicken broth

Instructions:

1. Place the turkey, meaty side up, in your slow cooker sprayed with a non-fat cooking spray
2. Squeeze half of lemon over turkey. Sprinkle with lemon pepper and garlic salt.
3. Place lemon leaves under turkey.
4. Cover. Cook on low 7-8 hours or just until turkey is tender.
5. Remove turkey. Discard lemons.
6. Allow turkey to rest 15 minutes before slicing.

Turkey Enchiladas

(To serve 4-6)

Preparation Time: 20 minutes

Cooking Time: 3-4 hours

Ideal slow-cooker size: 3-qt.

Ingredients:

- 10-12 corn tortillas
- 10-oz. can low sodium tomato sauce
- 4-oz. can chopped green chilies

- 1 cup chopped red onions
- 2 Tbsp. Worcestershire sauce
- 1-2 Tbsp. garlic powder
- 1 cup leftover turkey, diced
- 3 cups of shredded cheese, your choice of flavor

Instructions:

1. Spray the bottom of your slow-cooker with non-stick spray
2. Cover the bottom of your slow-cooker with 3-4 of the corn tortillas.
3. Combine tomato sauce, chilies, onions, Worcestershire sauce, chili powder, and garlic powder. Stir in turkey,
4. Pour half of this mixture into the layer of tortillas. Sprinkle with 1/3 of the shredded cheese. Repeat this step again, finishing with a layer of tortillas and cheese on top.
5. Cover. Cook on low for 3-4 hours.
6. Turn off your slow cooker & let stand for about 10-15 minutes before serving.

4-Bean Turkey Chili

(To serve 10)

Preparation Time: 30 minutes

Cooking Time: 4-5 hours

Ideal slow-cooker size: 4-qt

Ingredients:

- Remaining leftover turkey, chopped
- One large onion, chopped
- 6-oz. low sodium tomato paste
- 2 Tbsp. Chili powder
- 12-oz. can chili beans, undrained
- 12-oz. can kidney beans, undrained
- 12-oz. can black beans, undrained
- 12-oz. can pinto beans, undrained
- 12-oz. can low-sodium tomatoes with juice
- 1 Tbsp. Chopped fresh parsley, optional

Instructions:

1. Combine leftover turkey, onion, and tomato paste in slow cooker.
2. Add chili powder, beans, and tomatoes. Mix well.
3. Cover. Cook on low 4-5 hours.
4. Serve with grated low-fat cheddar cheese.
5. Sprinkle individual serving with fresh parsley, if you wish.

Slow-Cooker Fresh Veggie Lasagna

(To serve 4-6)

Preparation Time: 30 minutes

Cooking Time: 4-5 hours

Ideal slow-cooker size: 4-qt.

Ingredients:

- 1½ cups shredded mozzarella cheese
- ½ cup ricotta cheese
- 1/3 cup shredded parmesan cheese
- One egg, lightly beaten
- One tsp. Dried oregano
- ¼ tsp. garlic powder
- 1 cup marinara sauce, divided, plus more for serving
- One medium zucchini, diced, divided
- Four no-boil lasagna noodles
- 4 cups baby spinach, divided
- 1 cup mushroom, sliced, divided

Instructions:

1. Combine mozzarella, ricotta, parmesan, egg, oregano, and garlic powder in a bowl. Set aside.
2. Spread 2 Tbsp. Marinara sauce in the slow cooker.
3. Sprinkle with ½ of the diced zucchini and 1/3 of the cheese mixture.
4. Break two noodles into large pieces to cover cheese layer
5. Spread 2 Tbsp. Sauce, ½ of the spinach, and ½ of the mushrooms atop cheese.
6. Repeat layers, ending with the cheese mixture and sauce. Press layer down firmly
7. Cover and cook on low 4-5 hours. Let it rest for twenty minutes before cutting and serving. Serve with extra sauce

Super Easy Chicken

(To serve 5-6)

Preparation Time: 5 minutes

Cooking Time: 5-6 hours

Ideal slow-cooker size: 4-qt.

Ingredients:

- Ten boneless, skinless chicken breast halves
- Two pkg. Dry Italian dressing mix
- 1½ cups warm water or chicken stock

Instructions:

1. Place chicken in slow cooker. Sprinkle with dressing mix. Pour water or stock around chicken.
2. Cover. Cook for around five to six hours on low, or until the juices run clear.

Wild Soup Rice

(To serve 8)

Preparation Time: 25 minutes

Cooking Time: 3-4 hours

Ideal slow-cooker size: 4-qt.

Ingredients:

- 2 Tbsp. butter
- ½ cup dry wild rice
- 6 cups fat-free, low-sodium chicken stock
- ½ cup minced fresh onions
- ½ cup minced celery
- ½ lb. winter squash, peeled, seeded, cut into ½ -inch cubes
- 2 cups leftover chicken, chopped
- ½ cup browned, slivered almonds

Instructions:

1. Melt butter in a small skillet. Add rice and sauté 10 minutes over low heat. Transfer to slow cooker.
2. Add remaining ingredients apart from the chicken & the almonds.
3. Cover. Cook on low 3-4 hours, or until vegetables are cooked to your liking. One hour before serving, stir in chicken.
4. Top with browned slivered almonds before serving.

Company Casserole

(To serve 6)

Preparation Time: 15-25 minutes

Cooking Time: 2-6 hours

Ingredients:

- Ideal slow-cooker size: 4- or 5-qt
- 1¼ cups uncooked rice

- 2 Tbsp. Butter, melted
- 3 cups fat-free, low-sodium chicken broth
- 1 cup water
- Remaining leftover chicken, chopped
- Two 4-oz. Cans sliced mushrooms, drained
- 1/3 cup light soy sauce
- 12-oz. Pkg. Shelled frozen shrimp, thawed
- Eight green onions, chopped, 2Tbsp. reserved
- 2/3 cups slivered almonds

Instructions:

1. Combine rice and butter in a slow cooker. Stir to coat rice well.
2. Add remaining ingredients apart from shrimp, almonds, and 2 Tbsp. Green onions.
3. Cover. Cook for about five to six hours on low or on high for about two to three hours, until the rice is tender.
4. Fifteen minutes prior to the end of cooking time, stir in shrimp.
5. Sprinkle almonds and green onions over the top before serving.

Week 7

This week's menu

Sunday: Tex-Mex Luau

Monday: Chicken, Sweet Chicken

Tuesday: Asian Chicken Salad

Wednesday: Slow-Cooked Pork Chops with Green Beans

Thursday: Chicken Broccoli Alfredo

Friday: Pork-Veggie Stew

Saturday: BBQ Pork with Sandwiches

Recommended Side Dish: Carrot Raisin Salad

Special Dessert: Peanut Butter Fudge cake

Tex-Mex Luau

(To serve 6)

Preparation time: 20 minutes

Cooking time: 2-3 hours

Ideal slow-cooker size: 3- or 4-qt.

Ingredients:

- 1½ lbs. frozen firm-textured fish fillets, thawed
- Two medium onions, thinly sliced

- Two lemons, divided
- 2 Tbsp. Butter, melted
- Two tsp. salt
- One bay leaf
- Four whole peppercorns
- 1 cup water

Instructions:

1. Cut fillets into serving portions
2. Combine onion slices and one sliced lemon in butter, along with salt, bay leaf, and peppercorns.
3. Place fillets on top of onion and lemon slices. Add water.
4. Cover. Cook on high 2-3 hours or until fish is flaky.
5. Before serving, carefully remove fish fillets with a slotted spoon. Place on a heatproof plate.
6. Sprinkle with juice of half of the second lemon. Garnish with remaining lemon slices.
7. Serve hot or chill and serve cold.

Chicken, Sweet Chicken

(To serve 8-10)

Preparation Time: 15 minutes

Cooking Time: 5-6 hours

Ideal slow-cooker size: 3-qt.

Ingredients:

- Two medium sweet potatoes, they should be peeled and cut into ¼ -inch thick slices
- Ten boneless, skinless chicken thighs
- 8-oz. jar orange marmalade
- ¼ cup water
- ¼-½ tsp. Salt
- ½ tsp. pepper

Instructions:

1. Place sweet potato slices in slow cooker.
2. Rinse and dry chicken pieces. Arrange on top of the potatoes.
3. Spoon marmalade over the chicken and potatoes.
4. Pour water over all. Season with salt and pepper.
5. Cover and then cook for around one hour on high, later turn to low & cook for four to five hours, or until potatoes and chicken are both tender.

Asian Chicken Salad

(To serve 4)

Preparation time: 20 minutes

Ingredients:

- One head lettuce, shredded
- 1 cup shredded Brussels sprouts
- ½ cup shredded carrots
- 2 cups leftover chicken, chopped or sliced into thin strips

Dressing:

- ½ cup grape seed oil
- ½ cup rice wine vinegar
- One tsp. Low-Sodium Soy Sauce
- Two tsp. honey
- One tsp. ginger
- ½ tsp. gram masala

Toppings:

- ½ cup slivered almonds
- 1 cup chow Mein noodles

Instructions:

1. Mix the lettuce, Brussels sprouts, and carrot and divide between plates or bowls.
2. Mix the dressing ingredients drizzle over each salad.
3. Top each salad with slivered almonds and chow Mein noodles.

Slow-Cooked Pork Chops with Green Beans

(To serve 10-12)

Preparation time: 10 minutes

Cooking time: 4-8 hours

Ideal slow-cooker size: 3-qt.

Ingredients:

- 10-12 boneless pork chops

- Salt and pepper to taste
- 2 cups green beans, frozen or fresh
- Two slice bacon, cut up
- ½ cup water 1 Tbsp. lemon juice

Instructions:

1. Place pork chops in bottom of slow cooker. Add salt and pepper to taste.
2. Top with the remaining ingredients following the order listed.
3. Cover and cook on low 4-8 hours, or until meat and green beans are tender but not dry or overcooked.

Chicken Broccoli Alfredo

(To serve 4)

Preparation Time: 30 minutes

Cooking Time: 1-2 hours

Ideal slow-cooker size: 3-qt.

Ingredients:

- 8-oz. Pkg. Noodles, or spaghetti (half a 16-oz. pkg.)
- 1½ cups fresh or frozen broccoli
- 2 cups leftover chicken, cubed
- 10¾-oz. can cream of mushroom soup
- ½ cup grated mild cheddar cheese

Instructions:

1. Cook noodles according to package directions, adding broccoli during the last 4 minutes of the cooking time. Drain.
2. Combine all ingredients in your slow cooker.
3. Cover & cook for around one to two hours on low, or until it is heated through & until cheese is melted.

Pork-Veggie Stew

(To serve 4)

Preparation Time: 15 minutes

Cooking Time: 6 hours

Ideal slow-cooker: 4-qt.

Ingredients:

- 3-4 leftover pork chops, diced
- Four medium potatoes, peeled and cut into 2-inch pieces
- Three large carrots, peeled and cut into 2-inch pieces
- ½ cup ketchup
- 1¼ cups water, divided

Instructions:

1. Lightly spray slow cooker with non-stick cooking spray.
2. Place all ingredients except ketchup and ¼ cup water in the slow cooker.

3.   Cover and cook on high 5 hours. One hour before serving, combine ketchup with ¼ cup water pour over stew. Cook one more hour.

BBQ Pork Sandwiches

(To serve 4-6)

Preparation Time: 5 minutes

Cooking Time: 3 hours

Ideal slow-cooker size: 2-qt

Ingredients:

- Remaining leftover pork, chopped
- ¾ cup ketchup
- 2 Tbsp. Brown sugar
- 1 Tbsp. Worcestershire sauce
- 1 Tbsp. Apple cider vinegar
- One tsp. Garlic powder
- One tsp. Onion powder
- ½ tsp. Salt
- ½ tsp. Ginger
- ¼ tsp. Dry mustard
- 1/8 tsp. pepper
- Four dashes of hot sauce
- Hamburger buns
- Sliced jalapenos, optional

Instructions:

1. Place all ingredients except sliced jalapenos in your slow cooker and stir.
2. Cook on low for 3 hours
3. Serve on buns with jalapeno slices on top.

Week 8

This week's menu

Sunday: Cheeseburger Pie

Monday: Lazy Cabbage Rolls

Tuesday: Chicken with Feta

Wednesday: Open-Face Italian Beef Sandwiches

Thursday: Lemon Rice Soup

Friday: Italian Beef Hoagies

Saturday: Barbecued Lentils

Recommended Side Dish: Greek Pasta Salad

Special Dessert: Gooey Cookie Dessert

Cheeseburger Pie

(To serve 4-6)

Preparation Time: 20 minutes

Cooking Time: 4 hours

Ideal slow-cooker size: 3-4 qt.

Ingredients:

- 2 lbs. ground turkey
- One medium onion

- Two tsp. Garlic powder
- Two tsp. Onion powder
- 12-oz. shredded cheddar cheese
- ¼ cup mayonnaise
- ¼ cup plain Greek yogurt
- ½ cup cream
- 2 eggs

Toppings:

- Lettuce
- Pickles
- Onion, sliced into rings
- Sliced tomatoes

Instructions:

1. Brown the turkey & onion together in a skillet. Set aside half of the turkey and refrigerate for later this week.
2. Grease interior of slow-cooker crock
3. Pour the turkey at the bottom of your slow cooker. Top with 6-oz. of the shredded cheese.
4. Mix the mayonnaise, Greek yogurt, cream, and eggs. Pour this on top of the turkey and cheese.
5. Top with the rest of the cheese
6. Cover. Cook on low for 4 hours.
7. Served on top of a piece of lettuce and top with pickles, onions, and tomato slices, if desired.

Lazy Cabbage Rolls (To serve 6)

Preparation Time: 36 minutes

Cooking Time: 2- 5½ hours

Ideal Slow-Cooker Size: 5- or 6-qt.

Ingredients:

- Leftover browned turkey
- Salt and pepper, to taste
- One large onion, chopped
- One clove garlic, minced
- 1 lb. cabbage head chopped into 1- inch squares
- 2/3 cup uncooked brown rice
- 16-oz. can tomato sauce

Instructions:

1. Grease interior of slow-cooker crock.
2. Crumble cooker over the bottom of cooker. Season with salt and pepper. (Season each layer with salt and pepper, except tomatoes and tomato sauce.
3. Add a layer of the onion. Follow that with garlic, and then cabbage.
4. Spread uncooked rice over cabbage.
5. Pour tomatoes and sauce on top. Cook for around two to three hours on high, or on low for 4-5½ hours, or until the cabbage and rice are tender
6. Allow it stand for fifteen minutes before serving to let the dish firm up.

Chicken with Feta

(To serve 15)

Preparation Time: 15 minutes

Cooking Time: 4 hours

Ideal Slow-Cooker Size: 4- or 5-qt.

Ingredients:

- Eight boneless, skinless chicken thighs
- 2 Tbsp. Lemon juice, divided
- 3-4 oz. feta cheese, crumbled
- One red or green bell pepper, chopped

Instructions:

1. Grease interior of slow cooker crock.
2. Place thighs on the bottom of the crock. If you need to create a second layer, stagger the thighs so they don't completely overlap each other.
3. Sprinkle with 1 Tbsp. Lemon juice.
4. Crumble feta cheese evenly over thighs. (If you've made two layers, lift up to the top layer and sprinkle cheese over those underneath.
5. Top with remaining lemon juice.
6. Cover. Cook for around four hours on low, or until instant-read meat thermometer registers 160-165 degrees when inserted in thighs.
7. Sprinkle chicken with chopped bell pepper just before serving

Open-Face Italian Beef Sandwiches

(To serve 10)

Preparation Time: 20-30 minutes

Cooking Time: 6-8 hours

Ideal Slow-Cooker Size: 5- or 6-qt.

Ingredients:

- 3-lb. boneless beef chuck roast, partially frozen
- 1½ cups sliced onions
- 19-oz. can tomato-basil soup
- 2 Tbsp. cornstarch
- 2 Tbsp. Brown sugar
- ¼ tsp. Dried oregano
- ¼ tsp. Dried basil
- 1/8 tsp. cayenne pepper
- 2 Tbsp. Worcestershire sauce
- 10½-inch-thick slices Italian bread
- 10 slices provolone cheese
- 2 Tbsp. Chopped fresh parsley

Instructions:

1. Grease interior of slow cooker crock.
2. Slice the beef in a diagonal manner across the grain into thin slices. Put the beef in the crock along with the onions.
3. In a medium bowl, combine soup, cornstarch, brown sugar, oregano, basil, cayenne pepper, and Worcestershire sauce, Mix until smooth.

4. Pour sauce over beef and onions. Stir well so that all pieces of meat are covered with sauce.
5. Cover. Cook on low 6-8 hours, or until beef is tender.
6. For every serving, put a slice of bread on the plate. Pot with I slice o cheese. Sprinkle with parsley and serve immediately.

Lemon Rice Soup

(To serve 4)

Preparation Time: 5 minutes

Cooking Time: 3 hours, 10 minutes

Ideal Slow-Cooker Size: 3-qt.

Ingredients:

- 6 cups chicken broth
- ¾ cup long-grain rice
- ¼ cup diced carrots
- ¼ cup diced celery
- ¼ cup chopped onions
- 1 cup leftover chicken, chopped
- One tsp. salt
- ½ tsp. pepper
- Three egg yolks, beaten
- ¼ cup lemon juice

Instructions:

1. Place broth, rice, carrots, celery, onion, leftover chicken, salt, and pepper into slow cooker. Cook on low for 3 hours.
2. Remove 1 cup of the broth. Slowly whisk in the egg yolks and lemon juice. Return this slowly to the crock, whisking the whole time. Continue to cook on low for ten more minutes.

Italian Beef Hoagies

(To Serve 4)

Preparation Time: 10 minutes

Cooking Time: 15 minutes

Ingredients:

- Four hoagie rolls
- Leftover beef, warmed
- Four deli slices, mozzarella cheese
- 12 basil leaves
- 1 cup baby arugula
- One beefsteak tomato, sliced
- ½ cup balsamic vinegar
- Two tsp. honey

Instructions:

1. Pre-heat the oven to 400 degrees.
2. On a foil-lined baking sheet, place each hoagie roll, open-faced.

3. On one side, place beef and the other side a slice of mozzarella cheese.

4. Cook for around ten minutes or till cheese is melted.

5. Meanwhile, bring the balsamic vinegar honey to boil on the stove. Reduce to simmer till it turns thick and reduces to about a ¼ cup.

6. When you take your hoagies out of the oven, top each with three basil leaves, a bit of arugula, a few slices of tomato, and drizzle the balsamic reduction over the top.

Barbecued Lentils

(To serve 8)

Prep. Time: 5 minutes

Cooking Time: 6-8 hours

Ideal Slow-Cooker: 4-qt

Ingredients:

- 2 cups barbecue sauce
- 3½ cups water
- 1 lb. dry lentils
- One pkg. Vegetarian hot dogs, sliced

Instructions:

1. Combine all ingredients in slow cooker.
2. Cover. Cook on low 6-8 hours.

Week 9

This week's menu

Sunday: Tasty Drumsticks

Monday: Chickenetti

Tuesday: Just Peachy Ribs

Wednesday: Texas Cottage Pie

Thursday: Macaroni and Cheese

Friday: Beer Brats

Saturday: Sausage Beef Spaghetti Sauce

Recommended Side Dish: Sour cream potatoes

Special Dessert: Peaches and cream dessert

Tasty Drumstick

(To serve 8)

Prep. Time: 20 minutes

Cooking Time: 6 hours

Ideal slow-cooker size: 5-qt.

Ingredients:

- 5-6 lbs. chicken drumsticks, skin removed
- 8-oz. can tomato sauce

- ½ cup soy sauce
- ½ cup brown sugar
- Two tsp. Minced garlic
- 3 Tbsp. Cornstarch
- ¼ cup cold water

Instructions:

1. Place drumsticks in slow cooker
2. Combine the tomato sauce, garlic, soy sauce, and brown sugar in a bowl
3. Pour over drumsticks, making sure that each drumstick is sauced
4. Cover. Cook for around six hours on low, or until chicken is tender
5. Remove chicken with tongs to a platter and keep warm.
6. Drain juices in a sauce pan.
7. In a bowl blend cornstarch & water till it becomes smooth
8. Add cornstarch mixture to saucepan.
9. Bring mixture to a boil, stirring continuously
10. Stir for two minutes until thickened

Chickenetti

(To serve 5)

Prep. Time: 25 minutes

Cooking Time: 2-3 hours

Ideal Slow-cooker Size: 6- or 7-qt.

Ingredients:

- ½ cup chicken broth
- 8-oz. spaghetti. Cooked
- Leftover chicken, chopped
- 10¾-oz. can cream of mushroom soup, or otherwise cream of celery soup
- ½ cup water
- 1/8 cup green bell pepper, chopped
- ¼ cup diced celery
- ½ tsp. pepper
- One small onion, grated
- ¼ lb. White, or Yellow, American cheese, cubed

Instructions:

1. Put chicken broth into a slow cooker. Add spaghetti and meat.
2. I a medium-sized bowl, combine soup and water until smooth. Stir in remaining ingredients, and then pour into slow cooker.
3. Cover. Cook on low 2-3 hours

Just Peachy Ribs

(To serve 6-8)

Prep. Time: 10 minutes

Cooking Time: 8-10 hours

Ideal Slow-Cooker Size: 4qt.

Ingredients:

- 6 lbs. boneless pork spareribs
- ½ cup brown sugar
- ¼ cup ketchup
- ¼ cup white vinegar
- One garlic clove, minced
- One tsp. salt
- One tsp. pepper
- 2 Tbsp. Soy sauce
- 15-oz. can spiced cling peaches, cubed, with juice

Instructions:

1. Cut ribs into serving-size pieces and brown in a broiler or in a saucepan in oil. Drain. Place In the slow cooker.
2. Combine remaining ingredients. Pour over ribs.
3. Cover. Cook on low 8-10 hours.

Texas Cottage Pie

(To serve 6)

Prep. Time: 25-30 minutes

Baking Time: 30-35 minutes

Ingredients:

- 1 Tbsp. oil
- Leftover pork, chopped
- ½ tsp. Salt

- ½ tsp. Cumin
- ½ tsp. paprika
- One tsp. Chili powder
- ¼ tsp. Black pepper
- ¼ tsp. cinnamon
- One tsp. Chopped garlic
- 15-oz. can black beans, drained and rinsed
- 1 cup, frozen corn
- 14½-oz. can diced tomatoes with green chilies
- 3 cups mashed potatoes
- ½ cup milk
- 1 cup shredded pepper jack cheese, divided

Instructions:

1. In a skillet, add the leftover pork, salt, seasoning, and garlic until warmed.
2. Cook 2 minutes more on medium heat.
3. Add black beans, corn, and tomatoes with chilies. Stir well.
4. Cover. Cook no low heat 15 minutes.
5. Meanwhile, warm mashed potatoes mixed with ½ cup milk in microwaveable bowl I microwave (2 minutes, covered, on power 8), or in saucepan or stovetop (covered and over Fresh
6. Stir ½ cup cheese in warmed mashed potatoes.
7. Transfer meat into greased seven by 10-inch baking dish.
8. Top with mashed potatoes, spreading in an even layer of baking dish.
9. Sprinkle with the remaining ½ cup cheese.

10. Bake it at 350 degrees Fahrenheit for thirty to thirty-five minutes.

Macaroni and Cheese

(To serve 6)

Prep. Time: 30 minutes

Cooking Time: 3-4 hours

Ideal Slow-Cooker Size: 4-qt.

Ingredients:

- 8-oz. Pkg. Dry macaroni, cooked
- 2 Tbsp. Oil of your choice
- 13-oz. can evaporated milk (Fat-free will work)
- 1½ cups milk
- One tsp. salt
- 3 cups (about ½ lb.) shredded cheese: cheddar, or American, or Velveeta, or a combination
- 2-4 Tbsp. butter, melted
- 2 Tbsp. Finely chopped onion
- Four hot dogs, sliced, optional

Instructions:

1. In a slow cooker, toss cooked macaroni in oil. Stir in remaining ingredients except for hot dogs.
2. Cover. Cook on low 2-3 hours.
3. Add hot dogs if you wish. Cover. Cook 1 hour longer on low (whether you've added hotdogs or not).

Beer Brats

(To serve 8-10)

Prep. Time: 10 minutes

Cooking Time: 6-7 hours

Ideal slow-cooker size: 4-qt.

Ingredients:

- Ten fresh bratwurst
- Two cloves garlic, minced
- 2 Tbsp. Olive oil
- 12-oz. can beer

Instructions:

1. Brown sausage and garlic in olive oil in skillet. Pierce sausage casings and cook five more minutes. Transfer to slow cooker.
2. Pour beer into cooker to cover sausages.
3. Cover. Cook on low 6-7 hours.

Sausage Beef Spaghetti Sauce

(To serve 8-10)

Prep. Time: 15 minutes

Cooking Time: 6 hours

Ideal slow-cooker size: 5-qt.

Ingredients:

- Leftover brats, chopped
- 28-oz. can crushed tomatoes
- 14-oz. water
- One tsp. Garlic powder
- ½ tsp. pepper
- 1 Tbsp. or more parsley flakes
- 1 Tbsp. Dried oregano
- 12-oz. can tomato paste
- 12-oz. can tomato puree
- Spaghetti

Instructions:

1. Place all ingredients but the spaghetti in the slow cooker.
2. Cover. Cook on low for 6 hours.
3. Serve over cooked spaghetti.

Week 10

This week's menu

Sunday: Big Juicy Burgers

Monday: Hope's Simple Italian Meat Loaf

Tuesday: Mile-High Shredded Beef Sandwiches

Wednesday: Twenty-Clove Chicken

Thursday: Green Chile Shredded Beef Stew

Friday: Hot Chicken Salad

Saturday: Chicken Tortilla Casserole

Recommended Side Dish: Mozzarella/Tomato/Basil salad

Special Dessert: Gooey chocolate pudding cake

Big Juicy Burgers

(To serve 8)

Preparation Time: 15 minutes

Cooking Time: 7-9 hours

Ideal Slow-Cooker Size: 4- or 5_qt.

Ingredients:

- 1 cup chopped onions
- ¼ cup chopped celery

- 4 lbs. ground beef
- 1½ tsp. salt, divided
- One tsp. pepper
- 2 cups tomato juice
- Two tsp. Minced garlic
- 1 Tbsp. ketchup
- One tsp. seasoning
- Hamburger buns

Instructions:

1. Put the chopped onions & celery in your slow cooker
2. Place the beef, one tsp. Salt & pepper in a large mixing bowl. Using your hands mix the salt & pepper into the beef. Divide the mixture in half. Wrap up half tightly and place in the refrigerator to use later this week. Divide the remaining dough into eight balls, each the same size
3. Flatten the eight balls of beef, so that they can look like the hamburger patties. Put the patties in your slow cooker over the onions & celery. Don't stack them. In case you have to, stagger them so that they don't lie exactly on top of each other. Wash your hands well.
4. In your medium mixing bowl, stir together the tomato juice, minced garlic, ketchup, Italian seasoning and ½ tsp. salt. Put this sauce over the patties in your slow-cooker.
5. Cover your slow cooker. Cook the burger on low for 7-9 hours.
6. Serve each big juicy burger on a hamburger bun.

Hope's Simple Italian Meat Loaf

(To serve 6-8)

Preparation Time: 5 minutes

Cooking Time: 7-9 hours

Ideal Slow-Cooker Size: 4-qt.

Ingredients:

- ½ cup chopped onion
- Two eggs, beaten
- 1 cup Italian bread crumbs
- Leftover ground beef mixture
- 3 Tbsp. ketchup
- 1 Tbsp. Brown sugar

Instructions:

1. Grease your slow cooker and make a foil basket out of foil strips.
2. Add the onion, egg, and bread crumbs to the turkey mixture into a loaf and place into the slow cooker.
3. Cook on low for 7-9 hours.
4. Mix the ketchup and brown sugar. Spread it on top of the loaf the last 30 minutes of cooking.

Mile-High Shredded Beef Sandwiches

(To serve 8)

Prep. Time: 35 minutes

Cooking Time: 7-9 hours

Ideal Slow-Cooker Size: 4-qt.

Ingredients:

- 3-lb. chuck roast, or otherwise round steak, trimmed of fat
- 2 Tbsp. Oil of your choice
- 1 cup chopped onions
- ½ cup sliced celery
- 2 cups reduced-sodium, 98% fat-free beef broth
- One garlic clove
- ¾ cup ketchup
- 2 Tbsp. Brown sugar
- 2 Tbsp. vinegar
- One tsp. Dry mustard
- ½ tsp. Chili powder
- 3 drops Tabasco sauce
- One bay leaf
- ¼ tsp. Paprika
- ¼ tsp. Garlic powder
- One tsp. Worcestershire sauce
- Eight sandwich rolls

Instructions:

1. In a skillet brown the two sides of meat in oil. Add onions and celery and sauté briefly. Transfer into slow cooker and broth.

2.   Cover & cook for around six to eight hours on low, or till tender. Evacuate the meat from your cooker & cool. Shred the beef.

3.   Evacuate the vegetables from cooker and drain, reserving 1½ cups broth. Mix the vegetables & meat together.

4.   Return the shredded meat & the vegetables to the cooker. Add broth and the remaining ingredients and combine well.

5.   Cover. Cook on high 1 hour. Remove bay leaf. Pile into a sandwich roll and serve.

Twenty-Clove Chicken

(To serve 8-10)

Prep. Time: 20 minutes

Cooking Time: 5-6 hours

Ideal Slow-Cooker Size: 5- or 6-qt

Ingredients:

- ½ cup dry white wine
- Four Tbsp. Dried parsley
- Four tsp. dried basil
- Two tsp. Dried oregano
- Pinch of crushed red pepper flakes
- 20 cloves of garlic(About two bulbs)
- 4 Ribs celery, chopped
- Ten boneless, skinless chicken breast halves

- Two lemons, juice and zest
- Fresh herbs, optional

Instructions:

1. Combine wine, dried oregano, and dried red pepper flakes in large bowl.
2. Add garlic cloves and celery. Mix well.
3. Transfer garlic and celery into the slow cooker with the slotted spoon.
4. Add chicken to herb mixture one piece at a time. Coat well. Place the chicken over the vegetables in slow cooker.
5. Sprinkle lemon juice and zest over chicken. Add any remaining herb mixture
6. Cover. Cook for about five to six hours on low, or until chicken is no longer pink in the center.
7. Garnish with fresh herbs if desired.

Green Chile Shredded Beef Stew

(To serve 6-7)

Prep. Time: 10 minutes

Cooking Time: 6-7 hours

Ideal Slow-cooker Size: 4- to 5-qt

Ingredients:

- 5 cups beef stock
- 1 cup red wine

- 1 bay leaf
- 1 medium onion, chopped
- 2 carrots, chopped
- 8-oz. can mild green chilies
- 1 jalapeno, seeded and diced
- Leftover beef

Instructions:

1. Add all ingredients to the slow cooker.
2. Cook on low for 6-7 hours.

Hot Chicken Salad

(To serve 6-8)

Prep. Time: 15-30 minutes

Cooking Time: 1½ hours

Ideal Slow-Cooker Size: 4qt.

Ingredients:

- 10¾ -oz. can cream of chicken soup
- 10¾ -oz. can cream of mushroom soup
- 1 cup mayonnaise
- 1 small onion, chopped
- ½ tsp. salt
- ¼ -½ tsp. salt
- 4 cups leftover chicken, cubed
- 1 can water chestnuts, drained and chopped

- 1 cup sour cream
- 1 cup cooked and drained fettuccine pasta
- Two cups of shredded cheese, your favorite flavor
- Potato chips, crushed

Instructions:

1. Combine soup, mayonnaise, chopped onion, salt, and pepper In the slow cooker. Mix until smooth.
2. 2 stir in leftover cubed chicken and water chestnuts.
3. Fold in sour cream and fettuccine.
4. Cover. Cook on high until bubbly, about 1½ hours.
5. Ten minutes before the end of cooking time and before serving, sprinkle with shredded cheese and crushed potato chips. Continue cooking, uncovered.

Chicken Tortilla Casserole

(To serve 4-5)

Preparation Time: 30 minutes

Cooking Time: 3-6 hours

Ideal Slow-Cooker Size: 5- or 6-qt.

Ingredients:

- 6-oz. chicken broth
- Five 6-inch flour tortillas, cut into strips about ½ *2 inches, divided
- Remaining leftover chicken
- One medium onion, chopped

- ½ tsp. canola oil
- 10 ¾ oz. Can mild green chilies, chopped
- 1 egg
- ½ cup grated low-fat cheddar cheese

Instructions:

1. Put the reserved chicken broth in your slow cooker sprayed with nonfat cooking spray.
2. Scatter half the tortillas strips in the bottom of the slow cooker.
3. Blend the remaining ingredients together, except the second half of the tortilla strips and the cheese.
4. Layer half of the chicken mixture into your cooker, followed by the rest of the chicken mix.
5. Cover. Cook for around four to six hours on low or on high 3-5 hours.
6. Add cheese to the top of the dish during last 20-30 minutes of cooking.
7. Uncover & allow the casserole to rest for 15 minutes before serving.

Week 11

This week's menu

Sunday: Chicken in Piquant Sauce

Monday: Three-Cheese Chicken Bake

Tuesday: Sharon's Chicken and Rice Casserole

Wednesday: Tomato Spaghetti Sauce

Thursday: Easy Sausage Sandwiches

Friday: Triple-Decker Tortilla

Saturday: Slow-Cooker Pizza

Recommended Side Dish: Picnic pea salad

Special Dessert: Tapioca Treat

Chicken in Piquant Sauce

(To serve 4-6)

Prep. Time: 10-15 minutes

Cooking Time: 3-4 hours

Ideal Slow-Cooker Size: 3- or 4-qt.

Ingredients:

- 16-oz. jar Russian or creamy French, salad dressing
- 12-oz. jar apricot preserves

- One envelope dry onion soup mix
- Six boneless, skinless chicken breast halves

Instructions:

1. In a bowl, mix the dressing, preserves, and dry onion soup mix.
2. Place the chicken breasts in your slow cooker.
3. Pour sauce on top of the chicken.
4. Cover and cook on high3 hours, or on low 4 hours, or until chicken is tender but not dry.

Three-Cheese Chicken Bake

(To serve 8-10)

Prep. Time: 25 minutes

Baking Time: 45 minutes

Ingredients:

- ½ lb. Lasagna noodles, divided
  Mushroom sauce:
- ½ cup of chopped onion
- ½ cup of chopped green bell pepper
- 3 Tbsp. butter
- 10¾-oz. can cream of chicken soup.
- 1/3 cup milk
- ¼ lb. fresh mushroom, sliced or
- 4-oz. Can mushroom pieces, drained
- ¼ cup chopped pimentos

- ½ tsp. Dried basil
- 12-oz. creamed cottage cheese, divided
- 3 cups leftover diced chicken, divided
- 2 cups shredded cheddar cheese, divided
- ½ cup grated parmesan cheese, divided

Instructions:

1. Cook noodles until just tender in a large amount of boiling water. Drain and rinse in cold water.
2. Prepare the mushroom sauce by cooking the onion & green pepper in butter in a medium-sized saucepan.
3. Stir soup, milk, mushrooms, pimentos, and basil into sautéed vegetables.
4. Grease 9*13-inch baking dish.
5. Put half of the noodles at the bottom of the baking dish.
6. Cover with half of the mushroom sauce.
7. Top with half the cottage cheese.
8. Top with half the chicken.
9. Top with half the cheddar and parmesan cheese. Repeat layers, using all remaining ingredients.
10. Bake at 350 degrees Fahrenheit for 45 minutes.

Sharon's Chicken and Rice Casserole

(To serve two)

Prep. Time: 5 minutes

Cooking Time: 4-6 hours

Ideal Slow-Cooker Size: 2½ hours

Ingredients:

- 10¾-oz. can cream of celery soup
- 2-oz. can sliced mushrooms, undrained
- ½ cup raw long-grain rice
- Remaining leftover chicken
- 1 Tbsp. Dry onion soup mix

Instructions:

1. Combine soup, mushroom, and rice in greased slow cooker. Mix well.
2. Layer chicken breasts on top of mixture. Sprinkle with onion soup mix.
3. Cover. Cook on low 4-6 hours

Tomato Spaghetti Sauce

(To serve 8-10)

Prep. Time: 10 minutes

Cooking Time: 10½-12½ hours

Ideal Slow-Cooker Size: 2½-qt.

Ingredients:

- 2 cups finely chopped onions
- Four cloves garlic, minced
- 4 lbs. fresh tomatoes, peeled and chopped, or 28-oz. can tomatoes, cut up, with juice
- 12-oz. can tomato paste

- 2 Tbsp. sugar
- Four tsp. instant beef bouillon granules
- Two tsp. dried oregano
- One tsp. dried basil
- Two large bay leaves
- Salt, to taste
- Pepper to taste
- 8-oz. can sliced mushrooms
- 4 Tbsp. corn starch
- 4 Tbsp. cold water

Instructions:

1. Combine all ingredients except mushrooms, cornstarch, and water in slow cooker.
2. Cover. Cook on low 10-12 hours.
3. Remove bay leaves. Stir in mushrooms.
4. Combine cornstarch and water. Stir into sauce.
5. Cover. Cook on high till thickened & bubbly, about 25 minutes.

Easy Sausage Sandwiches

(To serve 4)

Prep. Time: 10 minutes

Cooking Time: 5½-8 hours

Ideal Slow-Cooker Size: 5-qt.

Ingredients:

- Four pieces of sausages of your choice, sub-roll length
- Water
- 1½ cups leftover spaghetti sauce
- 1-2 cups shredded mozzarella cheese
- Four sub rolls

Instructions:

1. Place sausage pieces in slow cooker. Add 1-2 inches water.
2. Cover and cook for about 5-7 hours on low. Drain water
3. Stir in spaghetti sauce
4. Cover and cook 30-60 minutes more until sauce is heated through.
5. Serve on rolls topped with mozzarella cheese.
6. Tip: Serve with sautéed peppers and onions as condiments for topping the sandwiches.

Triple-Decker Tortilla

(To serve 6)

Prep. Time: 5-10 minutes

Baking Time: 15 minutes

Ingredients:

- 2 cups cooked pinto beans, divided
- 1 cup salsa, divided
- Four small flour tortillas
- ½ cup canned corn, or frozen

- ½ cup shredded Monterey jack or cheddar cheese, divided
- Avocado, sliced, optional
- Cilantro, chopped, optional

Instructions:

1. Drain, rinse, and slightly mash pinto beans
2. Grease a 9-inch pie plate. Heat oven to 450 degrees Fahrenheit.
3. Layer in this order: ¼ cup salsa, one tortilla, 1 cup beans, one tortilla, ½ cup corn, ¼ cup cheese, ¼ cup salsa, one tortilla, the remaining 1 cup beans, the last tortilla, and ½ cup salsa.
4. Cover with foil.
5. Bake for 12 minutes. Uncover and sprinkle with remaining ¼ cup cheese. Bake 3 minutes more. Top with avocado and cilantro if you wish. Cut into wedges to serve.

Slow-Cooker Pizza

(To serve 8-10)

Prep-Time: 30 minutes

Cooking Time: 2-3 hours

Ideal Slow-Cooker Size: 4-qt.

Ingredients:

- 12-oz. bag kluski, or other sturdy noodles

- 1½ lbs. ground beef
- Remaining leftover spaghetti sauce
- 16-oz. mozzarella cheese, shredded
- 8-oz. pepperoni, thinly sliced

Instructions:

1. Cook noodles per directions on package. Drain.
2. As the noodles are cooking, brown the ground beef in a non-stick skillet. Drain off drippings
3. Meanwhile, grease interior of the slow cooker.
4. Pour in ¼ of spaghetti sauce. Follow with half the noodles, and then half the browned ground beef. Top with 1/3 of the shredded cheese. Follow with half the pepperoni.
5. Repeat the layers, beginning with 1/3 of the sauce, followed by the rest of the noodles, and the rest of the pepperoni.
6. Top with the remaining spaghetti sauce. Finish with the rest of the cheese.
7. Cover & then cook for around two to three hours on low, or until heated through and until cheese has melted.

Week 12

This week's menu

Sunday: Sloppy Joes

Monday: Carne Asada

Tuesday: Sloppy Joe and Macaroni Casserole

Wednesday: Carne Asada Soup

Thursday: BBQ Balls

Friday: Slow-Cooker Ratatouille

Saturday: Hash Brown Dinner

Recommended Side Dish: Fresh corn and tomato salad

Special Dessert: Perfectly peachy cake

Sloppy Joes

(To serve 8-12)

Prep. Time: 10-15 minutes

Cooking Time: 2-6 hours

Ideal Slow-cooker Size: 4- to 5-qt.

Ingredients:

- 2 lbs. ground beef
- One large onion, chopped

- ½ cup chopped green bell pepper.
- 2 14½-oz. cans diced tomatoes
- 1/3 cup brown sugar
- Four tsp. Worcestershire sauce
- 1 Tbsp. Ground cumin
- Two tsp. Chili powder
- One tsp. salt

Instructions:

1. Brown the beef in a skillet, stirring in to break into small pieces.
2. Add onion and pepper to meat in skillet, cooking a few more minutes. Drain off dripping.
3. Transfer meat mixture to slow cooker
4. Stir in tomatoes, brown sugar, Worcestershire sauce, and seasoning.
5. Cover and cook until flavors are well blended, 2 hours on high or 6 hours on low.

Carne Asada

(To Serve 6-8)

Prep. Time: 5 minutes

Marinade time: 12-24 hours

Cooking Time: 3-4 hours

Ideal Slow-Cooker Time: 3-qt.

Ingredients:

- 4-5 lbs. flank steak.

  Marinade:

- ½ tsp. sea salt
- ¼ tsp. pepper
- ½ tsp. ground cumin
- ½ tsp. chili powder
- Six cloves garlic, crushed
- Three lime, juiced
- One orange, juiced
- One tsp. Red wine vinegar
- ½ cup olive oil
- 12-14 white corn tortillas

Toppings:

- Avocado slices
- Chopped fresh cilantro
- Lime wedges, for juice
- Crumble quesco fresco

Instructions:

1. Place the flank steak in your slow cooker.
2. Mix all the marinade ingredients. Pour them over the flank steak, coating all sides
3. Cover your crock with plastic wrap and let the steak marinade 12-24 hours.

4.   Cook on low for 3 -4 hours, or until the desired doneness

5.   Remove flanks steak from slow cooker and let rest for 10 minutes.

6.   Slice thinly.

7.   Serve in warmed white corn tortillas with desired toppings

Soppy Joe and Macaroni Casserole

(To serve 4-6)

Prep. Time: 10 minutes

Cooking Time: 2-3 hours

Ideal Slow-Cooker Size: 5-qt.

Ingredients:

- Leftover sloppy joe meat
- 1 cup beef broth
- 12 oz. half cooked macaroni
- 2 cups shredded cheddar cheese

Instructions:

1.   Mix the leftover sloppy joe meat and broth. Gently stir in the pasta.

2.   In a greased slow cooker, place the meat/pasta mixture. Top with the shredded cheese.

3.   Cover. Cook on low for 2-3 hours.

Carne Asada Soup

(To serve 4)

Prep. Time: 5 minutes

Cooking Time: 4-6 hours

Ideal Slow-Cooker Size: 3-qt.

Ingredients:

- 5 cups beef stock
- One medium onion, chopped
- One can pinto beans, with juices
- ½ cup frozen corn
- One tsp. Sea salt
- ¼ tsp. Pepper
- ½ tsp. Ground cumin
- ½ tsp. Chili powder
- Leftover Carne Asada meat
- Crumbled quesco fresco
- Avocado, sliced
- Fresh cilantro, chopped

Instructions:

1. Place the beef stock, onion, pinto beans, corn and spices in slow cooker
2. Cover and cook on low for 4-6 hours. Add in the leftover meat during the final cooking hour.
3. Serve in bowls with some crumbled quesco fresco, avocado slices, and fresh cilantro sprinkled over the top.

BBQ Balls

(To serve 10)

Prep. Time: 40 minutes

Cooking Time: 2 hours

Ideal Slow-Cooker Size: 4-qt.

Ingredients:

- 2 lbs. 99% fat-free ground turkey
- 4 eggs
- 2 cups uncooked instant rice
- Two medium onions, chopped
- Two 1-lb. Cans cranberry sauce
- 2 14-oz. bottles ketchup
- 4 Tbsp. Worcestershire sauce
- One tsp. Garlic powder
- Rice

Instructions:

1. Blend ground turkey, eggs, instant rice, and onion. Form into ¾-inch balls.
2. Bake at 400 degrees Fahrenheit for 20 minutes or until brown. Drain.
3. Combine cranberry sauce, and garlic powder in a small bowl.
4. Place meatballs in slow cooker. Pour sauce over the top. Stir to coat.
5. Cover. Cook on low two hours.

6.   Serve over Rice.

Slow-Cooker Ratatouille

(To serve 6)

Preparation Time: 35-40 minutes

Cooking Time: 6-7 hours

Ideal Slow-Cooker Size: 5-qt.

Ingredients:

- 1 Tbsp. Olive oil
- One large onion chopped
- Six large cloves garlic, minced
- One green bell pepper, cut into strips
- One red bell pepper cut into strips
- One medium eggplant, cubed, peeled
- 2 cups mushroom, thickly sliced
- Four tomatoes, cubed
- 1 cup low-sodium tomato puree
- ¼ cup dry red wine, or wine
- Vinegar
- 1 Tbsp. Lemon juice
- Two tsp. Dried thyme
- One tsp. Dried oregano
- One tsp. Ground cumin
- One tsp. salt
- ½ tsp. black pepper

- 4 Tbsp. Minced fresh basil
- ¼ cup fresh parsley, chopped

Instructions:

1. Turn slow cooker on high 2 minutes.
2. Put oil into the slow cooker and add remaining ingredients, except fresh basil and parsley.
3. Cover. Cook for around two hours on high, then on low for four to five hours.
4. Stir in fresh basil. Sprinkle with parsley. Serve.

Hash Brown Dinner

(To serve 6-8)

Prep. Time: 15-30 minutes

Cooking Time: 4½ hours

Ideal Slow-Cooker Size: 5-qt.

Ingredients:

- Leftover BBQ Balls, chopped up
- ½ cup, chopped onions
- 3 cups frozen hash brown potatoes, thawed
- ½ tsp. Salt
- ½ tsp. pepper
- 1-lb. Pkg. Frozen California Blend vegetables
- 10¾-oz. can cream of chicken soup.
- 1 cup milk
- ¾ lb. cheese of your choice, cubed

Instructions:

1. Place chopped meatballs and onion in lightly greased slow cooker
2. Spoon potatoes over the top.
3. Sprinkle with salt and pepper.
4. Top with vegetables.
5. Put together soup & milk in a small bowl.
6. Pour over vegetables.
7. Cover. Cook on low 4 hours.
8. Top with cheese.
9. Cover. Cook for an extra thirty minutes, or until the cheese is melted.

Week 13

This week's menu

Sunday: Teriyaki Salmon

Monday: Salmon Cheese Casserole

Tuesday: Herby Chicken

Wednesday: Perfect Pork Chops

Thursday: Green Enchiladas

Friday: Chops and Beans

Saturday: Chicken Tortilla Soup

Recommended Side Dish: summer salad

Special Dessert: Slow cooker Berry cobbler

Teriyaki Salmon

(To serve 4)

Prep. Time: 10 minutes

Cooking Time: 1-2 hours

Ideal Slow-Cooker Size: 3- or 4-qt.

Ingredients:

- Four salmon fillets
- 4 Tbsp. Teriyaki sauce

- 4 Tbsp. Hoisin sauce
- 1 Tbsp. Low-Sodium Soy Sauce
- 1 Tbsp. Brown sugar
- Two tsp. Ground ginger
- 1/8 tsp. pepper

Instructions:

1. Lay out six pieces of foil, big enough to wrap in the salmon fillets. Lay the salmon fillets on top of each of them.
2. Mix all the remaining ingredients. Divide this mixture evenly over each salmon filet and spread to coat evenly.
3. Close the packets up tightly and place them in the crock.
4. Cover & cook on low for 1-2 hours. The fish should flake easily when done.

Salmon Cheese Casserole

(To serve6)

Prep. Time: 5 minutes

Cooking Time: 3-4 hours

Ideal Slow-Cooker Size: 2-qt.

Ingredients:

- 4-oz. can mushrooms, drained
- Leftover salmon, flaked

- 1½ cups bread crumbs
- Two eggs, beaten
- 1 cup grated cheese of your choice
- 1 Tbsp. Lemon juice
- 1 Tbsp. Dried minced onion

Instructions:

1.   Flake fish in a bowl, removing bones. Stir in remaining ingredients. Pour into slightly greased slow-cooker.
2.   Cover. Cook on low 3-4 hours.

Herby Chicken

(To serve 8-10)

Prep. Time: 10 minutes

Cooking Time: 5-7 hours

Ideal Slow-Cooker Size: 7-qt.

Ingredients:

- 6-lb. whole roaster chicken
- One lemon, cut into wedges
- One bay leaf
- 2-4 sprigs fresh thyme, or ¾ tsp. dried thyme
- Salt and pepper to taste

Instructions:

1. Remove giblets from chicken.
2. Put lemon wedges and bay leaf in the cavity.
3. Place the whole chicken in your slow cooker.
4. Scatter sprigs of thyme over the chicken. Sprinkle with salt and pepper.
5. Cover and cook for around five to seven hours on low, or until chicken is tender
6. Tip: Serve hot with pasta or rice or debone and freeze for your favorite casserole.

Perfect Pork Chops

(To serve 2)

Prep. Time: 20 minutes

Cooking Time: 3-4 hours

Ideal Slow-Cooker Size: 4-qt.

Ingredients:

- One large onion
- 3½ lb. boneless, center loin pork chops, frozen
- Fresh ground pepper, to taste.
- 1½ tsp. reduced-sodium bouillon granules of your choice
- ½ cup hot water
- 4 Tbsp. Prepared mustard with white wine
- Fresh parsley sprigs, or lemon slices, optional

Instructions:

1. Cut off ends of onion and peel. Cut onion in half crosswise to make four solid wheels. Place in bottom of your slow cooker.
2. Sear the two sides of the frozen chops in a heavy skillet. Place in slow-cooker on top of onions. Sprinkle with pepper.
3. Dissolve bouillon cube in hot water. Stir in mustard. Pour into slow cooker.
4. Cover. Cook for around three to four hours on high.
5. Serve while topped with fresh parsley sprigs or lemon slices, if desired.

Green Enchiladas

(To serve 8)

Prep. Time: 5-7 minutes

Cooking Time: 2-4 hours

Ideal Slow-Cooker Size: 3-qt.

Ingredients:

- 2 10-oz. cans green enchiladas
- Eight large tortillas, divided
- 2 cups leftover chopped chicken, divided
- 1½cups divided mozzarella cheese

Instructions:

1. Pour a little enchilada sauce at the bottom of your slow cooker.

2. Layer 1 tortilla, ¼ cup of chicken, and ¼ cup of sauce into slow cooker

3. Repeat the layers till all ingredients are completely used.

4. Sprinkle mozzarella cheese over the top.

5. Cover and cook on low 2-4 hours.

Chops and Beans

(To serve 6)

Prep. Time: 20 minutes

Cooking Time: 4-5 hours

Ideal Slow-Cooker Size: 4-qt.

Ingredients:

- Leftover pork, chopped
- Two 1-lb. Cans pork and beans
- ¼ cup plus 2 Tbsp. No-Salt-Added ketchup
- Two slices bacon, browned and crumbled
- ½ cup chopped onions, sautéed
- 1 Tbsp. Worcestershire sauce
- 2 Tbsp. Brown sugar
- Two tsp. Prepared mustard
- One lemon, sliced

Instructions:

1. Place all ingredients in the slow-cooker. Stir well.

2. Cover. Cook on low 4-5 hours.

Chicken Tortilla Soup

(To serve 4)

Prep. Time: 15 minutes

Cooking Time: 5-6 hours

Ideal Slow-Cooker Size: 3-qt

Ingredients:

- 15-oz. can no-salt-added black beans, undrained
- 15-oz. can Mexican stewed tomatoes
- ½ cup salsa of your choice
- 4-oz. can chopped green chilies
- 6-oz. can no-salt-added tomato sauce
- Remaining leftover chicken
- 1 oz. tortilla chips
- ½ cup fat-free cheddar cheese

Instructions:

1. Combine all ingredients except chicken, chips, and cheese in a large slow-cooker.
2. Cover. Cook on low 5-6 hours. Add leftover chicken in the last hour of cooking.
3. To serve, put a handful of chips in each soup bowl. Ladle soup over chips. Top with cheese.

FALL

Week 1

This week's menu

Sunday: Barbara Jean's junior beef

Monday: Teriyaki chicken

Tuesday: Your choice of vegetable soup

Wednesday: Teriyaki chicken Tacos

Thursday: Apple Raisin Ham

Friday: Sweet potatoes, ham, and oranges

Saturday: Lemon Dijon fish

Recommended Side Dish: Winter squash with herbs and butter

Special Dessert: Triple chocolate lava cake

Barbara Jean's junior beef

(To serve 4-6)

Prep. Time: 10 minutes

Cooking Time: 5-6 hours

Ideal Slow-cooker size: 4-qt.

Ingredients:

- 2 cups grated cheddar or Swiss cheese
- 5 lb. Beef roast
- ½ lb. Fresh mushroom, sliced and sautéed
- ½ tsp. salt
- 4-6 hamburger rolls
- One medium onion, chopped
- Four dill pickles, chopped
- ½ tsp. Black pepper
- Juice from 1 qt. Jar of dill pickles
- One tsp. Seasoned salt
- ½ tsp. Cayenne pepper

Instructions:

1. Combine all ingredients except rolls, cheese, and mushrooms in slow cooker
2. Cover. Cook on high 4-5 hours
3. Shred meat using two forks. Minimize heat to low & then cook for around one hour, or until the meat is very tender
4. Serve on hamburger buns with sautéed mushrooms and grated cheddar or Swiss cheese

Teriyaki chicken

(To serve 4)

Prep. Time: 6-7 hours

Ideal Slow-Cooker Size: 4-qt

Ingredients:

- Two cloves garlic, minced
- Eight skinless chicken thighs
- 2 tbsp. grated fresh ginger
- ½ cup soy sauce
- 2 tbsp. brown sugar

Instructions:

1.   Wash and dry chicken. Arrange in the slow cooker.
2.   Combine remaining ingredients in a bowl. Pour over chicken
3.   Cover. Cook for around one hour on high. Minimize the cooker's heat to low & cook for around five to six hours, or until chicken is fork-tender
4.   Serve over rice with a fresh salad

Your favorite vegetable soup

(To serve 4)

Prep. Time:10 minutes

Cooking Time: 6 hours

Ideal slow-cooker size: 4- or 5-qt.

Ingredients:

- 1/8 cup uncooked long-grain rice or small pearl barley, or ¼ cup cooked orzo or small shells
- 3 cups vegetable, beef, or chicken stock
- One bay leaf
- 3 cups vegetables

- 15 oz. can diced tomatoes
- Leftover beef

Instructions:

1.   Combine your ingredients in the slow cooker apart from pasta, barley or rice
2.   Cover. Cook on low 6 hours
3.   An hour before the cooking time ends, stir in rice or barley or 30 minutes before end of cooking time, stir in cooked pasta

Teriyaki chicken tacos

(To serve 4)

Prep. Time: 10 minutes

Cooking Time: 5 minutes

Ingredients:

- Leftover teriyaki chicken
- 2 cups coleslaw or broccoli slaw
- 16 corn tortillas
- Dressing:
- ½ tsp. garlic powder
- 1/8 cup olive oil
- One tsp. Brown sugar
- 1/8 cup rice vinegar
- ½ tsp. sesame oil
- One tsp. Low sodium soy sauce

- ¼ tsp. salt

Instructions:

1. Warm the leftover chicken and corn tortillas
2. Meanwhile, mix the ingredients for the dressing. Pour it over the coleslaw or broccoli slaw and mix well
3. Fill each taco with some teriyaki chicken and top with slaw

Apple raisin ham

(To serve 6)

Prep. Time: 10-15 minutes

Cooking Time: 4-5 hours

Ideal slow cooker size: 4-qt.

Ingredients:

- 2 ½ lb. fully cooked boneless ham
- 2 tbsp. water
- 1/3 cup orange juice
- 21 oz. can apple pie filling
- ¼ tsp. ground cinnamon
- 1/3 cup golden raisins

Instructions:

1. Cut ham into six equal slices
2. In a mixing bowl combine pie filling, raisins, cinnamon, orange juice and water

3. Place one slice of ham in your slow cooker. Spread 1/6 of the apple mixture over the top
4. Repeat layers until you have used all the ham and apple mixture
5. Cover and cook on low 4-5 hours

Sweet potatoes, ham, and oranges

(To serve 4)

Prep. Time: 15 minutes

Cooking Time: 4-5 hours

Ideal Slow Cooker Size: 3- or 4-qt.

Ingredients:

- 1 tbsp. cornstarch
- 2-3 sweet potatoes sliced and peeled
- 1/8 tsp. pepper
- ¼ inch thick ham slice, cut into four pieces from leftover ham
- ½ cup brown sugar
- Three seedless oranges, peeled and sliced
- ¼ tsp. ground allspice
- 3 tbsp. orange juice concentrate
- 3 tbsp. honey

Instructions:

1. Place sweet potatoes in slow cooker
2. Arrange ham and orange slices on top

3.   Combine remaining ingredients. Drizzle over ham and oranges

4.   Cover. Cook on low 4-5 hours, or just until the sweet potatoes are as tender as you like them

Lemon Dijon fish

(To serve 4)

Prep. Time: 10 minutes

Cooking time: 3 hours

Ideal slow cooker size: 2-qt.

Ingredients:

- 1 tbsp. lemon juice
- 1 ½ lbs. orange roughy fillets
- 3 tbsp. melted butter
- One tsp. Worcestershire sauce
- 2 tbsp. Dijon mustard

Instructions:

1.   Cut fillets to fit in slow cooker
2.   In a small bowl, combine the fixings that remained together. Pour sauce over the fish
3.   Cover and cook on low for 3 hours, or until fish flakes easily but is not dry or overcooked

Week 2

This week's menu

Sunday: Baked Ziti

Monday: Mexican Haystacks

Tuesday: Simple chicken thighs

Wednesday: Mexican haystack nachos

Thursday: Chicken rice soup

Friday: Autumn brisket

Saturday: Baked rice dinner

Recommended Side Dish: Beets with capers

Special Dessert: Pumpkin Bread pudding

Baked ziti

(To serve 8-10)

Prep. Time: 15-20 minutes

Cooking Time: 4 hours

Standing time: 15 minutes

Ideal slow cooker size: 5-qt.

Ingredients:

- ½ lb. mozzarella grated cheese
- 14 oz. jar of your favorite spaghetti sauce, divide
- 1 lb. cottage cheese
- One tsp. Dried minced garlic
- 1 egg
- 1 lb. uncooked ziti
- 2 tbsp. parmesan cheese
- 1/8 tsp. salt
- One tsp. Parsley flakes
- 1/8 tsp. pepper

Instructions:

1. Blend together cottage cheese, garlic, egg, parsley, salt parmesan cheese, and pepper
2. Pour 2 cups of spaghetti sauce in your greased slow cooker
3. Put 1/3 of uncooked ziti over the spaghetti sauce
4. Spoon 1/3 of the cottage cheese mixture over the ziti
5. Repeat the layers twice. You should have a cup of spaghetti sauce left
6. Pour the remaining tomato sauce over top
7. Cover. Cook on low four hours
8. Thirty minutes before the cooking time ends, sprinkle the top of the ziti mixture with mozzarella cheese. Do not cover. Continue cooking 30 more minutes
9. Let stand 15 minutes before serving to let everything firm up

Mexican Haystacks

(To serve 10-12)

Prep. Time: 20 minutes

Cooking Time: 1-3 hours

Ideal slow-cooker size: 5-qt.

Ingredients:

- Cooked rice or baked potatoes
- 2 lbs. ground beef
- 2 10 oz. cans tomato sauce
- One small chopped onion
- Pepper
- 2 15 oz. cans chili beans with chili gravy or red beans
- One tsp. Garlic salt
- 2 10 oz. cans mild enchilada sauce or mild salsa
- ½ tsp. chili powder
- Condiments:
- Chopped tomatoes
- Raisins
- Shredded lettuce
- Diced apples
- Fresh pineapple chunks
- Shredded coconut
- Corn chips
- Shredded Monterey Jack cheese

Instructions:

1. Brown beef in the skillet. Using a slotted spoon, lift it out of the drippings and into the slow cooker. Discard drippings
2. Stir onion, garlic salt, enchilada sauce, tomato sauce, chili powder, chili beans and pepper into the beef in the slow cooker
3. Cover. Cook on low for 2-3 hours or on high for 1 hour
4. Serve over baked potatoes or rice. Then add as many condiments on top as you want

Simple chicken thighs

(To serve 4-6)

Prep. Time: 10 minutes

Cooking Time: 4-6 hours

Prep. Time: 4-6 hours

Cooking Time: 3-12 hours

Ideal slow-cooker size: 4-qt

Ingredients:

- ¼ cup chopped fresh parsley
- 4 lbs. bone-in chicken thighs, skin removed
- One garlic clove, minced
- 3 tbsp. olive oil
- ¼ cup honey
- ½ tsp. freshly ground pepper

- ¼ cup soy sauce
- 4 tbsp. red wine vinegar
- Cornstarch

Instructions:

1. Place chicken in a shallow glass pan in a single layer
2. In a small bowl, combine oil, vinegar pepper, honey, garlic, parsley and soy sauce
3. Pour over chicken. Marinate the chicken in your fridge for a minimum of 3 hours and a maximum of 12
4. Place chicken in marinade slow cooker. Cover and cook for around four to six hours on low for 4-6 hours
5. Either lift the chicken thighs out of the sauce with a mixture of 1 tbsp. Cornstarch and 3 tbsp. Water whisked together and then whisked through the hot sauce. Serve thickened sauce as a gravy on the side

Mexican haystack nachos

(To Serve 6)

Prep. Time: 8 minutes

Cooking Time: 10-15 minutes

Ingredients:

- ½ cup chopped onions
- Leftover Mexican haystacks chili
- Tortilla chips

- 8 oz. shredded cheese

Additional toppings:

- Guacamole
- Sour cream or Greek yogurt
- Green chopped onions

Instructions:

1. Warm the leftover Mexican haystacks chili
2. Preheat your oven to 400 degrees Fahrenheit
3. Spray your baking sheet with nonstick spray then arrange as many chips as you wish and cover with shredded cheese
4. Bake for 10-15 minutes, or until cheese is melted
5. Top with any additional toppings you want

Chicken rice soup

(To serve 4-6)

Prep. Time: 4-5 minutes

Cooking time: 4-8 hours

Ideal slow cooker size: 4-qt.

Ingredients:

- Leftover chicken
- ¼ cup uncooked wild rice
- One tsp. Dried thyme leaves
- ¼ cup long grain rice, uncooked

- 1/8 tsp. red pepper flakes
- One medium chopped onion
- One tsp. Vegetable oil
- ¾ cup celery, chopped into ½ inch thick pieces
- 3 ¼ cups chicken broth

Instructions:

1.   Mix wild and white rice with oil in slow cooker.
2.   Cover. Cook on high for 15 minutes
3.   Add broth, vegetables, and seasonings
4.   Cover. Cook for around four to five hours on high or 7-8 hours on low. 1 hour before serving, add the chicken

Autumn brisket

(To serve 8)

Prep. Time: 20-30 minutes

Cooking time: 4-9 hours

Ideal slow cooker size: 6-qt.

Ingredients:

- Two tsp. Caraway seeds
- Salt and pepper
- 1 cup of water
- One large onion cut in wedges
- 3 lb. boneless beef brisket
- 1 lb. head cabbage, cut into wedges

- One medium granny smith apple, cored and cut into eight wedges
- One large sweet potato, peeled and cut into 1-inch pieces
- 2 10 ¾ oz. cans cream of celery soup

Instructions:

1. Place brisket in slow cooker
2. Shake salt & pepper over the meat to taste
3. Top with onion, sweet potato, and cabbage
4. Season to taste with salt and pepper
5. Place apple wedges over vegetables
6. In a medium-sized bowl combine soup, water, and caraway seeds if you wish
7. Spoon mixture over brisket and vegetables

Baked rice dinner

(To serve 4)

Prep. Time: 15 minutes

Baking time: 2 hours

Ideal slow cooker size: 3-qt.

Ingredients:

- ¾ stick butter
- 2-3 cups bite-sized pieces of leftover brisket
- 10 ¾ oz. can beef consommé
- 1 cup long grain uncooked rice
- 10 ¾ oz. can French onion soup

Instructions:

1. Butter 1-1 ½ qt. Baking dish. Cut remaining butter into chunks. Place in baking dish
2. Add soup, consommé, meat and rice
3. Cover. Bake at 350 degrees Fahrenheit for 1-1 ½ hours or until liquid is absorbed

Week 3

This week's menu

Sunday: Zucchini hot dish

Monday: Easy chicken

Tuesday: Stuffed ground beef

Wednesday: Basic meat curry sauce

Thursday: Stuffed acorn squash

Friday: Italian sausage dinner

Saturday: Edie's Paella

Recommended Side Dish: Saucy Mushrooms

Special Dessert: Extra crisp apple crisp

Zucchini hot dish

(To serve 4)

Prep. Time: 15-20 minutes

Cooking time: 2-3 hours

Ideal slow cooker size: 2-qt.

Ingredients:

- 1-2 cups shredded cheddar cheese
- 2 ½ lbs. ground beef, divide

- 10 ¾ oz. can cream of mushroom soup
- One large onion, chopped
- 4-5 6-inch long sliced zucchini
- Salt and pepper

Instructions:

1. Brown ground beef with onions, along with salt and pepper, in a nonstick skillet until crumbly. Drain. Put ½ lb. away for the stuffed ground beef later this week and 1 lb. away for the stuffed Acorn squash later this week

2. Layer the zucchini & beef mixture alternately in your slow cooker

3. Top with soup. Sprinkle with cheese

4. Cover & cook for around two to three hours on low, or until the zucchini is done to your liking

Easy chicken

(To serve 8)

Prep. Time: 5 minutes

Cooking time: 8 hours

Ideal slow cooker size: 3-qt.

Ingredients:

- 4 lbs. frozen chicken breasts
- 1 ½ cups warm water, chicken broth or white wine
- Two pkgs. Dry Italian dressing mix

- ½ cup chopped onion

Instructions:

1. Place the frozen chicken in your slow cooker & sprinkle with dry Italian dressing and onion
2. Warm liquid and pour over chicken
3. Cook on low for 8 hours

Stuffed ground beef

(To serve 4)

Prep. Time: 10 minutes

Cooking time: 6 hours

Ideal slow cooker size: 4-qt.

Ingredients:

- ½ lb. leftover ground beef
- 2 cups cabbage, shredded
- Salt and pepper, to taste
- 2 cups dry bread cubes
- 2 cups tomato juice

Instructions:

1. Take the ½ lb. Ground beef out of the refrigerator you browned earlier this week
2. Spray the inside of the cooker with nonstick cooking spray. Layer the ingredients in slow cooker in this

order: ground beef, cabbage, salt and pepper, bread filling

3. Pour tomato juice over top
4. Cook on low 4-6 hours, or until cabbage is just tender

Basic meat curry sauce

(To serve 8)

Prep. Time: 20-30 minutes

Cooking time: 2-3 hours

Ideal slow cooker size: 3-qt.

Ingredients:

- 1-2 cups leftover chicken, chopped into bite-sized pieces
- Two large chopped onions
- Rice
- 2 tbsp. lemon juice
- 1-2 cloves minced garlic
- 2-4 tsp. curry powder

Instructions:

1. Grease interior of slow-cooker crock
2. Mix lemon juice, onions, garlic and curry powder in crock
3. Stir in the chicken until all pieces are well coated
4. Cover. Cook on low 2-3 hours, or until onions are as tender as you like them

5. If you would like a thickened sauce, mix 2 tbsp. Flour into meat and sauce at the end of cooking time. Cook on high for 10 minutes, or until sauce bubbles and thickens

6. Serve over steamed rice

Stuffed Acorn Squash

(To serve 8)

Prep. Time: 20 minutes

Cooking time: 2-3 hours

Ideal slow cooker size: 3-qt.

Ingredients:

- ½ lb. cubed sharp cheddar cheese
- Two acorn squash
- ½ tsp. ginger
- 1 lb. leftover ground beef
- Four tsp. Curry powder
- Scant ½ tsp. Black pepper
- One small chopped onion
- ½ tsp. cardamom
- 5 cups chopped, unpeeled apples, divided
- Scant ½ tsp. Ground nutmeg
- 6 tbsp. apricot preserves
- 2 tbsp. butter
- Scant ½ tsp. Ground cinnamon
- ¼ tsp. salt

Instructions:

1. Wash the squash & later cut it in half from top to bottom. Scrape out the seeds and stringy stuff. Cut each half in half again

2. Put four quarters into the bottom of the slow cooker side by side, cut side up. Set the other four quarters on to, but staggered so that they are not sitting inside the four pieces on the bottom. Add about 2 tbsp. Water to the cooker. Cover. Turn the cooker to low and let it go for 3-6 hours, or until you can stick a fork in the skin of the squash halves with very little resistance

3. Sometime during those 3-6 hours, warm the leftover 1 lb. Ground beef and stir 2 cups chopped apples into beef and onions

4. Mix in curry powder, ginger, black pepper and cardamom

5. Add the cubed cheese, salt, and apricot preserves. Stir together gently. Set aside until squash is done softening up

6. When squash is tender, divide the meat mixture among the eight quarters evenly

7. Put the filled quarters back into the cooker in staggered layers

8. Cover. Cook on high for 45-60 minutes or until the stuffing is heated through and the cheese is melted

9. Sauté the remaining 3 cups apple slices in butter just until they are tender. Season lightly with cinnamon and nutmeg

10. Remove the filled squash from the cooker. Place a quarter on each serving plate. Top each with sautéed apples

Italian sausage dinner

(To serve 8)

Prep. Time: 5 minutes

Cooking time: 4-9 hours

Ideal slow cooker size: 4-qt.

Ingredients:

- ½ cup chicken stock or broth
- 1-pint grape tomatoes
- 1 tbsp. olive oil
- Salt and pepper
- 1 lb. fingerling potatoes
- One tsp. Garlic powder
- 8-10 Italian sausage links
- 1 ½ tsp. Italian seasoning
- One large quartered red onion

Instructions:

1. If desired, brown sausages in a skillet. In the bottom of the crock, place the grape tomatoes, potatoes, onion pieces and sausage links on top
2. Drizzle the olive oil above the contents of the crock and sprinkle with the Italian seasoning, salt, pepper,

and garlic powder. Pour the chicken stock/ broth in last

3.   Cook on low for 6 hours

Edie's paella

(To serve 8)

Prep. Time: 5 minutes

Cooking time: 6 hours

Ideal slow cooker size: 4-qt.

Ingredients:

- 15 ½ oz. can of the great northern beans, rinsed & drained
- One large chopped onion
- 4-5 chopped tomatoes
- 15 ½ oz. can of the black beans, rinsed & drained
- 2 tbsp. olive oil7 ½ cups chicken broth/stock
- 15 ½ oz. can of the pinto beans, rinsed & drained
- Leftover chicken
- ¾ tsp. salt
- 1 ½ cups instant rice
- ½ tsp. black pepper
- Leftover Italian sausage cut into chunks
- 1 ½ tsp. Fresh rosemary leaves or ½ tsp. dried

Instructions:

1.   Grease interior of slow-cooker crock

2.   Add onion, great mother beans, tomatoes, black beans, chicken broth, pinto beans, salt, and pepper. Stir together until well mixed

3.   Cover. Cook on low for 4 hours. An hour before cooking time is up, add in leftover chicken, leftover sausage and stir in rosemary and rice

Week 4

This week's menu

Sunday: Butterfly Steaks

Monday: Snowmobile soup

Tuesday: King Turkey

Wednesday: Favorite Tetrazzini

Thursday: Apricot salsa salmon

Friday: Country-style ribs

Saturday: rib and rice bowls

Recommended Side Dish: cheesy creamed corn

Special Dessert: chocolate blueberry dessert

Butterfly steaks

(To serve 8)

Prep. Time: 20-30 minutes

Cooking time: 4 hours

Ideal slow cooker size: 6-qt.

Ingredients:

- Rice
- 1/3 cup olive oil

- One tsp. Ground ginger
- lb. butt beef, or venison, tenderloin
- ½ cup soy sauce
- One tsp. Dry mustard
- 1 tbsp. salt
- ½ tsp. garlic powder, divided
- ¾ cup canola oil
- Two tsp. Celery seeds
- One tsp. Black pepper
- ½ cup apple cider vinegar

Instructions:

1. Cut tenderloin into ¾-1 inch-thick slices. Cut each slice through the center but not the whole way through. Flatten into a butterfly-shaped steak and lay in large glass baking dish

2. In a bowl, mix four tsp. Garlic powder, celery seeds, vinegar, canola oil for marinade, salt, and pepper. Pour over steaks in a glass pan

3. Cover, and then marinate in your fridge for two hours stirring occasionally

4. Meanwhile, grease interior of slow cooker crock

5. Place marinated steaks on broiler pan and broil at 400 degrees Fahrenheit just until lightly browned. Place steaks in the slow cooker. Stagger the pieces so they do not directly overlap each other

6. Mix soy sauce, olive oil, dry mustard, and remaining ½ tsp. Garlic powder. Pour over meat, making sure to spoon sauce on any steaks on the bottom layer

7. Cook on low 2-4 hours

8.   Serve with rice

Snowmobile soup

(To serve 8)

Prep. Time: 20-30 minutes

Cooking time: 4-9 hours

Ideal slow cooker size: 6-qt.

Ingredients:

- One small chopped onion
- Leftover steak
- One soup can milk
- Five large potatoes, julienned French fries
- ¼ tsp. pepper
- 10 ¾ oz. can cream of mushroom soup
- One tsp. salt
- 2 lbs. shredded cheddar cheese

Instructions:

1.   Stir onion, milk, salt, onion, cheese, potatoes and pepper into your slow cooker
2.   Cover cook on low for 5-6 hours, or until potatoes are as soft as you like them. Before the cooking time ends, add in the leftover steak

King Turkey

(To serve 8)

Prep. Time: 20-30 minutes

Cooking time: 4-9 hours

Ideal slow cooker size: 6-qt.

Ingredients:

- 1 cup white wine
- 5-6 lb. Turkey breast, bone in and skin on
- 1 cup chicken broth
- A sprinkling of lemon pepper
- One medium chopped onion
- 4 tbsp. melted butter
- One rib chopped celery
- A good shower of salt

Instructions:

1. Wash turkey breast. Pat dry. Put onion and celery in the cavity. Place in greased slow cooker
2. Pour melted butter over turkey. Season with salt and lemon pepper
3. Pour broth and wine around Turkey
4. Cover. Cook on low 5-7 hours or just until meat thermometer registers 165 degrees Fahrenheit
5. Let stand 15 minutes before carving

Favorite tetrazzini

(To serve 8)

Prep. Time: 20-30 minutes

Cooking time: 4-9 hours

Ideal slow cooker size: 6-qt.

Ingredients:

- 4 oz. broken spaghetti
- 1 cup cheddar cheese grated
- 4 oz. jar chopped pimento, drained
- One medium chopped onion
- Parmesan cheese grated
- 1/3 cup milk
- One medium green bell pepper, chopped
- 8 oz. can mushroom stems, drained
- 10 ¾ oz. can cream of chicken soup
- 3-4 cups diced leftover turkey
- 1 cup plain fat-free yogurt
- 8 oz. sliced ripe olives, drained

Instructions:

1. Cook spaghetti according to package directions. Drain well
2. Sauté onion and green pepper in nonstick skillet until soft
3. Mix soup, yogurt, and milk together in a large mixing bowl until smooth
4. Stir into soup mixture the onion and green pepper, olives, meat, pimento, spaghetti, and mushrooms. Fold together until well mixed
5. Pour this in your greased 9 by 13-inch baking dish

6.   Bake at 350 degrees Fahrenheit for 30 minutes, or until bubbly

7.   If you wish, sprinkle with Parmesan cheese. Then sprinkle with shredded cheddar cheese. Bake 10 more minutes

Apricot salsa salmon

(To serve 8)

Prep. Time: 10 minutes

Cooking time: 4 hours

Ideal slow cooker size: 6-qt.

Ingredients:

- ¼ cup apricot jam
- 12 oz. frozen salmon fillets
- ¼ cup roasted salsa verde

Instructions:

1.   Grease the interior of your slow-cooker crock

2.   Do not forget not to thaw the salmon. Place frozen salmon skin side down in bottom of the cooker

3.   Mix jam and salsa. Spread mixture over salmon

4.   Cover. Cook on low for 1 ½ hours or until an instant-red meat thermometer registers 135 degrees Fahrenheit when stuck into center of fillet

Country style ribs

(To serve 6-8)

Prep. Time: 17 minutes

Cooking time: 3-9 hours

Ideal slow cooker size: 4-qt.

Ingredients:

- 2 tbsp. Worcestershire sauce
- 5-6 lbs. pork shoulder ribs
- One tsp. Salt
- ¾ cup ketchup
- 2 tbsp. apple cider vinegar
- ¾ cup water
- One tsp. coarsely ground black pepper dash cayenne pepper
- 1 tbsp. chopped and dried chili pepper

Instructions:

1. Grease interior of slow cooker crock
2. Place ribs in the crock. If you need to make a second layer, stagger pieces so they don't directly overlap each other
3. Mix all other ingredients in a bowl
4. Spoon mixture over ribs, making sure that those on the bottom get covered with some sauce, too
5. Cover. Cook for around five to seven hours on low, or on high 3-4 hours or until instant red meat thermometer registers 145-150 degrees Fahrenheit when stuck in center of ribs

Rib and rice bowls

(To serve 8)

Prep. Time: 20-30 minutes

Cooking time: 4-9 hours

Ideal slow cooker size: 6-qt.

Ingredients:

- Leftover rib meat, cut up
- Four servings of rice, cooked according to package directions
  Sauce:
- 2-3 scallions, chopped
- 4 tbsp. Red chili paste
- Two tsp. sugar
- Two tsp. Sesame oil
- Two tsp. Sesame seeds
- Four cloves minced garlic
- 2 tbsp. low-sodium soy sauce
- 2 tbsp. rice vinegar

Instructions:

1. Warm up rib meat and cook rice according to the package directions
2. Mix all the ingredients except the scallions for the sauce. If it becomes too spicy for you, add in some ketchup to cut it down

3. In 4 bowls, divide up the rice. Place a portion of rib meat on top of each. Drizzle the sauce over the top of each bowl. Top with some scallions

4. Add some or other mixed veggies to each bowl to get your veggies in

Week 5

This week's menu

Sunday: Italian Chicken Fajita wraps

Monday: Apple and onion beef pot roast

Tuesday: Italian chicken Quesadillas

Wednesday: Creamy vegetable beef stew

Thursday: Sweet and saucy pork tenderloin

Friday: Chili Rellenos Casserole

Saturday: Pork fried rice

Recommended Side Dish: Boston brown bread

Special Dessert: Pumpkin pie pudding

Italian chicken fajita wraps

(To serve 8)

Prep. Time: 20-30 minutes

Cooking time: 4-9 hours

Ideal slow cooker size: 6-qt.

Ingredients:

- 2 tbsp. sugar
- One tsp. salt

- 3 lbs. Boneless, skinless chicken breasts
- ½ tsp. Celery seeds
- One tsp. Dried thyme
- 2 tbsp. dried parsley
- Four cloves garlic, sliced thinly
- Two tsp. Dried basil
- 4 tbsp. dried oregano
- 10 10-inch-flour tortillas
- One tsp. Freshly ground pepper
- One large onion, sliced in rings
- 2 cups salsa
- Two green bell peppers, sliced in ribs
- 2 16 oz. bottles of Italian salad dressing
- Two red bell peppers, sliced in ribs

Toppings:

- Freshly grated Parmesan cheese
- Chopped fresh basil
- Fresh mozzarella cheese slices
- Chopped olives
- Chopped tomatoes
- Hot sauce or pickled Italian hot peppers
- Lemon wedges
- Shredded lettuces

Instructions:

1. Cut chicken into thin strips. Place in large mixing bowl

2.   Add garlic, salad dressing, herbs, salsa, salt, herbs, sugar, and pepper. Mix. Cover & marinate it for four to eight hours or overnight in your fridge

3.   Pour the chicken & the marinade into your slow cooker. Cook on low for 2-4 hours until chicken is white in the middle & tender

4.   Spoon your chicken together with its sauce into an ovenproof serving dish or a rimmed baking sheet. Later, add in vegetables. Slide it under a broiler for a short time until some browned spots are seen on the chicken & the vegetables

5.   Serve it with tortillas and toppings and lots of napkins

Apple and onion beef pot roast

(To serve 6-7)

Prep. Time: 25 minutes

Cooking time: 4-9 hours

Ideal slow cooker size: 6-qt.

Ingredients:

- 3 lb. boneless beef roast, cut in half
- 2 tbsp. water
- 2 tbsp. cornstarch
- Oil of your choice
- One large sliced onion
- 1 cup water
- One large quartered tart apple
- One tsp. Seasoning salt

- ½ tsp. Worcestershire sauce
- ¼ tsp. Garlic powder
- ½ tsp. Soy sauce

Instructions:

1. Brown the roast on all sides in an oil in skillet. Transfer roast to slow cooker
2. Add water to skillet. Stir with wooden spoon to loosen browned bits
3. Sprinkle with seasoning salt, Worcestershire sauce, soy sauce and garlic powder.
4. Top with apple and onion
5. Cover. Cook on low 5-6 hours
6. Remove roast, onion and apple pieces. Let stand for 15 minutes
7. To make gravy, put the juices from the roast into a saucepan and then simmer until it is reduced to 2 cups
8. Mix cornstarch and water until smooth in small bowl
9. Stir into the broth. Bring to boil. Cook and then stir for 2 minutes, or until thickened
10. Slice pot roast and serve with gravy

Italian Chicken Quesadillas

(To serve 4-8)

Prep. Time: 25 minutes

Cooking time: 4-9 hours

Ideal slow cooker size: 5-qt.

Ingredients:

- 8 oz. shredded cheddar cheese
- 10-12 10 inch flour tortillas
- Leftover chicken

Toppings:

- Salsa
- Sour cream
- Chopped onion
- Guacamole
- Chopped green or black olives
- Diced tomatoes
- Diced cucumbers
- Shredded lettuce

Instructions:

1. Warm the leftover chicken
2. In the skillet or on a griddle, place a tortilla and then add some chicken and any other toppings of your choice. Finish with more cheese so the two sides stick together and top with another tortilla
3. Flip the quesadilla when the first side is barely toasted. Cook on the second side until all the cheese is melted
4. Serve with any additional toppings you choose
5. Creamy vegetable beef stew

Creamy vegetable beef stew

(To serve 6-8)

Prep. Time: 20 minutes

Cooking time: 5-7 hours

Ideal slow cooker size: 4-qt.

Ingredients:

- 2-3 cups leftover shredded pot roast
- 4 cups tomato juice
- Two tsp. salt
- ½ cup chopped onion
- 4 cups tomato juice
- ½ tsp. dried basil
- 1 cup diced potatoes
- ¼ tsp. pepper
- 1 cup diced tomatoes
- White sauce:
- 1 1/3 cups milk
- 2 tbsp. butter
- 2 tbsp. flour

Instructions:

1. Place tomato juice, carrots, basil, onion, pepper, potatoes and salt in slow cooker
2. Cover. Cook on low for 4-6 hours. 1 hour before serving, stir in the leftover pot roast. Then, make white sauce

3.   In a saucepan, melt butter. Whisk in the flour & cook, stirring until flour and butter are bubbly

4.   Pour in milk gradually whisking and whisk until smooth. Stir over low heat until sauce thickens

5.   Pour white sauce into soup, stirring. Cook an additional hour on low.

6.   Sweet and saucy pork Tenderloins

(To serve 8)

Prep. Time: 20-30 minutes

Cooking time: 2-5 hours

Ideal slow cooker size: 3-qt.

Ingredients:

- ½ cup sweet barbecue sauce
- 4-5 lb. pork tenderloin
- 21 oz. can apple pie filling
- Salt and pepper

Instructions:

1.   Place pork tenderloin in the bottom of your crock and sprinkle with salt and pepper

2.   Cover your tenderloin with apple pie filling and pour the barbecue sauce on top of that

3.   Cover & cook for around seven to eight hours on low

Chili Rellenos Casserole

(To serve 8)

Prep. Time: 20-30 minutes

Cooking time: 4-9 hours

Ideal slow cooker size: 6-qt.

Ingredients:

- ¾ shredded Monterey Jack Cheese, divided
- Six eggs, beaten slightly
- 4 oz. can chopped green chilies
- 1 ½ cups low-fat cottage cheese
- ¾ cup shredded cheddar cheese, divided
- 20 buttery crackers, crushed

Instructions:

1. Grease interior of slow cooker crock
2. In a bowl, mix eggs, half the cheddar, cottage cheese, chilies, crackers and Monterey Jack cheese
3. Cover. Cook on high for 1 ¼ hours. Check to see whether the mixture is completely set. If not, cook another 15 minutes and check again
4. Uncover and sprinkle dish with remaining cheese
5. Cook, uncovered until cheese melts
6. Let stand 5 minutes before serving

Pork fried rice

(To serve 7)

Prep. Time: 20-25 minutes

Cooking time: 4-9 hours

Ideal slow cooker size: 7-qt.

Ingredients:

- ½ tsp. salt
- 1 cup leftover pork, diced
- ½ tsp. sesame oil
- 2 tbsp. olive oil, divided
- Two green chopped onions
- Two eggs, beaten
- 2 tbsp. low sodium soy sauce
- 4 cups cooked rice

Instructions:

1. In a wok or a skillet, add ½ tbsp. of the olive oil and warm up the pork. Set it aside in a bowl.
2. Heat another ½ tbsp. of olive oil and scramble the eggs. Place these in a bowl with the pork
3. Heat the rest of your oils and heat up your rice, stirring it around and breaking up any clumps. Do this until it is heated through
4. Add in the green onions and let them heat for a moment
5. Add in the soy sauce and heated pork and scrambled eggs and salt. Stir till everything becomes coated and heated through

Week 6

This week' menu

Sunday: Eye popping ribs

Monday: slow cooker spaghetti sauce

Tuesday: Dawns sausage and peppers

Wednesday: Spicy chili

Thursday: Turkey thighs, Acorn squash, and apples

Friday: Brunswick soup mix

Saturday: Tuna noodle casserole

Recommended Side Dish: Stuffed Acorn squash

Special Dessert: Apple caramel dessert

"Eye-popping" ribs

(To serve 5)

Prep. Time: 20 minutes

Cooking time: 4-9 hours

Ideal slow cooker size: 6-qt.

Ingredients:

- 2 lbs. boneless country ribs
- Brew, or other red wine

- ¼ cup brown sugar
- 2 cups Leelanau Cellars Witches
- Two apples, "eyeballs" cut out with a melon baller
- 1 tbsp. garlic powder
- 1 tbsp. onion powder

Instructions:

1. Place the ribs in the crock
2. Add the brown sugar, onion and garlic powder and top with the apple "eyeballs"
3. Lastly, pour the Witches Brew over the ribs and apple "eyeballs"
4. Cook on low for 8 hours
5. Slow cooker spaghetti sauce

Slow cooker spaghetti sauce

(To serve 6-8)

Prep. Time: 15 minutes

Cooking time: 7 hours

Ideal slow cooker size: 4-qt.

Ingredients:

- Two tsp. Dried basil
- One medium onion, chopped
- ½-1 tsp. dried thyme
- One tsp. salt
- 1 tbsp. brown sugar

- 2 14 oz. cans diced tomatoes, with juice
- Leftover rib meat, shredded or diced
- 1 bay leaf
- Cooked spaghetti
- 6 oz. tomato paste
- Four cloves minced garlic
- 8 oz. can tomato sauce
- Two tsp. Dried oregano

Instructions:

1. Add your ingredients to your slow cooker apart from the rib meat and pasta
2. Cover. Cook on low 7 hours. Before the cooking time ends, add in the leftover rib meat. If the sauce seems too runny, keep the lid off during last hour of cooking
3. Serve over spaghetti

Dawn's sausage and peppers

(To serve 4)

Prep. Time: 10 minutes

Cooking time: 4 hours

Ideal slow cooker size: 2-qt.

Ingredients:

- 3 medium onions, sliced
- 1 sweet red bell pepper, sliced

- 3 lbs. sweet Italian sausage, cut into 3-inch pieces
- 1 sweet yellow bell pepper, sliced
- 1 tsp. salt
- Four cloves minced garlic
- ½ tsp. Crushed red pepper flakes
- 1 tbsp. oil of your choice
- 28 oz. can chopped tomatoes

Instructions:

1. Sauté onions, garlic and onions in oil in skillet. When just softened, place in slow cooker (or skip this step, but check that the vegetables are cooked as per your wish at the end of the 6-hour cooking time)
2. Add tomatoes, salt, and crushed red pepper. Mix well
3. Add sausage pieces
4. Cover. Cook on low for 6 hours
5. Serve o rolls, or over pasta or baked potatoes

Spicy chili

(To serve 3-5)

Prep. Time: 10 minutes

Cooking time: 1-2 hours

Ideal slow cooker size: 3-qt.

Ingredients:

- ½ tsp. salt
- Leftover sausage, cut into bite-sized pieces

- ½ tsp. Dried oregano
- ½ lb. Ground beef
- ½ tsp. sugar
- ¼ tsp. Pepper
- ½ cup chopped onions
- ½ tsp. Worcestershire sauce
- 16 oz. Can tomato juice
- ½ lb. sliced mushroom
- 1 cup salsa
- 6 oz. can tomato paste
- 1/8 cup chopped green bell peppers
- ¼ tsp. dried basil
- 1 lb. ground beef

Instructions:

1. Brown ground beef and onions in skillet. Stir it frequently in order to break up clumps of meat
2. During last 3 minutes of browning, add mushrooms, celery, and green peppers. Continue cooking: then drain off drippings
3. Spoon meat and sautéed vegetables into the cooker. Stir in remaining ingredients except for the leftover sausage
4. Cover. Cook on low 4-6 hours. Before the cooking time ends, add in the leftover sausage

Turkey thighs, acorn squash, and apples

(To serve 8)

Prep. Time: 20-30 minutes

Cooking time: 4-9 hours

Ideal slow cooker size: 6-qt.

Ingredients:

- ½ tsp. ground allspice
- ½ cup apple juice, or cider
- One tsp. Ground cinnamon
- 2 lbs. acorn squash, peeled, seeded & then cut into 1 inch thick rings
- Salt and pepper
- 1 tbsp. apple brandy
- Six medium Granny Smith, or other tart, apples, cored and cut into ½ inch thick rings
- One shallot, or small onion, chopped
- Four turkey thighs, skin and excess fat removed
- 3 tbsp. brown sugar

Instructions:

1. Spray inside of slow cooker with nonstick spray. Layer in squash, followed by apple rings
2. Place the turkey thighs on the top. Sprinkle it with salt, pepper, & onion or shallot
3. In a small bowl, combine apple juice, brown sugar, allspice, brandy, and cinnamon. Pour over turkey
4. Cover. Cook on low for 6-8 hours, or just until turkey and squash are tender

Brunswick soup mix

(To serve 8)

Prep. Time: 25 minutes

Cooking time: 2-3 hours

Ideal slow cooker size: 5-qt.

Ingredients:

- Leftover turkey, chopped up
- ¼ tsp. Worcestershire sauce
- 1 medium chopped onion
- 1/8 cup sugar
- ½ tsp. pepper
- 2 cups frozen, cubed, hash browns, thawed
- 4 cups chicken broth
- 15 ¼ oz. can corn
- 14 ½ oz. can diced tomatoes
- 15 ¼ oz. can lima beans, drained

Instructions:

1. Combine all ingredients except the turkey in large slow cooker
2. Cover. Cook on low 7 hours. The last of cooking, add in leftover turkey
3. Serve when turkey is heated through

Tuna noodle casserole

(To serve 4)

Prep. Time: 20 minutes

Cooking time: 4 hours

Ideal slow cooker size: 4-qt.

Ingredients:

- 1 cup frozen cheese
- 2 ½ cups dry noodles
- ¼ cup almonds
- 1 tsp. salt
- ½ cup shredded Swiss or sharp cheddar cheese
- Half soup can of water
- ½ cup finely chopped onion
- 10 ¾ oz. can cream of mushroom soup
- 6 or 12 oz. can tuna, according to your taste preference

Instructions:

1. Combine all ingredients in slow cooker except peas
2. Cover. Cook for around two to three hours on high, or on low for 4 hours, while stirring occasionally
3. 20 minutes before the cooking time ends, stir in peas & reduce heat to low if cooking on high

Week 7

This week's menu

Sunday: Spanish beef

Monday: Hot Spanish beef and gravy open-faced sandwiches

Tuesday: Cozy Kielbasa

Wednesday: Easy veggie-beef soup

Thursday: Mix it and rub chicken

Friday: Sauerkraut sausage bean soup

Saturday: Scalloped chicken

Recommended Side Dish: Seasoned mashed potatoes

Special Dessert: Easy Autumn cake

Spanish beef

(To serve 6-8)

Prep. Time: 20minutes

Cooking time: 3-9 hours

Ideal slow cooker size: 4-qt.

Ingredients:

- 2 cups of salsa, just as mild or as hot as you like
- 3-4 lb. boneless beef chuck roast

- Two tsp. Seasoning salt
- One tsp. Garlic powder
- Two large onions, thinly sliced
- Four beef bouillon cubes
- 2 4 oz. chopped green chilies, undrained
- 1 tbsp. dry mustard
- Water

Instructions:

1. Combine all your ingredients apart from salsa in the slow cooker. Add just enough water to cover the meat
2. Cover the cooker & cook for around ten to twelve hours on low, or until the beef is tender but not dry. Lift meat out of cooker into the bowl. Reserve liquid in cooker
3. Shred the beef using two forks to pull it apart
4. Combine the beef, salsa and enough of the reserved liquid to have the consistency you want. Save the remaining liquid for making gravy tomorrow
5. Use as filling for burritos, chalupas, quesadillas or tacos

Hot Spanish Beef and Gravy Open-faced Sandwiches

(To serve 8)

Prep. Time: 20-30 minutes

Cooking time: 4-9 hours

Ideal slow cooker size: 6-qt.

Ingredients:

- 1 lb. leftover beef, shredded bread
- Cooking liquid from the Spanish beef
- ¼ tsp. Salt
- ½ tsp. Soy sauce
- Cornstarch or flour
- 1/8 tsp. Pepper
- ¼ tsp. Salt
- ½ tsp. Worcestershire

Instructions:

1. To make the gravy, heat the cooking liquid from the Spanish beef, Worcestershire sauce, soy sauce, salt and pepper in a pot on the stove over medium-low heat

2. When the liquid is simmering, whisk in the cornstarch or flour. Whisk briskly so you don't get chunks, and add only a little at a time. The amount you add will depend on the thickness you desire and the amount of liquid you are working with

3. When your desired thickness is reached, turn the stove off and remove the gravy from the heat

4. Meanwhile, warm the leftover beef

5. To serve, take a piece of bread, place some of the beef, on it and ladle some of the gravy over the top

Cozy Kielbasa

(To serve 4-6)

Prep. Time: 12 minutes

Cooking time: 4 hours

Ideal slow cooker size: 4-qt.

Ingredients:

- 3 lbs. smoked kielbasa
- 3 medium onions, sliced
- 2 cups unsweetened applesauce
- ¼ cup brown sugar

Instructions:

1. Slice kielbasa into ¼ inch slices. Brown in skillet. Stir often to make sure all sides brown. Drain the kielbasa of any drippings
2. Combine applesauce and brown sugar in slow cooker
3. Stir in the kielbasa and onions
4. Cover. Cook on low 4 hours

Easy Veggie-Beef stew

(To serve 8)

Prep. Time: 20 minutes

Cooking time: 4 hours

Ideal slow cooker size: 4-qt.

Ingredients:

- 1 lb. leftover beef
- 2 cups sliced carrots
- 10 ¾ oz. can cream of celery soup
- 1 tbsp. sugar
- 1 lb. frozen green beans, thawed
- 1 tbsp. dried minced onion
- 14 ½ oz. can corn, drained, or 16 oz. bag frozen corn, thawed
- 1 tbsp. sugar
- 3 cups beef, or vegetable, broth
- 3 tsp. instant beef bouillon
- 28 oz. can diced tomatoes
- Two tsp. Worcestershire sauce

Instructions:

1. Add all ingredients except leftover beef and mix well
2. Cook on low 7-8 hours or on high 4 hours. Before the cooking time ends, stir in the leftover beef.
3. Serve once the beef is heated through

Mix it and run chicken

(To serve 4-6)

Prep. Time: 10 minutes

Cooking time: 4-5 hours

Ideal slow cooker size: 3-qt.

Ingredients:

- ½ tsp. salt
- 2 15 oz. cans cut green beans, undrained
- Eight boneless, skinless chicken breast halves
- 2 10 ¾ oz. cans cream of mushroom soup

Instructions:

1. Drain beans, reserving the juice in a medium-sized mixing bowl
2. Stir soups into bean juice, blending thoroughly. Set aside
3. Place the beans in the slow cooker. Sprinkle with salt
4. Place chicken in cooker. Sprinkle with salt
5. Top with soup
6. Cover & cook for around eight to ten hours on low, or until chicken is tender, but not dry or mushy

Sauerkraut sausage bean soup

(To serve 8-10)

Prep. Time: 10 minutes

Cooking time: 2-3 hours

Ideal slow cooker size: 4-qt.

Ingredients:

- Leftover kielbasa, cut into bite-sized pieces
- 3 15 oz. cans white beans, undrained
- ½ cup ketchup
- 16 oz. can sauerkraut, drained and rinsed

Instructions:

1.   Combine all ingredients in slow cooker except the kielbasa

2.   Cover. Cook on high for 2-3 hours. Before the cooking time ends, add in the kielbasa

Scalloped chicken

(To serve 4-6)

Prep. Time: 10 minutes

Cooking time: 2-3 hours

Ideal slow cooker size: 3-qt.

Ingredients:

- 1 cup frozen peas
- 4 cups leftover cooked chicken
- 1 cup water
- 2 eggs
- 1 ½ cups milk
- 1 box stuffing mix for chicken

Instructions:

1.   Combine chicken and dry stuffing mix. Place in slow cooker

2.   Beat eggs, milk, and water together in a bowl. Pour over chicken and stuffing

3.   Cover. Cook on high for around two to three hours

4.   Before the cooking time ends, add in the frozen peas

Week 8

This week's menu

Sunday: Apple corned beef and cabbage

Monday: Autumn harvest loin

Tuesday: Reuben Casserole

Wednesday: Kale and friends soup

Thursday: Cheesy Macaroni's

Friday: Peppercorn roast beef

Saturday: Vegetable and beef borscht

Recommended Side Dish: Dressed up Acorn squash

Special Dessert: Carrot cake

Apple Corned beef and cabbage

(To serve 6-8)

Prep. Time: 15 minutes

Cooking time: 8-10 hours

Ideal slow cooker size: 5-qt.

Ingredients:

- 1 cup brown sugar
- 5 lb. corned beef brisket, cut into 6-8 pieces

- 1 qt. pure apple juice
- 1 small cabbage head cut into thin wedges
- 2-3 cups baby carrots, or sliced full sized carrots
- 3-4 medium potatoes, cut into chunks

Instructions:

1. Place corned beef in slow cooker
2. Place vegetables around and on top of meat
3. Pour apple juice over everything. Sprinkle with brown sugar
4. Cover & cook for around eight to ten hours on low, or until meat and vegetables are tender but not overcooked

Autumn Harvest loin

(To serve 4-6)

Prep. Time: 30 minutes

Cooking time: 4 ½-5 1/2 hours

Ideal slow cooker size: 5-qt.

Ingredients:

- 1/3 cup brown sugar
- 1 ½ whole butternut squash, peeled and cubed
- Salt and pepper
- 3 lb. pork loin
- Two large Granny Smith apples, peeled and quartered
- 1 cup cider or cider juice

- ¼ tsp. Dried sage
- ¼ tsp. Ground cinnamon
- ¼ tsp. Dried thyme

Instructions:

1. Put peeled & cubed squash into your slow cooker. Pour in cider. Cover and cook on low 1 ½ hours

2. Sprinkle the pork loin with salt & pepper on all sides. Settle into slow cooker on top of the squash

3. Lay apple quarters around the meat

4. Sprinkle everything with brown sugar, cinnamon, sage and thyme

5. Cover. Cook on low for 3-4 hours. Place your instant-read thermometer into the loin's center. The meat is ready the minute the thermometer reads 140 degrees Fahrenheit

6. Remove pork from the cooker. Cover with foil to keep warm. Continue cooking the squash and apples if they are not as tender as you like them

7. You can cut the loin into ½ inch thick slices after it has stood 10-15 minutes. Keep covered until ready to serve

8. Serve topped with apples and squash. Pass the cooking juices in a small bowl to spoon over the meat, squash, and apples

Reuben Casserole

(To serve 4)

Prep. Time: 10 minutes

Cooking time: 2-4 hours

Ideal slow cooker size: 2-qt.

Ingredients:

- 4 cups dry packaged stuffing mix, divided
- 2 cups leftover corned beef, chopped up, divide
- ¼ cup thousand island salad dressing, divided
- 15 oz. can sauerkraut, drained, divided
- ½ cup shredded, or 8 slices, Swiss cheese, divided

Instructions:

1. Spray slow cooker with nonstick cooking spray
2. Layer half of each ingredient in the order listed
3. Repeat layers
4. Cover and cook on low 2-4 hours, until casserole is cooked through and cheese has melted

Kale and friends soup

(To serve 6)

Prep. Time: 20 minutes

Cooking time: 8 hours

Ideal slow cooker size: 5 1/2-qt.

Ingredients:

- ½ bunch kale, torn into bite-sized pieces
- ¼ tsp. dried rosemary

- ½ cup diced, leftover cooked pork
- ½ tsp. dried basil
- 15 oz. can cannellini beans, drained and rinsed
- ½ butternut squash, peeled and cubed
- 3-4 cups chicken broth
- Salt and pepper
- ¼ tsp. dried thyme

Instructions:

1. Combine all ingredients in slow cooker
2. Cover & cook for around eight hours on low
3. Taste to correct seasonings. Add more broth if too thick, or you are trying to stretch the soup

Cheesy Macaronis

(To serve 10-12)

Prep. Time: 30 minutes

Cooking time: 3 hours

Ideal slow cooker size: 6-qt.

Ingredients:

- 1 lb. dry macaroni
- 2 lbs. Velveeta cheese, cubed or sharp cheese, shredded
- 12 oz. can evaporated milk
- 3 cups milk

Instructions:

1. Cook macaroni according to package directions. Drain

2. Put both kinds of milk in the slow cooker. Add cheese to milk

3. Stir in cooked macaroni

4. Cover & cook for around three hours on low

Peppercorn Roast Beef

(To serve 6-8)

Prep. Time: 10-15 minutes

Cooking time: 8-10 hours

Ideal slow cooker size: 4-qt.

Ingredients:

- 3-4 lb. chuck roast
- 2 cups water
- 1 tsp. garlic powder
- 3-4 peppercorns
- ½ cup soy sauce
- 1 bay leaf

Optional ingredients:

- ½ cup flour
- 1 tsp. thyme
- ½ cup water

Instructions:

1.   Place roast in slow cooker
2.   In a mixing bowl, combine all other ingredients and pour over roast
3.   Cover and cook on low for 8-10 hours
4.   Remove your meat to a platter & let it rest before slicing or shredding

Vegetable beef borscht

(To serve 8)

Prep. Time: 20-30 minutes

Cooking time: 4-9 hours

Ideal slow cooker size: 6-qt.

Ingredients:

- ½ tsp. pepper
- Half a small head of cabbage, sliced thin
- Two tsp. salt
- 1 large diced onion
- 2 cups tomato juice
- Water
- 1 cup corn
- Four sliced carrots
- ¼ tsp. garlic powder
- 2 cups beef broth
- ¼ tsp. dill seed
- Leftover roast beef, cut into bite-sized pieces or shredded
- 1 cup green beans

- Sour cream
- 3 medium diced potatoes
- 1 cup diced tomatoes

Instructions:

1. Grease interior of slow cooker crock
2. Mix all ingredients except water, sour cream, and leftover roast beef. Add water to fill slow cooker three-quarters full
3. Cover. Cook for around six to eight hours on low, or until vegetables are as soft as you like them. The last hour of cooking add the leftover roast beef.
4. Pass sour cream around the table so individuals can add a dollop to their bowels if they wish.

Week 9

This week's menu

Sunday: French chicken

Monday: Chicken cordon bleu casserole

Tuesday: Losta beans chili

Wednesday: Seven layer casserole

Thursday: Apple cider sausage

Friday: Sweet pepper Burritos

Saturday: Ruth's split pea soup

Recommended Side Dish: Green bean tomato sauté

Special Dessert: Raisin nut stuffed apples

French chicken

(To serve 6)

Prep. Time: 5 minutes

Cooking time: 5 hours

Ideal slow cooker size: 6-qt.

Ingredients:

- 1 tsp. dried basil
- 1 ½ tsp. salt
- 1 lb. baby carrots
- Two ribs sliced celery
- 4 lbs. skinless, bone-in chicken thighs
- Two medium sliced onions
- Four cloves peeled garlic
- ½ cup white cooking wine, or chicken stock
- ½ tsp. Black pepper
- 2 Tbsp. Chopped fresh parsley
- ½ tsp. Dried marjoram

Instructions:

1. Place carrots, onions, celery, and garlic in bottom of slow cooker.
2. Lay chicken thighs on top. Pour wine or broth over chicken.
3. Sprinkle with salt, pepper, basil, and marjoram.
4. Cover. Cook on slow 4 ½-5 ½ hours, until chicken registers 165 degrees Fahrenheit on thermometer and carrots are tender.
5. Sprinkle with fresh parsley before serving.

Chicken Cordon Bleu Casserole

(To serve 5)

Prep. Time: 20 minutes

Cooking time: 5-6 hours

Ideal slow cooker size: 5-qt.

Ingredients:

Fillings:

- 1 lb. chipped ham
- 1 small chopped onion
- 8 cups cubed bread
- ¼ tsp. pepper
- 3 Tbsp. butter
- ½ tsp. salt
- 1 ½ cups diced celery
- 1 ¾ cups milk
- 3 Tbsp. butter
- 2-3 cups cooked, diced leftover chicken
- 10 ¾ oz. can cream of chicken soup
- ½ lb. grated Swiss cheese
- ½ cup milk

Instructions:

1. Prepare filling by sautéing celery and onion in butter in saucepan until soft
2. Place cubed bread in large mixing bowl

3. Pour sautéed vegetables, eggs, 1 ¾ cups milk, salt and pepper over bread
4. Grease 2 9 by 13-inch baking pans
5. Layer half of ham, cheese and filling into each pan
6. Layer half of chicken into each pan, distributing evenly over top of filling mixture
7. In a mixing bowl, blend soup and ½ cup milk together
8. Pour soup mixture over top of chicken
9. Bake it at a temperature of 350° F for one hour

Losta beans chili

(To serve 5)

Prep. Time: 20 minutes

Cooking time: 5-6 hours

Ideal slow cooker size: 5-qt.

Ingredients:

- 2 15 oz. cans green beans, drained
- 2 lbs. ground beef
- ½ cup sugar
- 1 ½ lbs. Diced bacon
- ½ tsp. salt
- 1 ½ cup chopped onion
- ½ cup ketchup
- ½ tsp. pepper
- Two tsp. Dry mustard

- ½ cup brown sugar
- 2 16 oz. cans kidney beans, rinsed and drained
- 2 14 ½ oz. cans baked beans
- 2 15 oz. cans drained butter beans

Instructions:

1. Brown ground beef and bacon in the skillet. Drain. Reserve 1 lb. of the browned beef in the refrigerator
2. Combine all ingredients in slow cooker
3. Cover. Cook on high 1 hour. Reduce heat to low and cook 8-9 hours

Seven-Layer Casserole

(To serve 5)

Prep. Time: 20 minutes

Cooking time: 5-6 hours

Ideal slow cooker size: 5-qt.

Ingredients:

- 6-8 slices lean bacon
- ½ cup uncooked rice
- 1/8-1/4 tsp. pepper, as you like
- 12 oz. can whole kernel corn, undrained
- ½ tsp. salt
- ¼ cup chopped onion
- 8 oz. can tomato sauce, divided
- ¼ cup chopped green bell pepper

- ½ cup water, divided
- 1 lbs. leftover browned ground beef

Instructions:

1. Grease your slow cooker well. Spread uncooked rice over the bottom of your cooker. Spoon the corn over top of the rice, including the juice from the corn
2. In a bowl, mix one can of tomato sauce with ½ cup water. Spoon over the corn. Sprinkle with the onion and green pepper
3. Place the browned ground beef over the vegetables
4. Combine the remaining can of tomato sauce with ½ cup water. Stir in the salt and pepper. Spoon over the meat
5. Cut the bacon slices into fourths and arrange over top
6. Cover. Cook on low 4-6 hours, or until the vegetables are as tender as you like them. Uncover the cooker during the last 15 minute so that the bacon gets a bit crispy

Apple cider sausage

(To serve 3-4)

Prep. Time: 20 minutes

Cooking time: 1 hour

Ideal slow cooker size: 5-qt.

Ingredients:

- 10 sweet Italian sausage links

- Hot dog buns
- Two apples, peeled and cut into wedges
- 1 tsp. maple syrup
- ¾ cup apple cider
- 1 red onion, quartered

Instructions:

1. Place the sausage links in the crock
2. Add in the apples and onions, then pour the apple cider and maple syrup over the top
3. Cover & cook for around six hours on low
4. Serve in hot dog buns

Sweet Pepper Burritos

(To serve 5)

Prep. Time: 20 minutes

Cooking time: 2-3 hours

Ideal slow cooker size: 5-qt.

Ingredients:

- Salsa, just as mild or hot as you wish
- ¾ cup uncooked brown rice
- 1 ½ cups cheddar cheese, shredded
- 1 medium sweet green bell pepper, diced
- 3 oz. Pkg. Cream cheese, cubed
- 1 ¼ cups water
- Six whole wheat tortillas, about 6 inches in diameter

- ½ tsp. Black pepper
- 1 medium sweet red bell pepper, diced
- 1 medium chopped onion
- 1 medium sweet yellow bell pepper, diced
- Two tsp. Ground cumin

Instructions:

1. Grease interior of slow-cooker crock
2. Place raw brown rice, water, black pepper, onion and cumin in the crock. Stir until well mixed
3. Cover. Cook for around 1 ¾ hours on high, or until rice is nearly tender
4. Stir in diced sweet bell peppers at the end of cooking time, along with cheddar cheeses
5. Cover. Continue cooking on high 30 minutes more or until rice and peppers are as tender as you like them
6. Spoon 2/3 cup rice-pepper-cheese mixture onto lower half of each tortilla. Fold in the sides. Then bring up the bottom & roll it up
7. Place each burrito, seam side down, in greased 9 by 13-inch baking pan
8. Cover. Bake at 425 degrees Fahrenheit 10-15 minutes
9. Let stand 4 minutes. Serve with salsa if you wish

Ruth's split pea soup

(To serve 5)

Prep. Time: 20 minutes

Cooking time: 5-6 hours

Ideal slow cooker size: 5-qt.

Ingredients:

- 1 bag dry split peas
- ½ tsp. pepper
- 6 cups water
- Leftover Italian sausage, cut into bite-sized pieces
- Two medium diced potatoes
- ½ tsp. Dried marjoram, or thyme
- 1 medium chopped onion

Instructions:

1. Wash and sort dried peas, removing any stones. Then combine all ingredients except the sausage in slow cooker

2. Cover. Cook for around twelve hours on low, or high for 6 hours. The last hour of cooking, add in the Italian sausage

Week 10

This week's menu

Sunday: Easy and elegant ham

Monday: Schnitz und knepp

Tuesday: Ham and broccoli

Wednesday: Pasta bean pot

Thursday: Turkey slow cooker

Friday: Turkey Cacciatore

Saturday: Turkey frame soup

Recommended Side Dish: Old-fashioned stuffing

Special Dessert: Slow-cooker pumpkin

Easy and elegant ham

(To serve 5)

Prep. Time: 20 minutes

Cooking time: 3-6 hours

Ideal slow cooker size: 5-qt.

Ingredients:

- 2 20 oz. cans sliced pineapple, divided
- 6 lb. fully cooked boneless ham, halved

- 12 oz. jar orange marmalade
- 6 oz. jar maraschino cherries, well drained

Instructions:

1. Drain pineapple, reserving juice. Set juice aside
2. Place half of pineapple in ungreased slow cooker
3. Top with ham. Add cherries, remaining pineapple and reserved juice
4. Spoon marmalade over ham
5. Cover. Cook for around six to seven hours or until heated through. Remove to serving platter and let stand for 10-15 minutes before slicing
6. Serve pineapple and cherries over sliced ham

Schnitz und Knepp

(To serve 5)

Prep. Time: 20 minutes

Cooking time: 1-2 hours

Ideal slow cooker size: 5-qt.

Ingredients:

Schnitz:

- 3/4 -1 lb. dried sweet apples
- 1 cinnamon stick
- 3 lbs. ham slices, cut into 2-inch cubes, from leftovers
- 2 tbsp. brown sugar

Knepp (dumplings)

- 4 tsp. Baking powder
- ¼ tsp. pepper
- 2 cups flour
- 1 egg, well beaten
- 1 tsp. salt
- 3 tbsp. melted butter
- Scant ½ cup milk

Instructions:

1. Cover apples with water in a large bowl and let soak for a few hours
2. Place ham cubes in slow cooker. Cover with water
3. Cover cooker. Cook on high 2 hours
4. Add in apples & water in which they have been soaking
5. Add brown sugar and cinnamon stick. Mix until sugar dissolves
6. Cover. Cook on low 3 hours
7. Combine dumpling ingredients in a bowl. Drop into hot liquid in cooker by tablespoonfuls
8. Turn cooker to high. Cover. Do not lift lid for 15 minutes
9. Serve piping hot on a large platter

Ham and Broccoli

Makes 6—8 servings

Prep. Time: 20 minutes

Cooking Time: 3¼—4¼ hours

Ideal slow-cooker size: 5-qt.

Ingredients:

- ¾ lb. Fresh broccoli, chopped, or 10-oz. Pkg. Frozen chopped broccoli
- 10¾-oz. can cream of mushroom soup
- 8-oz. jar cheese sauce
- 2 ½ cups milk
- 1¼ cups uncooked long-grain rice
- 1 rib celery, sliced
- 1/8 tsp. pepper
- 3 cups leftover cooked ham, cubed
- 8-oz. can water chestnuts, drained and sliced
- ½ tsp. paprika

Instructions:

1. Combine all ingredients except ham, water chestnuts, and paprika in slow cooker
2. Cover. Cook on High 3—4 hours
3. Stir in ham and water chestnuts. Cook 15—20 minutes, or until heated through. Let stand lo minutes before serving
4. Sprinkle with paprika just before serving.

Pasta Bean Pot

Makes 4—6 servings

Prep. Time: 10—15 minutes

Cooking Time: 4—5 hours

Ideal slow-cooker size: 4-qt.

Ingredients:

- ½ Tbsp. olive oil
- ½ medium onion, chopped
- 1 garlic clove, minced
- ½ tsp. vinegar of your choice
- 4 oz. uncooked elbow macaroni
- 14-oz. can stewed, or diced, tomatoes
- ½ of a 12-oz. can cannellini beans, undrained
- ½ of a 12-oz. can kidney beans, undrained
- 6 oz. chicken broth
- ½ tsp. dried oregano
- ½ tsp. dried parsley
- Dash red pepper

Instructions:

1. Put all ingredients in slow cooker. Mix well.
2. Cover. Cook for around four to five hours on Low, or until macaroni are tender but not mushy.

Turkey Slow Cooker

Makes 10—12 servings

Prep. Time: 5 minutes

Cooking Time: 8 hours

Ideal slow-cooker size: 7-qt.

Ingredients:

- 6-lb. turkey breast
- 1 envelope dry onion soup mix
- 16-oz. can whole berry cranberry sauce

Instructions:

1. Place turkey in slow cooker.
2. Combine soup mix and cranberry sauce in the bowl. Spread over turkey.
3. Cover. Cook on Low 8 hours.

Turkey Cacciatore

Makes six servings

Prep. Time: 20 minutes

Cooking Time: 4 hours

Ideal slow-cooker size: 4-qt.

Ingredients

- 2½ cups cut-up leftover cooked turkey
- 1 tsp. salt
- Dash of pepper
- 1 Tbsp. Dried onion flakes
- 1 green bell pepper, it should be seeded & finely chopped
- One clove garlic, finely chopped

- 15-oz. can whole tomatoes, mashed
- 4-oz. can sliced mushrooms, drained
- Two tsp. Tomato paste
- 1 bay leaf
- ¼ tsp. dried thyme
- 2 Tbsp. Finely chopped pimento

Procedure:

1. Combine all ingredients well in slow cooker
2. Cover. Cook on Low 4 hours.
3. Suggestion: Serve over rice or pasta. Or drain off the most liquid and serve in taco shells.

Turkey Frame Soup

Makes six servings

Prep. Time: 40 minutes

Cooking Time: 3¼—4½ hours

Ideal slow-cooker size: 6-qt.

Ingredients:

- 2 cups cooked leftover turkey, diced
- Two qts. Turkey broth
- 1 medium onion, diced
- ½-¾ tsp. salt, or to taste
- 8-oz. can chopped tomatoes
- 1 Tbsp. Chicken bouillon granules
- 1 tsp. dried thyme

- ¼ tsp. pepper
- 1½ tsp. dried oregano
- 3 cups chopped fresh vegetables (any combination of sliced celery, carrots, onions, rutabaga, broccoli, cauliflower, mushrooms, and more)
- 1½ cups uncooked noodles

Procedure:

1. Place turkey, broth, onion, salt, tomatoes, bouillon granules, thyme, pepper, oregano, and vegetables into slow cooker. Stir.
2. Cover. Cook on Low heat for around three to four hours or until vegetables are nearly ready.
3. About 15 to 30 minutes before serving time, stir in noodles and cover. Cook on Low heat. If noodles are thin and small, they'll cook in 15 minutes or less. If heavier, they may need 30 minutes to become tender.
4. Stir well before serving.

Week 11

This week's menu

Sunday: Butter and Sage Cornish hens

Monday: Chicken corn soup

Tuesday: Zucchini Torte

Wednesday: Dilled Pot Roast

Thursday: Spicy, scrumptious sausage

Friday: Chorizo and beef enchilada casserole

Saturday: Sausage Tortellini

Recommended Side Dish: Potato cheese puff

Special Dessert: Apple caramel pie

Butter and Sage Cornish Hens

(To serve 4-6)

Prep. Time: 10 minutes

Cooking time: 7-9 hours

Ideal slow cooker size: 6-7 qt.

Ingredients:

- 2-4 Tbsp. olive oil
- Salt and pepper, to taste

- 4-6 Cornish game hens
- ½-1 cup white wine, or chicken broth
- 4-8 Tbsp. butter, cut into pieces
- 2-4 Tbsp. olive oil
- Garlic powder and sage, to taste

Instructions:

1. 'Warm the olive oil in a skillet.
2. In the meantime, salt & pepper all sides of the Cornish hens.
3. Place the Cornish hens. Breasts down in the skillet and brown them a bit. Turn and brown the underside as well.
4. Pour your wine or chicken broth into your crock's bottom, and then place the hens in the crock as well.
5. Season them with the sage and garlic powder. Place the pieces of butter on top of your Cornish hens as well.
6. Cover & cook for around seven to eight hours on Low.

Chicken Corn Soup

(To serve 4-6)

Prep. Time: 15 minutes

Cooking time: 8-9 hours

Ideal slow cooker size: 4-qt.

Ingredients:

- 1 medium onion, chopped
- 1 garlic clove, minced
- Two carrots, sliced
- Two ribs celery, chopped
- ¼ tsp. pepper
- Two medium potatoes, cubed
- 1 tsp. mixed dried herbs
- 1/3 cup tomato sauce
- 12-oz. can cream-style corn
- 14-oz. can whole kernel corn
- 3 cups chicken stock
- Leftover diced Cornish hen meat
- ¼ cup chopped fresh Italian parsley
- 1 tsp. salt

Procedure:

1.   Combine your ingredients apart from parsley, salt, & pepper in your slow cooker.
2.   Cover. Cook for around eight to nine hours on Low, or until chicken is tender.
3.   Add parsley & seasonings thirty minutes before you serve.

Zucchini Torte

(To serve 8)

Prep. Time: 25minutes

Cooking time: 4-5 hours

Ideal slow cooker size: 4-qt.

Ingredients:

- 5 cups diced zucchini
- 1 cup grated carrots
- 1 small onion, diced finely
- 1½ cups biscuit baking mix
- ½ cup grated Parmesan cheese
- 4 eggs, beaten
- ¼ cup olive oil
- Two tsp. Dried marjoram
- ½ tsp. salt
- Pepper, to taste

Instructions:

1. Grease interior of slow-cooker crock.
2. Mix all ingredients. Pour into greased slow cooker.
3. Cover & cook for around four to five hours on Low, until set. Remove lid last 30 minutes to allow excess moisture to evaporate.
4. Serve hot or at room temperature.

Dilled Pot Roast

(To serve 6)

Prep. Time: 5 minutes

Cooking time: 7 ¼-9 1/4 hours

Ideal slow cooker size: 4-5 qt.

Ingredients:

- 3-3½-lb. beef pot roast
- 1 tsp. salt
- ¼ tsp. pepper
- Two tsp. Dried dill weed, divided
- ¼ cup water
- 1 Tbsp. Vinegar of your choice
- 3 Tbsp. flour
- ½ cup water
- 1 cup sour cream

Procedure:

1. Sprinkle the meat with the pepper, one tsp. Dill, & salt on all sides. Place in slow cooker. Add water and vinegar.
2. Cover. Cook for around seven to nine hours on Low, or until tender. Remove meat from pot. Turn to High.
3. Dissolve flour in water. Stir into meat drippings. Stir in additional 1 tsp. dill. Cook on High 5 minutes. Stir in sour cream. Cook on High another 5 minutes.

Spicy Scrumptious Sausage

(To serve 8)

Prep. Time: 5 minutes

Cooking time: 6 hours

Ideal slow cooker size: 4-qt.

Ingredients:

- Eight spicy Italian sausage links
- 16-oz. can red kidney beans, drained, rinsed
- 16-oz. can chili beans
- 4-oz. can mild or hot diced green chilies
- 14-oz. can diced tomatoes
- 1 medium onion, chopped
- 1 tsp. salt
- ¼ tsp. pepper
- Long-grain rice

Instructions:

1. Place all ingredients into the crock except the rice.
2. Cook on Low for 6 hours.
3. Serve over cooked rice.

Chorizo and Beef Enchilada Casserole

(To serve 8)

Prep. Time: 10 minutes

Cooking time: 4-6 hours

Ideal slow cooker size: 6-qt.

Ingredients:

- 9 small flour tortillas
- 2 cups leftover pot roast
- 1 medium onion, chopped

- 2 cups diced fresh tomato
- 12 oz. chorizo, browned
- 10-oz. can mild red enchilada sauce
- 2 cups shredded Mexican-blend cheese
- 10-oz. can mild green enchilada sauce

Instructions:

1. Spray your crock liberally with nonstick spray.
2. Place 3 tortillas into the bottom of your crock. You may need to cut them to make them fit.
3. Layer in half of the pot roast, half of the onions, half of the chorizo, & half of the tomatoes. Pour half of red enchilada sauce over the top. Top it with ½ a cup of the shredded cheese.
4. Repeat this whole procedure once again, then top it with a new layer of tortillas, the whole can of green enchilada sauce, & the remaining cup of shredded cheese.
5. Cover and cook on Low for 4—6 hours.

Sausage Tortellini

(To serve 8)

Prep. Time: 25-30 minutes

Cooking time: 1 ½-2 ½ hours

Ideal slow cooker size: 6-qt.

Ingredients:

- Leftover sausage
- 1 cup chopped onions
- Two cloves garlic, minced
- 5 cups beef or chicken broth
- ¾ cup water
- ¾ cup red wine
- 2 14¾-oz. cans diced tomatoes, undrained
- 1 cup thinly sliced carrots
- ¾ tsp. dried basil
- ¾ tsp. dried oregano
- 16-oz. Pkg. tortellini
- 3 Tbsp. Chopped fresh parsley
- 16-oz. can tomato sauce
- ¾ cup sliced zucchini, optional

Instructions:

1. Add leftover sausage, onions, garlic, broth, water, wine, tomatoes, carrots, basil, oregano, and tomato sauce to crock. Stir together well.
2. Add zucchini if you wish, and tortellini.
3. Cover and Cook on High for 1½-2½ hours or until pasta is as tender as you like it, but not mushy.
4. Stir in parsley and serve.

Week 12

This week's menu

Sunday: Balsamic glazed pork ribs

Monday: Enchilada Quinoa Casserole

Tuesday: Easy ranch chicken

Wednesday: White chicken chili

Thursday: Coney dogs

Friday: Pasta a la Carbonara

Saturday: Coney fries

Recommended Side Dish: Baked stuffed tomatoes

Special Dessert: Bay pound cake

Balsamic-Glazed Pork Ribs

(To serve 6-8)

Prep. Time: 30 minutes

Cooking time: 4-6 hours

Standing time: 2-12 hours

Ideal slow cooker size: 6-qt.

Ingredients:

- 2 Tbsp. Olive oil
- ½ tsp. dried rosemary
- 1 Tbsp. Kosher salt
- 1 Tbsp. Fennel seeds
- 1 tsp. freshly ground pepper
- ½ tsp. dried sage
- ¼ tsp. dried thyme
- 1 tsp. paprika
- Pinch—1 tsp. Crushed red pepper, according to your preferred heat
- ½ tsp. ground coriander
- ¼ tsp. ground allspice
- 3 lbs. pork ribs
- 3 Tbsp. Balsamic vinegar

Instructions:

1. In a small-sized bowl, mix olive oil, rosemary, salt, fennel seeds, pepper, sage, thyme, paprika, red pepper, coriander, and allspice.
2. Rub spice paste over the ribs & let it stand at room temperature for two hours, or refrigerate overnight.
3. Place ribs in slow cooker, cutting if needed to fit.
4. Cook on Low for 4—6 hours, until tender.
5. Remove the ribs from your slow cooker & place them on a rimmed baking sheet. Preheat the broiler. Smear the meaty side of the ribs with balsamic vinegar & broil 6 inches from heat until browned, for about two minutes.
6. Let it stand for five minutes, then cut between ribs, or serve in slabs.

Enchilada Quinoa Casserole

(To serve 4-6)

Prep. Time: 5 minutes

Cooking time: 4 hours

Ideal slow cooker size: 3-qt.

Ingredients:

- 30 oz. red enchilada sauce, divided
- 15-oz. can black beans, drained and rinsed
- 15-OZ. can corn, drained
- 14-oz. can diced tomatoes with
- 1 tsp. salt
- Green chilies
- 1 cup uncooked quinoa
- Leftover pork, chopped into bite-sized pieces
- 4 oz. cottage cheese (blended until smooth)
- 1 cup shredded Mexican-blend cheese

Optional Toppings:

- 1/8 tsp. pepper
- Avocado
- Chopped fresh cilantro
- Sour cream
- Diced tomatoes

Instructions:

1. Add half of the enchilada sauce, the beans, corn, diced tomatoes, quinoa, pork, blended cottage cheese, salt, and pepper to a greased slow cooker and stir.
2. Pour the remaining enchilada sauce over the top. Top with the shredded cheese.
3. Cover & cook for around four hours on Low.
4. Serve with any of the optional toppings your desire.

Easy Ranch Chicken

(To serve 8)

Prep. Time: 5 minutes

Cooking time: 6-7 hours

Ideal slow cooker size: 4-qt.

Ingredients:

- One medium onion, it should be cut in half & then sliced into half rings
- 3 lb. frozen boneless, skinless chicken breasts
- 1 pkg. dry ranch dressing mix
- 1½ cups warm water

Procedure:

1. Place the onion into the slow cooker, put the chicken on top, then sprinkle with the ranch dressing.
2. Pour the cup of warm water over the top, being careful not to wash off the dressing.
3. Cook on Low for 6—7 hours.

White Chicken Chili

(To serve 4)

Prep. Time: 10 minutes

Cooking time: 7-9 hours

Ideal slow cooker size: 4-6-qt.

Ingredients:

- 1 cup dry navy beans
- 4 cups water
- ½ cup chicken broth
- 16-oz. jar salsa
- 1 large onion, chopped
- 1 Tbsp. Ground cumin
- ½ tsp. salt
- ½ tsp. pepper
- 8 oz. pepper jack cheese, cut into chunks
- 8 oz. Monterey Jack cheese, cut into chunks
- Leftover chicken, chopped into bite-sized pieces
- Tortilla chips, optional

Instructions:

1. Soak navy beans in a large-sized bowl or pot overnight. Make sure to cover them with about 4 inches of water. During the morning, drain & rinse the beans.

2.   Put the beans & four cups of water into your slow cooker. Add in the chicken broth, salsa, onion, cumin, salt, and pepper to crock pot. Stir.

3.   Cook on Low for 6—8 hours.

4.   The last hour, add the chicken Monterey Jack and pepper jack cheese and stir.

5.   Switch your slow cooker to High for an hour.

6.   Stir & serve with the crushed tortilla chips on top or on the side if you wish.

Coney Dogs

(To serve 8-10)

Prep. Time: 30 minutes

Cooking time: 3 hours

Ideal slow cooker size: 4-qt.

Ingredients:

- 2 lbs. ground beef
- 2 cups diced onions
- Two cloves garlic, crushed
- 2 lbs. hot dogs or fresh or smoked
- Sausage, cut into 5-inch lengths
- 2 Tbsp. Chili powder
- 1½ Tbsp. prepared mustard
- 16-oz. can tomato sauce
- ¾ cup water
- Hot dog rolls

Instructions:

1. Grease interior of slow-cooker crock.
2. If you have time, brown beef, onion, and garlic together in a skillet.
3. When browned, place in crock.
4. If you're using fresh sausage, brown in drippings in skillet. Place in the crock.
5. Stir chili powder, mustard, tomato sauce, and water into meat in crock. Mix well.
6. Cover. Cook on Low for 2 hours.
7. Stir in hot dogs or fresh sausage. Cook on Low for another hour, uncovered so the sauce can reduce.
8. Serve in rolls.

Pasta à la Carbonara

(To serve 5)

Prep. Time: 10 minutes

Cooking time: 8 hours

Ideal slow cooker size: 4-6-qt.

Ingredients:

- 1 pkg. thick-cut bacon, sliced into bite-sized pieces
- 1 chicken bouillon cube
- Two tsp. Garlic powder
- 1 tsp. (or less depending on the level of heat you prefer) crushed red pepper flakes
- 1 lb. rotini pasta

- ¼ cup of pasta water (the water you cook the pasta in)
- Two egg yolks
- ½ tsp. pepper
- ¼ cup grated Parmesan cheese
- ½ cup flat-leaf parsley, chopped

Instructions:

1. Place the cut-up bacon in the bottom of your crock. Try to separate it as much as you can so the pieces are not all completely stuck together. Cover & cook for around seven hours on Low.

2. The last 30—45 minutes of the cooking time, turn the slow cooker up to High & add your bouillon cube, crushed red pepper flakes, & garlic powder. Give it a stir.

3. Cook your pasta according to the package instructions. When your pasta is done, reserve ¼ cup of water.

4. In a bowl, mix the egg yolks, pepper, and Parmesan cheese. Next, whisk in the ¼ cup pasta water to temper your egg yolks.

5. Pour your pasta into the slow cooker, pour the egg/Parmesan mixture over the top, and toss in the parsley. Mix all together.

Coney Fries

(To serve 6)

Prep. Time: 10 minutes

Cooking time: 30 minutes

Ingredients:

- 30-oz. bag of frozen fries (whatever cut/style you like)
- Leftover chili
- 2—4 cups shredded cheese, your choice of flavor
- Six slices bacon, cooked and chopped
- Two green onions, chopped

Instructions:

1. Cook the fries according to the package instructions.
2. Meanwhile, warm the leftover chili.
3. When the fries are cooked, top them with the chili and shredded cheese. Place them in a 400°F oven for 10—15 minutes, or until the cheese is all melted.
4. Top them with the bacon pieces and green onions.

Week 13

This week's menu

Sunday: Sausage breakfast casserole

Monday: Tarragon chicken

Tuesday: Italian wedding soup

Wednesday: BBQ meatloaf

Thursday: Turkey slow cooker

Friday: Chicken Alfredo

Saturday: BBQ burgers

Recommended Side Dish: Polenta in a crock

Special Dessert: Chocolate nut clusters from the crock

Sausage Breakfast Casserole

(To serve 8-10)

Prep. Time: 6 minutes

Cooking time: 4-8 hours

Ideal slow cooker size: 6-qt.

Ingredients:

- 32-oz. pkg. Frozen shredded hash brown potatoes
- 1 lb. bulk sausage, cooked and drained

- 2 cups shredded cheese of your choice
- 14-oz. can diced tomatoes, drained
- Six green onions, sliced
- ¼ cup diced red bell pepper
- 12 eggs
- ½ cup milk
- ½ tsp. salt
- ¼ tsp. ground black pepper

Instructions:

1. Place half of the potatoes in lightly greased slow cooker. Top with half the sausage, half the cheese, half the tomatoes, half the green onions and half the bell pepper.
2. Repeat layers.
3. Beat eggs, milk, pepper, and salt in a mixing bowl until well combined.
4. Pour evenly over potato-sausage mixture.
5. Cover & cook for around six to eight hours on Low or on High for 4 hours, until eggs have set and casserole is firm in the middle.

Tarragon Chicken

(To serve 6)

Prep. Time: 15-20 minutes

Cooking time: 4 hours

Ideal slow cooker size: 5-qt.

Ingredients:

- Eight boneless, skinless chicken thighs
- ¾ tsp. salt, divided
- ½ tsp. black pepper, coarsely ground
- 1 tsp. dried tarragon
- 2 Tbsp. Chopped onion
- ½ cup dry white wine
- 2 Tbsp. butter
- 2 Tbsp. flour
- 1 cup heavy cream
- 1 Tbsp. Chopped fresh tarragon

Instructions:

1. Grease interior of slow-cooker crock.
2. Place thighs in cooker. If you need to create a second layer, stagger the pieces so they don't directly overlap each other.
3. In a small bowl, mix ½ tsp. Salt, pepper, dried tarragon, chopped onion, and wine.
4. Spoon over thighs, making sure to top those on both levels with the sauce.
5. Cover. Cook for around four hours on Low, or until instant-read meat thermometer registers 160—165°F when stuck in the thighs.
6. Close to end of cooking time, melt butter in the skillet or small saucepan with the cooking juices. Blend in flour and 1/4 tsp. salt. Cook while stirring continuously over heat for 1—2 minutes to take the raw flour taste away.

7.   Gradually pour in cream, constantly stirring over medium heat until sauce thickens.

8.   To serve, place thighs on the platter. Spoon the sauce over. Sprinkle with chopped fresh tarragon leaves.

Italian Wedding Soup

(To serve 6)

Prep. Time: 30 minutes

Cooking time: 3-7 hours

Ideal slow cooker size: 3-4-qt.

Ingredients:

- 2 eggs
- ½ cup bread crumbs
- ¼ cup chopped fresh parsley
- 2 Tbsp. Grated Parmesan cheese
- 3 cloves garlic, minced
- ¼ tsp. red pepper flakes
- ½ lb. ground beef or turkey
- ½ lb. spicy pork sausage, casings removed
- 2 32-oz. cartons chicken broth
- Salt and pepper, to taste
- 2/3 cup uncooked pasta

Instructions:

1.   cup chopped fresh spinach

2. Mix eggs, breadcrumbs, parsley, Parmesan, garlic, red pepper flakes, ground meat, and sausage.
3. Form mixture into i-inch meatballs. Brown in skillet or oven.
4. Transfer meatballs to slow cooker. Add chicken broth, salt, pepper, and pasta.
5. Cook for around three to four hours on High, or on Low for around six to seven hours, adding spinach 30 minutes before the end of cooking.

BBQ Meat Loaf

(To serve 10)

Prep. Time: 30 minutes

Cooking time: 5-6 hours

Ideal slow cooker size: 6-qt.oval

Ingredients:

- 3 lbs. lean ground beef
- 1½ lbs. lean ground pork
- ¾ cup finely chopped onion
- ½-¾ cup almond, or all-purpose, flour
- 1 ½ tsp. salt
- 1 tsp. black pepper
- Two tsp. Garlic powder
- Two large eggs
- 1 cup of your favorite barbecue sauce

Instructions:

1. Grease interior of slow-cooker crock.

2. Make a tinfoil sling for your slow cooker so you can lift the cooked meat loaf out easily. Begin by folding a strip of tinfoil accordion-fashion so that it's about 1½-2 inches wide, and long enough to fit from the top edge of the crock, down inside & up the opposite side, plus a two-inch overhang on each side of the cooker. Make a second strip exactly like the first.

3. Place the one strip in the crock, running from end to end. Place the second strip in the crock, running from side to side. The two strips should form a cross in the bottom of the crock.

4. In a large bowl, mix all ingredients together, except barbecue sauce. Mix well using your hands till thoroughly combined. Set aside half of the mixture for later this week.

5. Form the remaining meat mixture into a loaf and place into your crock, centering it where the two foil strips cross.

6. Cover. Cook on Low 3—4 hours.

7. 30 minutes before the cooking time ends, brush top and sides of loaf with about ¼ cup barbecue sauce.

8. Use foil handles for lifting meat loaf out of the crock and onto a serving platter. Let stand 10-15 minutes to allow meat to gather its juices.

9. Slice and serve with remaining barbecue sauce.

Chicken Alfredo

(To serve 24)

Prep. Time: 5 minutes

Cooking time: 4-6 hours

Ideal slow cooker size: 2-3-qt.

Ingredients:

- 3½ cups chicken broth
- 2 cups heavy cream
- 1 stick of butter, unsalted
- Six cloves garlic, minced
- ½ cup flour or cornstarch
- 1 cup of grated Parmesan cheese or the Parmesan/Romano blend
- Leftover chicken, chopped into bite-sized pieces
- Pasta
- Fresh chopped parsley, optional

Instructions:

1. Spray your crock's interior with a nonstick spray, then add the chicken broth, cream, butter, and garlic.
2. Cook on Low for 4—6 hours.
3. Briskly whisk in the flour or cornstarch a very little at a time until it is thickened.
4. Add the chicken and cook for an additional 30—40 minutes, or until the chicken is warmed through.
5. Serve over cooked pasta. Garnish with fresh parsley if you wish.
6. Tip: Freeze the rest of this sauce to use another time.

BBQ Burgers

(To serve 6-8)

Prep. Time: 5 minutes

Cooking time: 4-5 hours

Ideal slow cooker size: 6-qt.

Ingredients:

- Extra meat loaf mixture from earlier this week
- Hamburger buns
- 1 cup barbecue sauce (whatever your favorite is)

Optional Toppings:

- Onions, sliced into rings
- Relish, sweet or dill
- Pickles, sweet or dill
- Ketchup
- Mustard
- Mayonnaise
- Cheese slices Lettuce

Instructions:

1. In the bottom of your crock, crumble up some foil. This will prop the burgers off the bottom of the crock so they're not sitting in grease.
2. Form the meatloaf mixture into 6—8 hamburger patties.
3. Place them in the crock. You may have to make two layers depending on the shape/size of your crock. If

so, make some foil strips and place them across the other burgers, then put the remaining patties on top of those.

4.   Cover. Cook on Low for 4—5 hours.

5.   Serve on buns together with the barbecue sauce & your favorite toppings.

Black Bean Burritos

(To serve 6-8)

Prep. Time: 20 minutes

Cooking time: 7-12 hours

Ideal slow cooker size: 5-qt.

Ingredients:

- 2 cups dried black beans
- 7 cups water
- Hot chilies, diced, to taste
- ½ cup chopped onion
- 1/3 cup salsa, as hot or mild as you like
- 3 cloves garlic, minced
- 1 tsp. dried oregano
- 1 tsp. chili powder
- Two tsp. salt
- ½ tsp. black pepper
- 6—8 flour tortillas
- Chopped lettuce
- Fresh tomatoes, chopped, or salsa

- 1½ cups shredded cheese of your choice

Instructions:

1. Grease interior of slow-cooker crock.
2. Sort and rinse dried beans.
3. Place in the crock. Add water.
4. Cover. Cook for around nine to ten hours on Low, or on High for 6—7 hours, or till the beans are as tender as you wish.
5. Drain off any cooking liquid.
6. Stir hot chilies, onion, salsa, garlic, oregano, chili powder, salt, and pepper into cooked beans in the crock.
7. Cover. Cook for an hour on High, or on Low 2 hours, or until veggies are as tender as you want.
8. Spoon filling down at the center of each tortilla. Top with lettuce, tomatoes or salsa, and cheese.
9. Fold top and bottom of each tortilla over filling. Roll up to serve.

WINTER

Week 1

This week's menu

Sunday: Raspberry-Glazed Ham

Monday: Ham 'n' Cabbage Stew

Tuesday: Creamy Hum Toppings (for baked potatoes)

Wednesday: Herby Beef Sandwiches

Thursday: Beef Dumpling Soup

Friday: Turkey Breast with Orange Sauce

Saturday: Zucchini and Turkey Dish

Raspberry-Glazed Ham

(To serve 16-20)

Preparation Time: 10-15 minutes

Cooking Time: 4 hours

Ideal Slow-Cooker Size: 6-qt.

Ingredients:

- Eight 10-lb. Boneless ham, fully cooked
- ¼ cup apple juice
- 2 Tbsp. Lemon juice

- Two tsp. cornstarch
- 1/3 cup seedless raspberry jam, divided
- 1 Tbsp. butter

Instructions:

1. Place ham in slow cooker. Cover. Cook on low 2 hours
2. While the ham is cooking, blend apple juice, lemon juice, and cornstarch together in the saucepan.
3. Stir in roughly half of jam after liquid is well blended
4. Cook and stir until hot and bubbly. Add butter. Stir in the remaining jam.
5. Spoon glaze above the ham after it has cooked 2 hours.
6. Cover. Cook 2 more hours on low.
7. Slice ham and serve.

Ham 'n' Cabbage Stew

(To serve 4-5)

Preparation Time: 25-30 minutes

Cooking Time: 4-6 hours

Ideal Slow-Cooker Size: 4-qt.

Ingredients:

- ½ lb. leftover ham cubed
- ½ cup diced onions
- One garlic clove, minced

- 4-oz. can sliced mushrooms, undrained
- 4 cups shredded cabbage
- 2 cups sliced carrots
- ¼ tsp. Pepper
- ¼ tsp. Caraway seed.
- 2/3 cup beef broth
- 1 Tbsp. cornstarch
- 2 Tbsp. water

Instructions:

1. Mix all ingredients apart from cornstarch and water in slow cooker.
2. Cover. Cook on low 4-6 hours, or until vegetables are cooked as you like them.
3. In a small-sized bowl, mix cornstarch with water until smooth. Stir into slow cooker during last hour to thicken stew slightly.

Creamy Ham Toppings (for baked potatoes)

(To serve 7)

Preparation Time: 10-15 minutes

Cooking Time: 4 hours

Ideal Slow-Cooker Size: 6-qt.

Ingredients:

- ½ stick butter
- ¼ cup milk

- 2 cups milk
- ¼ cup half and half
- 1 Tbsp. Chopped fresh parsley
- 1 Tbsp. Chicken bouillon granules
- ½ tsp. Italian seasoning
- 2 cups diced leftover ham
- ¼ cup Romano cheese, grated
- 1 cup sliced mushrooms
- Baking potatoes (enough to feed your family)
- Shredded cheese of your choice
- Sour cream.

Instructions:

1. Melt the butter in a saucepan over medium heat. Stir in flour. Add milk and half-and-half.
2. Continue stirring until the sauce thickens and becomes smooth.
3. Stir in remaining ingredients (except potatoes, shredded cheese, and sour cream). Pour in the slow cooker.
4. Cover. Cook on low 1-2 hours. Meanwhile, bake potatoes.
5. Serve toppings over baked potatoes. Top with shredded cheese and sour cream.

Herby Beef Sandwiches

(To serve 7-8)

Preparation Time: 10-15 minutes

Cooking Time: 4 hours

Ideal Slow-Cooker Size: 6-qt.

Ingredients:

- 3-4 lb. boneless beef chuck roast
- 3 Tbsp. Fresh basil, or 1 Tbsp. Dried basil
- 3 Tbsp. Fresh oregano, or 1 Tbsp. Dried oregano
- 1½ cups water
- Sandwich rolls
- Sliced cheese of your choice. Optional

Instructions:

1. Place roast in slow cooker.
2. Combine Basil, oregano, and water in a bowl. Pour over roast.
3. Sprinkle with onion soup mix.
4. Cover. Cook on low 7-8 hours.
5. Shred meat with a fork. Stir sauce through shredded meat.
6. Serve the shredded herby beef on sandwich rolls alone or with melted cheese.

Beef Dumpling Soup

(To serve 6-9)

Preparation Time: 10-15 minutes

Cooking Time: 4 hours

Ideal Slow-Cooker Size: 5-qt.

Ingredients:

- Two carrots, peeled and shredded
- One rib celery, finely chopped
- 1ntomato, peeled and chopped
- One envelope dry onion soup mix
- 6 cups hot water.
- 1 cup buttermilk biscuit mix
- 1 Tbsp. Finely chopped parsley
- 6 Tbsp. milk
- Leftover shredded beef

Instructions:

1. Add carrots, celery, and tomato, onion soup mix, and water to slow cooker.
2. Cover. Cook on low 4-5 hours, or until the vegetables are as tender as you like them. Add the leftover shredded beef and continue to cook for 1 hour.
3. Three combine biscuit mix and parsley in a bowl. Stir in milk with fork until moistened. Drop dumplings by teaspoonful into the cooker.
4. Cover. Cook on high 30 minutes.

Turkey Breast with Orange Sauce

(To serve 4-7)

Preparation Time: 10-15 minutes

Cooking Time: 4 hours

Ideal Slow-Cooker Size: 5-qt.

Ingredients:

- One large onion, chopped
- Three cloves Garlic
- One tsp. Dried rosemary
- ½ tsp. pepper
- 4-5 lb. boneless, skinless turkey breast
- 1½ cups orange juice

Instructions:

1. Place onions in your slow cooker.
2. Mix garlic, rosemary, & pepper in a small-sized bowl.
3. Make gashes in Turkey, about ¾ of the way through, at 2-inch intervals. Stuff in the herb mixture.
4. Pour juice over turkey.
5. Cover. Cook for around seven to eight hours on low, or until turkey is no longer pink in center.

Zucchini and Turkey Dish

(To serve 5-8)

Preparation Time: 10-15 minutes

Cooking Time: 4-7 hours

Ideal Slow-Cooker Size: 6-qt.

Ingredients:

- 3 cups sliced zucchini
- One small onion, chopped

- ¼ tsp. salt
- 1 cup cubed leftover turkey
- Two fresh tomatoes, sliced, or
- 14½-oz. can diced tomatoes
- ½ tsp. dried basil
- ¼ cup grated parmesan cheese
- ½ cup shredded provolone cheese
- ¾ cup dry stuffing mix

Instructions:

1. Combine zucchini, onion, salt, turkey, tomatoes, oregano, and dried basil in the slow cooker. Mix well.
2. Top with cheese and stuffing
3. Cover. Cook on low 4-5 hours.

Week 2

This week's menu

Sunday: Bavarian Beef

Monday: Tempting Beef Stew

Tuesday: Spicy Sweet Chicken

Wednesday: Chicken Rice Special

Thursday: Cranberry Pork

Friday: Macaroni and Cheddar/Parmesan Cheese

Saturday: Pork on Sweet Potatoes

Bavarian Beef

(To serve 5-8)

Preparation Time: 10-15 minutes

Cooking Time: 4-7 hours

Ideal Slow-Cooker Size: 6-qt.

Ingredients:

- 4-4½-lb. boneless beef chuck roast
- Oil of your choice
- 3 cups sliced carrots
- 3 cups sliced onions
- Two large kosher dill pickles, chopped

- 1 cup sliced celery
- ½ cup dry red wine, or beef broth
- 1/3 cup German-style mustard
- Two tsp. Coarsely ground black pepper
- Two bay leaves
- ¼ tsp. ground cloves
- 1 cup water

Instructions:

1. Brown roast on both sides in oil skillet. Transfer to slow-cooker.
2. Distribute carrots, onions, pickles, and celery around roast in slow cooker.
3. Combine wine, mustard, pepper, bay leaves, and cloves in a bowl. Pour over ingredients in slow cooker.
4. Cover. Cook for around six to seven hours on low, or until meat and vegetables are tender but not dry or mushy.
5. Remove the meat & vegetables to a large platter. Cover to keep warm.
6. Mix flour with 1 cup water in a bowl until smooth. Turn cooker to high. Stir in flour-water paste, constantly stirring until broth is smooth and thickened. Serve with broth alongside.

Tempting Beef Stew

(To serve 5-8)

Preparation Time: 10-15 minutes

Cooking Time: 4-9 hours

Ideal Slow-Cooker Size: 6-qt.

Ingredients:

- 1½ carrots/ thinly sliced
- ½ of a 1-lb. Frozen green peas with onions
- ½ of a 1-lb. Pkg. Frozen green beans
- 8-oz. can whole, stewed, tomatoes
- ¼ cup beef broth
- ¼ cup white wine
- ¼ cup brown sugar
- 2 Tbsp. Instant tapioca
- ¼ cup bread crumbs
- One tsp. salt
- One bay leaf
- Pepper to taste
- Leftover beef

Instructions:

1. Combine all ingredients except the leftover beef in slow cooker
2. Cover. Cook on low 7-8 hours, or until the vegetables are as tender as you wish. Add the leftover beef in the last hour.

Spicy Sweet Chicken

(To serve 5-8)

Preparation Time: 15-25 minutes

Cooking Time: 4-9 hours

Ideal Slow-Cooker Size: 6-qt.

Ingredients:

- 6 lbs. chicken breasts, thighs, and/or legs, skinned
- 1 Tbsp. Oil of your choice
- 16-oz. can whole berry cranberry sauce, divided
- ¼ cup spicy-sweet Catalina salad dressing
- 2 Tbsp. Dry onion soup mix
- 1 Tbsp. cornstarch

Instructions:

1. Rinse chicken. Pat dry. Brown in hot oil in skillet. Arrange in a slow cooker.
2. In a bowl, combine half of cranberry sauce and all of the salad dressing and soup mix. Pour over chicken.
3. Cover. Cook for around seven hours on low, or on high for 3½ hours.
4. Stir cornstarch into remaining cranberry sauce in a bowl. Stir into chicken mixture.
5. Turn slow cooker to high. Cover and cook 30-45 minutes more, or until thickened and bubbly.

Chicken Rice Special

(To serve 5-8)

Preparation Time: 25 minutes

Cooking Time: 4-7 hours

Ideal Slow-Cooker Size: 6-qt.

Ingredients:

- 1 lb. pork, or turkey, sausage
- Leftover chicken, chopped
- 4 cups chicken broth
- Half a large sweet green bell pepper chopped
- Four ribs celery, chopped
- 1 cup uncooked rice
- 2-oz. Pkg. Dry noodle soup mix
- ½ cup sliced almonds

Instructions:

1. Brown the sausage in skillet. Drain off any drippings. Place meat in slow-cooker.
2. Add all other ingredients, except almonds and pimentos, to slow cooker. Stir well.
3. Top with almonds and pimentos.
4. Cover. Cook on high 4-6 hours, or until rice is done and liquid has been absorbed.
5. Stir well 1 hour before serving.

Cranberry Pork

(To serve 5-8)

Preparation Time: 15 minutes

Cooking Time: 4-9 hours

Ideal Slow-Cooker Size: 5-qt.

Ingredients:

- 3-4 lb. boneless rolled pork loin roast.
- 2 Tbsp. Canola oil
- 14-oz. can whole berry cranberry sauce
- ¾ cup sugar
- ¾ cup cranberry sauce
- One tsp. Dry mustard
- One tsp. Pepper
- ¼ tsp. Ground cloves
- ¼ cup cornstarch
- ¼ cup cold water
- Salt to taste

Instructions:

1. In a Dutch oven, brown the roast in oil on all sides over medium- high heat. You may require cutting the roast in half to fit into your Dutch oven and/ or your slow cooker.
2. Place browned roast in slow cooker.
3. In a medium-sized bowl, combine cranberry juice, mustard, pepper, and cloves. Pour over roast.
4. Cover. Cook on low 6-8 hours, or until a meat thermometer reads 160 degrees Fahrenheit in the center of roast. Remove roast and keep warm. Keep sauce on low in slow cooker.
5. In a small-sized bowl, combine the cornstarch, water, and salt until smooth.

6. Turn cooker to high. Stir cornstarch-water mixture into cooking juices. Bring to a boil. Cook and stir until sauce thickens. Serve with slices of pork roast.

Macaroni and Cheddar/Parmesan Cheese

(To serve 5-8)

Preparation Time: 10-15 minutes

Cooking Time: 4-7 hours

Ideal Slow-Cooker Size: 6-qt.

Ingredients:

- 8-oz. pkg. elbow macaroni, cooked al dente
- 13-oz. can fat-free milk
- 1 cup fat-free milk
- Two large eggs, slightly beaten
- 4 cups grated fat-free sharp cheddar cheese, divided
- ¼ tsp. salt
- 1/8 tsp. white pepper
- ¼ cup grated fat-free Parmesan cheese

Instructions:

1. Spray inside of cooker with a nonfat cooking spray. Then, in the slow cooker, combine lightly cooked macaroni, evaporated milk, milk, eggs, 3 cups cheddar cheese, salt, and pepper.
2. Top with remaining cheddar and parmesan cheese.
3. Cover. Cook on low 3 hours.

Pork on Sweet Potatoes

(To serve 4-7)

Preparation Time: 15 minutes

Cooking Time: 4-8 hours

Ideal Slow-Cooker Size: 5-qt.

Ingredients:

- Two average sweet potatoes, peeled and cut into ½-inch-thick slices
- 1 small onion, chopped
- Two apples, cored, peeled or not, and sliced
- 1 Tbsp. Brown sugar
- ¼ tsp. Ground cinnamon
- ¼ tsp. salt
- 1/8 tsp. coarsely ground black pepper
- Leftover pork
- 15-oz. can sauerkraut, drained

Instructions:

1. Grease interior of slow cooker crock.
2. Arrange the sweet potato parts over the bottom of slow cooker.
3. Sprinkle chopped onion over potatoes.
4. Cover with apple slices
5. In a small-sized bowl, mix brown sugar, cinnamon, salt, and pepper. Sprinkle over apple slices.

6.   Top with leftover pork. If you require to make a second layer, stagger the pieces so they don't directly overlap each other.

7.   Spoon drained sauerkraut over top of the leftover pork, including any on the bottom layer.

8.   Cover. Cook on low 4½-5 hours or on high 2-3 hours.

Week 3

This week's menu

Sunday: Succulent Steak

Monday: Garlic Beef Stroganoff

Tuesday: Chicken and Dumplings

Wednesday: Chianti-Braised Short Ribs

Thursday: Chicken and Rice Casserole

Friday: Hearty Beef and Cabbage Soup

Saturday: Fully-Loaded Baked Potato Soup

Succulent Steak

(To serve 4-7)

Preparation Time: 15 minutes

Cooking Time: 4-8 hours

Ideal Slow-Cooker Size: 5-qt.

Ingredients:

- ¼ cup plus 2 Tbsp. flour, divided
- 1 tsp. Salt
- ½ tsp. paprika
- 3-lb. round steak, trimmed of fat
- Two medium onions, sliced

- 4-oz. can sliced mushrooms, drained
- ½ cup beef broth
- Two tsp. Worcestershire sauce
- 3 Tbsp. water

Instructions:

1. Mix well together ¼ cup flour, salt, pepper, and paprika.
2. Cut steak into 5-6½-¾-inch-thick pieces. Dredge the steak pieces in seasoned flour until lightly coated.
3. Layer half of onions, half of steak, and half of the mushrooms into the cooker. Repeat.
4. Combine beef broth and Worcestershire sauce. Pour over mixture in slow cooker.
5. Cover. Cook on low 8-10 hours.
6. Transfer steak to your serving platter, and keep it warm. Mix together 2 Tbsp. Flour and water. Stir into the drippings & cook on high till it becomes thickened, about 10 minutes. Pour over steak and serve.

Garlic Beef Stroganoff

(To serve 4-8)

Preparation Time: 15 minutes

Cooking Time: 4-6 hours

Ideal Slow-Cooker Size: 5-qt.

Ingredients:

- Two tsp. Sodium-Free beef bouillon granules
- Two 4½-oz. Jars sliced mushrooms, drained, with juice reserved
- Mushroom juice, with warm water added to make full cup
- 10¾-oz. can 98% fat-free, reduced-sodium cream of mushroom soup
- 1 large onion, chopped
- Three cloves garlic, minced
- 1 Tbsp. Worcestershire sauce
- Leftover steak, chopped up noodles
- 6-oz. Fat-free cream cheese, cubed and softened

Instructions:

1. Dissolve bouillon in the mushroom juice & water in your slow-cooker.
2. Add soup, mushroom, onion, garlic, and Worcestershire sauce
3. Cover. Cook on low 4-5 hours. Add the leftover steak and cook for 1 more hour.
4. Turn off heat.
5. Stir in cream cheese until smooth.
6. Serve over noodles

Chicken and Dumplings

(To serve 4-6)

Preparation Time: 15 minutes

Cooking Time: 4-6 hours

Ideal Slow-Cooker Size: 6-qt.

Ingredients:

- 3 lbs. boneless, skinless chicken
- Breast, cut into 1-inch cubes
- 1.lb frozen vegetables of your choice
- 1 medium onion, diced
- 24-oz. fat-free low- sodium chicken broth divided.
- 1½ cups low-fat buttermilk biscuit mix

Instructions:

1. Blend chicken, vegetables, onion, & chicken broth (reserve ½ cup, plus 1 Tbsp., broth) in slow cooker
2. Cover. Cook on high 2-3 hours.
3. Mix biscuit mix with the reserved broth until moistened. Drop by tablespoonfuls over hot chicken and vegetable.
4. Cover. Cook on high 1 minutes.
5. Uncover. Cook on high 20 minutes more.

Chianti-Braised Short Ribs

(To serve 4-7)

Preparation Time: 15 minutes

Cooking Time: 4-8 hours

Ideal Slow-Cooker Size: 5-qt.

Ingredients:

- 5lbs. meaty beef short ribs on the bone
- Salt, to taste
- Pepper, to taste
- 1 Tbsp. Vegetable oil
- 1 medium onion, finely chopped
- 2 cups Chianti wine
- Two tomatoes, seeded and chopped
- 1 tsp. tomato paste

Instructions:

1. Season ribs with salt and pepper.
2. Add vegetable oil to large skillet. Brown half the ribs 7-10 minutes, turning to brown all sides. Drain and remove to slow cooker.
3. Repeat browning with the second half of ribs. Drain and transfer to a slow cooker.
4. Drain off all but one tablespoon drippings from skillet.
5. Sauté onion in skillet, scraping up any browned bits, until lightly softened, about 4 minutes.
6. Add wine and tomatoes to skillet. Bring to a boil.
7. Carefully pour hot mixture into slow-cooker.
8. Cover. Cook for around six hours on low, or until ribs are tender.
9. Transfer ribs to serving plate and cover to keep warm.
10. Strain cooking liquid from slow-cooker into a measuring cup. Skim off as much fat as possible.
11. Pour remaining juice into skillet used to brown ribs. Boil sauce until reduced to one cup.

12.   Stir in tomato paste until smooth. Season to taste with salt and pepper

13.   Serve sauce over ribs or on the side.

Chicken and Rice Casserole

(To serve 6-8)

Preparation Time: 20 minutes

Cooking Time: 5-7 hours

Ideal Slow-Cooker Size: 5-qt.

Ingredients:

- 1 cup uncooked long-grain rice
- 3 cups water
- Two tsp. Low-Sodium Chicken
- Bouillon granules
- 10¾-oz. can fat-free, low-sodium cream of chicken soup
- Leftover chicken
- ¼ tsp. Garlic powder
- 1 tsp. onion salt
- 1 cup grated, fat-free cheddar cheese
- 16-oz. bag frozen broccoli, thawed

Instructions:

1.   Mix all ingredients apart from broccoli in slow cooker

2.   One hour before the end of cooking time, stir in broccoli.

3.   Cook on high a total of 2-3 hours or on low a total of 4-6 hours.

Hearty Beef and Cabbage Soup

(To serve 6-8)

Preparation Time: 20 minutes

Cooking Time: 5-7 hours

Ideal Slow-Cooker Size: 5-qt.

Ingredients:

- 1 medium onion
- 28-oz. can crushed tomatoes
- 15-oz. can crushed tomatoes
- 15-oz. can kidney beans
- 2 cups water
- 1 tsp. Salt
- ½ cup chopped celery
- ½ tsp. pepper
- 1 Tbsp. Chili powder
- 2 cups thinly sliced cabbage
- Leftover ribs meat, off the bone and chopped up.

Instructions:

1.   Combine all ingredients except cabbage and leftover rib meat in slow-cooker
2.   Cover. Cook on low 3 hours.

3.   Add cabbage and leftover rib meat. Cook on high 60 minutes longer.

Fully-Loaded Baked Potato Soup

(To serve 6-8)

Preparation Time: 20 minutes

Cooking Time: 5-7 hours

Ideal Slow-Cooker Size: 5-qt.

Ingredients:

- Three large potatoes, baked
- 1 Tbsp. butter
- 1 small onion, chopped, or 4 scallions, sliced
- 1 clove garlic, minced
- 3 Tbsp. All-Purpose flour
- 1 tsp. salt
- 1 tsp. dried basil
- ½ tsp. pepper
- 3 cups vegetable broth
- 1½ cups milk
- Shredded cheese of your choice, for garnish
- Chopped fresh parsley, for garnish
- Sour cream for garnish

Instructions:

1.   Peel the baked potatoes if you wish. Cube the baked potatoes. Place in slow cooker.

2. In a skillet, melt butter and sauté onion and garlic.

3. Stir in flour, salt, basil, and pepper. Add broth, whisking continuously. Heat and stir until hot.

4. Pour over potatoes in slow cooker.

5. Cook on low for 2 hours.

6. Add milk. Cook an addition 30-40 minutes on low

7. Garnish with cheese, parsley, and sour cream.

Week 4

This week's Menu

Sunday: CC Roast

Monday: Cowtown favorite

Tuesday: Chicken in a pot

Wednesday: Sauerkraut and kielbasa

Thursday: Barley and chicken soup

Friday: Wanda's chicken and rice casserole

Saturday: Election lunch

CC Roast

(To serve 8)

Preparation Time: 25 minutes

Cooking Time: 5-7 hours

Ideal Slow-Cooker Size: 5-qt.

Ingredients:

- 3lb. boneless pot roast.
- 2 Tbsp. flour
- 1 Tbsp. Prepared mustard
- 1 Tbsp. Chili sauce
- 1 Tbsp. Worcestershire sauce

- 1 tsp. apple cider vinegar
- 1 tsp. sugar
- Four medium potatoes sliced
- 2 medium onions, sliced

Instructions:

1. Place pot roast in slow cooker.
2. Prepare a paste with the flour, mustard, chili sauce, Worcestershire sauce, vinegar, and sugar. Spread over roast.
3. Top with potatoes and then the onions.
4. Cover. Cook on low 6-8 hours.

Cowtown Favorite

(To serve 6-8)

Preparation Time: 20 minutes

Cooking Time: 5-7 hours

Ideal Slow-Cooker Size: 5-qt.

Ingredients:

- 1 medium onion
- Three large potatoes, peeled and chopped
- 3 cups carrots cut into ½-inch slices
- 1 rib celery, chopped
- 2 cups green beans
- 2 14-oz. cans low-sodium stewed tomatoes, undrained
- 10¾-oz. can low-sodium tomato soup

- 2 Tbsp. Instant tapioca
- Leftover roast, chopped

Instructions:

1. Place onions, potatoes, carrots, celery, and green beans into the slow cooker.
2. Mix tomatoes, soup, and tapioca together. Pour over vegetables.
3. Cover. Cook for around three hours on high, or on low 4-5 hours.
4. Add in the leftover roast the last hour of cooking.

Chicken in a Pot.

(To serve 8)

Preparation Time: 25 minutes

Cooking Time: 5-7 hours

Ideal Slow-Cooker Size: 5-qt.

Ingredients:

- Six carrots, sliced
- Four medium onions, sliced
- Four ribs celery, cut into 1-inch pieces
- 6-8 lb. chicken pieces
- Two tsp. Salt
- ½ tsp. Coarse black pepper
- 1 tsp. dried basil
- 1 cup chicken broth, water, or white cooking wine

Instructions:

1. Place vegetables in bottom of slow cooker. Place chicken on top of vegetables. Add seasoning and water.
2. Cover. Cook for around eight to ten hours on low 8-10 hours, or on high 3-5 hours. (Use 1½ cups of liquid if cooking on high).

Sauerkraut and Kielbasa

(To serve 8)

Preparation Time: 5 minutes

Cooking Time: 5-6 hours

Ideal Slow-Cooker Size: 5-qt.

Ingredients:

- 1½ lbs. fresh or canned
- Sauerkraut, drained and rinsed, cut into 1-inch slices

Instructions:

1. Combine sauerkraut and turkey kielbasa in the slow cooker.
2. Cover. Cook on low 5-6 hours.
3. Stir before serving.

Barley and Chicken Soup

(To serve 5)

Prep. Time: 15-20 minutes

Cooking Time: 4 hours

Ideal slow cooker size: 6-qt.

Ingredients:

- ½ lb. dry barley
- Fresh celery, as desired
- Fresh parsley, as desired
- Fresh basil, as desired
- 7-8 cups water
- 2 cups leftover chicken, diced

Instructions:

1. Combine all ingredients in a slow cooker except chicken
2. Cover. Cook on low for 4 hours. Add in leftover chicken the last hour of cooking.
3. Continue cooking until barley is soft and chicken is heated through.

Wanda's Chicken and Rice Casserole

(To serve 4-6)

Preparation Time: 10 minutes

Cooking Time: 3-5 hours

Ideal Slow-Cooker Size: 5-qt.

Ingredients:

- 1 cup long-grain rice, uncooked
- 3 cups water
- Two tsp. Chicken bouillon granules
- 10¾-oz. can cream of chicken soup.
- 16-oz. bag frozen broccoli
- 2 cups chopped leftover chicken
- ¼ tsp. garlic powder
- 1 tsp. onion salt
- 1 cup grated cheddar cheese

Instructions:

1. Combine all ingredients in slow cooker.
2. Cook on high 3-4 hours
3. Tip: if casserole is too runny, remove the lid from your slow cooker for 15 minutes while continuing to cook on high.

Election Lunch

(To serve 4-6)

Preparation Time: 15 minutes

Cooking Time: 2-4 hours

Ideal Slow-Cooker Size: 5-qt.

Ingredients:

- 1 large onion, chopped

- 1 rib celery, sliced
- 1 Tbsp. Worcestershire sauce
- 1½ tsp. dry mustard
- ¼ cup honey
- 10-oz. can tomatoes with green chili peppers
- 16-oz. can lima, or butter or beans, drained with liquid reserved.
- 16-oz. can garbanzo beans, drained, with liquid reserved
- Leftover sausage, chopped into bite-sized chops

Instructions:

1. Place all ingredients into slow-cooker, combining well. Add reserved juice from lima, kidney, and garbanzo beans if there's enough room in the cooker(s)
2. Cover. Cook on low 2-4 hours.

Week 5

This Week's Menu

Sunday: Chicken Tikki Masala

Monday: Indian Chicken Curry

Tuesday: Three cheese broccoli soup

Wednesday: Saucy round steak supper

Thursday: Saucy round steak sandwiches

Friday: Rosemary pork loin

Saturday: Creamy pork and potato soup

Chicken Tikki Masala

(To serve 4-6)

Preparation Time: 15 minutes

Cooking Time: 3-5 hours

Ideal Slow-Cooker Size: 5-qt.

Ingredients:

- 4 lbs. boneless, skinless chicken thighs
- 1 medium onion, chopped
- Three cloves garlic, minced
- 1½ Tbsp. grated ginger
- 29-oz. can puree tomatoes

- 1 Tbsp. Olive oil
- 1 Tbsp. Garam masala
- ½ tsp. Ground cumin
- ½ tsp. paprika
- 1 cinnamon stick
- 1 tsp. salt
- 1½ tsp. cayenne pepper
- Two bay leaves
- ¾ cup plain Greek yogurt
- ½ cup cream
- 1½ tsp. cornstarch

Instructions:

1. Grease interior of slow-cooker crock
2. Lay thighs in the crock. If you need to make a second layer, stagger pieces so they don't directly overlap each other.
3. In a good-sized bowl, mix together onion, garlic powder, ginger, tomatoes, olive oil, garam masala, cumin, paprika, cinnamon stick, salt, cayenne pepper, and bay leaves.
4. Cover. Cook 4 hours on low, or until instant-read meat thermometer registers 165 degrees Fahrenheit when inserted in center of the thigh.
5. Remove the thighs and keep them warm on platter or bowl.
6. Mix Greek yogurt into sauce in cooker.
7. In a small-sized bowl mix cream & cornstarch until smooth. Mix into sauce in cooker.
8. Return chicken to cooker.

9.   Cover. Cook an additional 15-20 minutes or until sauce that thickened.

Indian Chicken Curry

(To serve 4-6)

Preparation Time: 10 minutes

Cooking Time: 3-5 hours

Ideal Slow-Cooker Size: 5-qt.

Ingredients:

- 2 Tbsp. Curry powder
- 1 tsp. ground coriander
- 1 tsp. ground cumin
- Three cloves garlic, minced
- 14-oz. Can coconut milk
- ½ tsp. Tabasco sauce
- 1 Tbsp. Tomato paste or ketchup.
- 15-oz. can garbanzo beans, drained
- 1 medium onion, chopped
- 1 green or red bell pepper, chopped
- 1 cup sliced carrots
- 1 cup sliced celery
- 1 sweet potato, peeled and chopped
- Leftover chicken, chopped

Instructions:

1. Grease interior of slow-cooker crock.
2. In the crock, combine curry powder, coriander, cumin, minced garlic, cumin, minced garlic, coconut milk, Tabasco, and tomato paste. Blend well.
3. Add in the beans, onion, bell pepper, carrots, celery and sweet potato.
4. Cover. Cook on low 5-6 hours or until the vegetables are as tender as you like them. Add the leftover chicken in the last hour of cooking. Stir well.
5. Tip: Serve Two rice.

Three-Cheese Broccoli Soup

(To serve 5-7)

Preparation Time: 15 minutes

Cooking Time: 4-6 hours

Ideal Slow-Cooker Size: 3-qt.

Ingredients:

- 4 cups chicken or vegetable broth
- 2 cups 2% milk
- 2 10-oz. Bags frozen broccoli florets
- ½ cup very finely diced white onion
- ½ tsp. Black pepper
- ½ tsp. Kosher salt
- ½ tsp. Ground nutmeg
- 3 cups three different grated cheese, preferably Jarlsberg, Gruyere, and sharp cheddar

Instructions:

1. In slow cooker, combine broth, milk, broccoli, onion, pepper, salt, and nutmeg.
2. Cook for around five to six hours on low, or high for 2-3, until onion is soft.
3. Add cheese 20 minutes before serving. Cheese may be stringy and stick to broccoli- that's fine.

Saucy Round Steak Supper

(To serve 6-7)

Preparation Time: 15 minutes

Cooking Time: 8-9 hours

Ideal Slow-Cooker Size: 3-qt.

Ingredients:

- 3 lbs. round steak, sliced diagonally into 1/8- inch strips(reserve meat bone)
- ½ cup chopped onion
- ½ cup chopped celery
- 8-oz. can mushrooms, stems including pieces, drained (reserve liquid)
- 1/3 cup French dressing
- ½ cup sour cream
- 1 tsp. Worcestershire sauce

Instructions:

1. Place steak in the slow cooker. Add onion, celery, and mushrooms.
2. Combine dressing, sour cream, Worcestershire sauce, and mushroom liquid. Pour over mixture in slow cooker.
3. Cover. Cook on low 8-9 hours.

Saucy Round Steak Sandwiches

(To serve 5-7)

Preparation Time: 15 minutes

Cooking Time: 4-6 hours

Ideal Slow-Cooker Size: 3-qt.

Ingredients:

- Leftover saucy round steak
- Bread rolls of your choice
- 6-8 Swiss cheese slices
- Horseradish sauce

Instructions:

1. Warm the leftover saucy round steak
2. Preheat the oven to 400 degrees Fahrenheit. Put the dough on a baking sheet & top with the warmed round steak. Place a slice or two of the Swiss cheese over the top. Bake till the cheese is melted, approximately 8-10 minutes.

3.   Before serving, top each sandwich with some horseradish sauce.

Rosemary Pork Loin

(To serve 5-7)

Preparation Time: 15 minutes

Cooking Time: 3-4 hours

Ideal Slow-Cooker Size: 3-qt.

Ingredients:

- 4-5 lb. pork loin
- 2 cups apple cider
- Two cloves garlic, minced
- 1 tsp. onion salt
- ¾ tsp. chopped fresh oregano, or ¼ tsp. dried
- 1 Tbsp. Fresh rosemary leaves, or 1 tsp. dried
- 1 bay leaf

Instructions:

1.   Place pork loin in baking pan.
2.   Mix together remaining ingredients in a bowl. Pour over roast.
3.   Cover. Refrigerate for at least 8 hours. When you think of it, spoon some of the marinades over the roast.
4.   Place roast in slow cooker. Pour marinade over roast.
5.   Cover. Cook on low 3-4 hours.

6. When the meat is finished cooking, lift out of cooker onto a platter. Cover with foil to keep it warm. Let stand 15 minutes before slicing.

7. Slice and serve topped with marinade. (Fish out the bay leaf before serving.)

Creamy Pork and Potato Soup

(To serve 6-8)

Preparation Time: 15 minutes

Cooking Time: 3-4 hours

Ideal Slow-Cooker Size: 5-qt.

Ingredients:

- 3 cups chopped potatoes, peeled or unpeeled
- 1 cup water
- ½ cup chopped celery
- ½ cup chopped carrots
- ¼ cup chopped onions
- 2 cubes chicken, or vegetable, bouillon
- 1 tsp. dried parsley
- ½ tsp. salt
- ¼ tsp. pepper
- 1½ cups 2% milk
- 2 Tbsp. flour
- Leftover pork
- ½ lb. cheese of your choice, shredded

Instructions:

1. Combine potatoes, water, celery, carrots, onion, bouillon, parsley, salt, and pepper in slow cooker.

2. Cover. Cook on high 3 hours, or until vegetables are tender. In a jar with tight-fitting lid, add milk to flour. Cover tightly and shake until flour dissolves in milk. When smooth, add mixture to vegetables in cooker. Stir well.

3. Add in leftover pork and stir again. Cover. Cook on high extra 15-30 minutes, or till the soup is thickened and smooth and pork is heated through. Stir occasionally to prevent lumps from forming.

Week 6

This Week's Menu

Sunday: Taters and beef

Monday: Another chicken in a pot

Tuesday: Green chili stew

Wednesday: Pasta with tomatoes, olives, and two cheeses

Thursday: Tangy Pork Chops

Friday: Asian pork soup

Saturday: Meatless Mexican Lasagna

Taters 'n Beef

(To serve 5-7)

Preparation Time: 20 minutes

Cooking Time: 5-6 hours

Ideal Slow-Cooker Size: 6-qt.

Ingredients:

- 2½ lbs. ground beef, browned
- 1 tsp. salt
- ½ tsp. pepper
- ¼ cup chopped onions
- 1 cup canned tomato soup

- Five potatoes, sliced
- 1 cup canned tomato soup
- Five potatoes, sliced
- 1 cup milk

Instructions:

1. Brown the ground beef in skillet. Set aside 1 lb. of this and place in the refrigerator for later this week.
2. Combine remaining beef, salt, pepper, onions, and soup.
3. Place a layer of potatoes in slow cooker. Cover with a portion of the meat mixture. Repeat layers until ingredients are done.
4. Cover. Cook for an average of four to six hours on low. Add the milk & cook on high 15-20 minutes.

Another Chicken in a Pot

(To serve 5-7)

Preparation Time: 20 minutes

Cooking Time: 5-6 hours

Ideal Slow-Cooker Size: 6-qt.

Ingredients:

- 1 lb. bag baby carrots
- 1 small onion, diced
- 14½-oz. can green beans
- 4-lb. whole chicken, cut into serving-size pieces

- Two tsp. Salt
- ½ tsp. Black pepper
- ½ cup chicken broth
- ¼ cup white wine
- ½-1 tsp. dried basil

Instructions:

1.   Put carrots, onions, and beans on bottom of slow cooker. Add chicken. Top with salt, pepper, broth, and wine. Sprinkle with basil.
2.   Cover. Cook for around eight to ten hours on low, or on high for 3-5 hours.

Green Chili Stew

(To serve 5-7)

Preparation Time: 20 minutes

Cooking Time: 6-8 hours

Ideal Slow-Cooker Size: 6-qt.

Ingredients:

- Leftover browned beef
- Six potatoes, peeled and cubed
- 1 medium onion sliced
- Salt and pepper, to taste
- ¾ cup chopped green chilies
- Optional ingredients:
- 1 tsp. garlic powder

- 1 beef bouillon cube

Instructions:

1. Add all ingredients to slow cooker. Stir together thoroughly.
2. Cover & cook for around six to eight hours on low, or until the vegetables are tender.

Pasta with Tomatoes, Olives, and Two Cheeses

(To serve 5-7)

Preparation Time: 20 minutes

Cooking Time: 3-5 hours

Ideal Slow-Cooker Size: 6-qt.

Ingredients:

- Leftover chopped chicken
- 1½ cups chopped onion
- 1 tsp. minced garlic
- 3 28-oz. cans Italian plum
- Tomatoes, drained
- Two tsp. Dried basil
- ¼-½ tap. Red pepper flakes
- 2 cups chicken broth
- Salt and black pepper, to taste
- 1 lb. uncooked penne or rigatoni
- 3 Tbsp. Olive oil
- 2½ cups Havarti cheese

- 1/3 cup sliced, pitted, brine-cured olives
- 1/3 cups grated parmesan cheese
- ¼ cup finely chopped fresh basil

Instructions:

1. Grease interior of slow-cooker crock.
2. Place chicken, onion, garlic, tomatoes, dried basil, and red pepper flakes in crock. Stir together well, breaking up tomatoes with back of spoon
3. Stir in chicken broth.
4. Season with salt and pepper.
5. Cover. Cook on high 2 hours.
6. Uncover. Continue cooking on high 1 hour, or until sauce is reduced to the consistency you like.
7. During 30 last minutes of cooking, prepare pasta according to package directions in a large stockpot until al dente.
8. Drain pasta and stir in olive oil. Cover and keep warm.
9. When the sauce has been cooked completely, pour over pasta and toss to blend.
10. Stir in harvati cheese and allow to melt.
11. Spoon into serving bowl. Top with olives and parmesan cheese
12. Sprinkle with fresh basil, and then serve immediately.

Tangy Pork Chops

(To serve 5-7)

Preparation Time: 20 minutes

Cooking Time: 5-6 hours

Ideal Slow-Cooker Size: 6-qt.

Ingredients:

- 6-inch-thick pork chops
- ½ tsp. salt
- Two medium onions
- 1/8 tsp. pepper
- Two ribs celery, chopped
- 1 large green bell pepper, sliced
- 14½-oz. can stewed tomatoes
- ½ Tbsp. ketchup
- 2 Tbsp. Apple cider vinegar
- 2 Tbsp. Brown sugar
- 2 Tbsp. Worcestershire sauce
- 1 Tbsp. Lemon juice
- 1 beef bouillon cube
- 2 Tbsp. cornstarch
- 2 Tbsp. water

Instructions:

1. Place chops in slow cooker. Sprinkle with salt and pepper.
2. Add the onions, celery, pepper, and tomatoes
3. Blend ketchup, vinegar, brown sugar, Worcestershire sauce, lemon juice, and bouillon. Pour over vegetables.
4. Cover. Cook on low 5-6 hours.

5.   Combine cornstarch and water until smooth. Stir into slow cooker.

6.   Cover. Cook on high for around 30 minutes, or until thickened

Asian Pork Soup

(To serve 5-7)

Preparation Time: 20 minutes

Cooking Time: 4-9 hours

Ideal Slow-Cooker Size: 5-qt.

Ingredients:

- Two cloves garlic, minced
- Two medium carrots, cut up
- Four green onions, cut into 1-inch pieces
- 2 Tbsp. Light soy sauce
- ½ tsp. fresh ginger, chopped
- 1/8 tsp. pepper
- 2 14½-oz. can chicken broth
- 2½ tsp. sodium-free chicken bouillon granules
- 2½ cups water
- Leftover pork, chopped
- 1 cup sliced mushroom
- 1 cup bean sprouts

Instructions:

1.   Combine all ingredients except leftover pork, mushroom, and sprouts in the slow cooker.
2.   Cover. Cook on low 7-9 hours or high 3-4 hours.
3.   Stir in leftover pork, mushrooms, and bean sprouts. Cover. Cook on low 1 hour.

Meatless Mexican Lasagna.

(To serve 5-6)

Preparation Time: 20 minutes

Cooking Time: 2-3 hours

Ideal Slow-Cooker Size: 6-qt.

Ingredients:

- 3 cups of frozen corn, it should be thawed
- 15-oz. can of black beans, they should be rinsed & drained
- 14½-oz. can of diced tomatoes having basil, oregano, & garlic, undrained
- 4-oz. can chopped green chilies
- Three green onions, sliced
- Two tsp. Dried oregano
- Two tsp. Ground cumin
- 4 6-inch corn tortilla, divided
- 1½ cups shredded Mexican-blend cheese, divided
- 6 Tbsp. Sour cream

Instructions:

1. In a dish, mix, corn, beans, tomatoes, green chilies, onions, oregano, and cumin.
2. Grease 5-qt. slow cooker. Place two tortillas in the crock.
3. Spread tortillas with half of the bean mixture.
4. Sprinkle with cheese
5. Repeat the layers.
6. Cook on high 2 hours or until heated through.
7. Let stand for 5 minutes.
8. Garnish with sour cream.

Week 7

This week's menu

Sunday: Beer braised chicken

Monday: Tasty Pork Tacos

Tuesday: White chicken chili

Wednesday: Mexican rice and beans

Thursday: Hearty pork and veggie soup

Friday: Barbecued ham steaks

Saturday: Potluck baked corn

Beer Braised Chicken

(To serve 6-8)

Preparation Time: 20 minutes

Cooking Time: 8-9 hours

Ideal Slow-Cooker Size: 6-qt.

Ingredients:

- 6-lb. whole chicken
- ½ stick butter, cut up
- 12-oz beer
- 1 medium onion, quartered

Rub:

- ½ tsp. salt
- 1/8 tsp. pepper
- 1 tsp. dried basil
- 1 Tbsp. Garlic powder

Instructions:

1. Take the giblets out of your chicken breast. Rinse the chicken and dry it. Place the chicken breast side down in your slow-cooker.
2. Fill it with your onion slices and put some butter under the skin and around the chicken.
3. Pour the beer over the top. Mix the rub ingredients & spatter over the top.
4. Cover and cook on low for 8-9 hours

Tasty Pork Tacos

(To serve 5-7)

Preparation Time: 20 minutes

Cooking Time: 5-6 hours

Ideal Slow-Cooker Size: 6-qt.

Ingredients:

- 6-lb. boneless pork butt roast
- Juice and zest of 3 limes
- 1 tsp. garlic powder

- 1 tsp. minced Garlic
- 1 tsp. salt
- 1-2 tsp. ground cumin
- 1 cup fresh chopped cilantro, divided
- Tortillas

Toppings:

- Salsa
- Chopped onions
- Chopped fresh tomatoes
- Sliced black olives
- Torn lettuce
- Shredded cheese, your choice of flavor
- Chopped jalapeno peppers
- Sour cream

Instructions:

1. Grease interior of slow cooker crock.
2. Place pork in crock
3. In a bowl, combine juice and zest of limes, garlic powder, salt, cumin, and ½ cup chopped cilantro.
4. Pour sauce over roast.
5. Cover. Cook on low 6 hours.
6. Remove roast from crock and place in a good sized bowl. Shred, using two forks
7. Stir shredded meat back into the crock. Add remainder of chopped cilantro.
8. Fill tortillas with shredded meat and add your favorite toppings.

White Chicken Chili

(To serve 5-7)

Preparation Time: 20 minutes

Cooking Time: 5-6 hours

Ideal Slow-Cooker Size: 6-qt.

Ingredients:

- Leftover chicken, chopped
- 2 cups chicken broth
- 2 14½-oz. can cannellini beans
- 14½-oz. can garbanzo beans
- ¼ cup chopped onions
- ¼ cup chopped bell pepper
- Two tsp. Ground cumin
- ½ tsp. Dried oregano
- ¼ tsp. Cayenne pepper.
- ¼ tsp. salt

Instructions:

1. Combine all ingredients in slow cooker
2. Cover and cook on low for 5-6 hours.
3. Tip: Serve with sour cream, shredded cheese, and tortilla chips

Mexican Rice and Beans

(To serve 4-6)

Preparation Time: 20 minutes

Cooking Time: 2-3 hours

Ideal Slow-Cooker Size: 6-qt.

Ingredients:

- 1 cup leftover shredded pork.
- 15-oz. can black beans, rinsed and drained
- 10-oz. pkg. frozen whole kernel corn
- 1 cup long-grain rice, uncooked
- 16-oz. jar thick & stout mild or medium salsa
- 1½ cups vegetable or tomato juice
- ½ tsp. Ground cumin
- ½ tsp. Dried oregano
- ½ tsp. Salt
- ¼ tsp. Black pepper
- ¾ cup shredded cheddar cheese

Instructions:

1. Grease interior of slow-cooker crock.
2. Combine all your ingredients, apart from cheese, in the crock.
3. Cover. Cook for around two to three hours on high, until rice is tender, stirring once half way through.
4. Scatter cheese over rice and beans.
5. Allow to stand, uncovered, until cheese melts.

Hearty Pork and Veggie Soup

(To serve 4-6)

Preparation Time: 20 minutes

Cooking Time: 3-4 hours

Ideal Slow-Cooker Size: 6-qt.

Ingredients:

- ½ of a 1.8-oz pkg. dry beef-flavored soup mix
- ½ 0f a 1.8-oz. pkg. tomato flavored soup mix.
- 4 cups water
- 2 cups diced potatoes
- 3 cups chopped vegetables(celery, carrots, peppers, onions)
- Leftover shredded pork

Instructions:

1. In slow cooker, blend powdered soup mix into water. Add vegetables.
2. Cover and cook for around one hour on high, and then on low 3 hours.
3. One half hour before the end of cooking time, stir in meat.

Barbecued Ham Steaks

(To serve 4-6)

Preparation Time: 20 minutes

Cooking Time: 3-4 hours

Ideal Slow-Cooker Size: 6-qt.

Ingredients:

- 1 small onion, chopped
- 7-oz. bottle 7up, sprite, or ginger ale
- ¼ cup ketchup
- 1 tsp. salt
- 1/8 tsp. black pepper
- Four whole cloves
- 3-4 lbs. ham steaks

Instructions:

1. Grease interior of slow-cooker crock.
2. Mix together chopped onion, soda, ketchup, mustard, salt, pepper, and whole cloves in the crock.
3. Submerge steaks in the sauce. Overlap steaks if you must, but as little as possible.
4. Cover. Cook for around three to four hours on low, or until meat is heated through but not dry.
5. Fish out cloves and discard.
6. Cut each steak into smaller pieces and serve topped with barbecue sauce.

Potluck Baked Corn

(To serve 4-6)

Preparation Time: 20 minutes

Cooking Time: 3-4 hours

Ideal Slow-Cooker Size: 6-qt.

Ingredients:

- 2 lbs. Frozen corn, thawed and drained
- Four eggs, beaten
- Two tsp. salt
- 1¾ cups 2% or whole milk
- 2 Tbsp. Butter, melted
- 3 Tbsp. sugar
- 6Tbsp. flour

Instructions:

1. Mix all your ingredients in the mixing bowl until well combined.
2. Pour into greased slow cooker.
3. Cover. Cook on high 3-4 hours until set in the middle and lightly browned at edges.

Week 8

This week's menu

Sunday: Super Sausage Supper

Monday: Pasta Fagioli

Tuesday: Low-Fat Glazed Chicken

Wednesday: Low-Fat Chicken Cacciatore

Thursday: Slow—Cooker Shrimp Marinara

Friday: French Dip

Saturday: Barbecued Beef

Super Sausage Supper

(To serve 4-6)

Preparation Time: 20 minutes

Cooking Time: 5-6 hours

Ideal Slow-Cooker Size: 5- or 6-qt.

Ingredients:

- Two 8-oz. pkgs. Hot or mild ground sausage
- 16 oz. pkg. Frozen mixed vegetables
- $10^{3}/_{4}$ -oz. can broccoli cheese soup

Instructions:

1. Brown the sausage in a pan. Reserve 8 oz. of it and place in the refrigerator for later this week. Place the remaining browned sausage in slow cooker.
2. Distribute frozen vegetables over the sausage.
3. Spread undiluted soup on top of the vegetables.
4. Cover and cook on High for 1 hour, or on Low 5—6 hours, or until meat is cooked and vegetables are tender.

Pasta Fagioli

(To serve 4-6)

Preparation Time: 20 minutes

Cooking Time: 8-10 hours

Ideal Slow-Cooker Size: 5- or 6-qt.

Ingredients:

- Leftover browned sausage
- 3 cups beef broth
- 2 14½ -oz. cans diced tomatoes with garlic and onion
- 1 cups water
- 15-oz. can tomato sauce
- 1/4 cup dried red kidney beans that have been soaked overnight, drained and rinsed
- 1/4 cup dry great northern beans, soaked overnight, drained and rinsed
- 1 tsp. garlic powder
- 1 tsp. onion powder

- 1 tsp. Italian Seasoning
- Salt and pepper, to taste
- 1 cup chopped carrots
- 1 cups peeled and chopped zucchini
- ½ red onion, chopped
- ¾ cups dry pasta of your choice
- Parmesan cheese, for garnish

Instructions:

1. Combine all ingredients (except the Parmesan) in the slow cooker and stir.
2. Cook on Low for 8-10 hours.
3. 45 minutes before you serve, add the pasta. Serve with a sprinkle of Parmesan cheese.

Low-Fat Glazed Chicken

(To serve 4-8)

Preparation Time: 20 minutes

Cooking Time: 3-4 hours

Ideal Slow-Cooker Size: 5- or 6-qt.

Ingredients:

- 6-oz. can frozen concentrated orange juice, thawed
- ½ tsp. dried marjoram
- ¼ tsp. ground nutmeg
- ¼ tsp. garlic powder
- Eight skinless chicken breast halves

- 1/4 cup water
- 2 Tbsp. cornstarch

Instructions:

1. Mix orange juice concentrate with marjoram, nutmeg, and garlic powder.
2. Dip chicken breasts in the sauce. Place in slow cooker.
3. Pour remaining orange juice mixture over chicken.
4. Cover and cook for around six hours on Low or on High 3-4 hours.
5. Remove chicken from slow cooker and keep warm on a platter.
6. Pour remaining liquid into a saucepan.
7. Combine the cornstarch with water & pour into a saucepan.
8. Cook until thickened, stirring continually.
9. Pour sauce over the chicken.
10. Suggestion: Serve with rice or noodles.

Low-Fat Chicken Cacciatore

(To serve 4-8)

Preparation Time: 20 minutes

Cooking Time: 5-6 hours

Ideal Slow-Cooker Size: 5- or 6-qt.

Ingredients:

- ¼ lb. fresh mushrooms

- ½ bell pepper, chopped
- 1 small onion, chopped
- 12-Oz. can low-sodium chopped tomatoes
- 3-oz. low-sodium tomato paste
- 6-oz. can low-sodium tomato sauce
- ¼ tsp. dried oregano
- ¼ tsp. dried basil
- ¼ tsp. garlic powder
- ¼ tsp. salt
- 1/8 tsp. black pepper
- Leftover chicken, chopped

Instructions:

1. Combine all ingredients in slow cooker, except leftover chicken.
2. Cover. Cook on Low 5—6 hours. The last hour of cooking, stir in the leftover chicken.
3. Suggestion: Serve over rice or whole wheat, or semolina, pasta.

Slow Cooker Shrimp Marinara

(To serve 6)

Preparation Time: 20 minutes

Cooking Time: 3-4 hours

Ideal Slow-Cooker Size: 5- or 6-qt.

Ingredients:

- 16-oz. can low-sodium chopped tomatoes
- 2 Tbsp. Minced fresh parsley
- 1 clove garlic, minced
- ½ tsp. dried basil
- ½ tsp. salt
- ¼ tsp. black pepper
- 1 tsp. dried oregano
- 6-oz. can tomato paste
- ½ tsp. seasoned salt
- 1 lb. shrimp, cooked and shelled
- 3 cups cooked spaghetti (about 6-oz. dry) grated Parmesan cheese, for garnish

Instructions:

1. Combine tomatoes, parsley, garlic, basil, salt, pepper, oregano, tomato paste, and seasoned salt in slow cooker.
2. Cover. Cook on Low 3—4 hours.
3. Stir shrimp into sauce.
4. Cover. Cook on High 10—15 minutes.
5. Serve over cooked spaghetti. Top with parmesan cheese.

French Dip

(To serve 4-8)

Preparation Time: 20 minutes

Cooking Time: 5-6 hours

Ideal Slow-Cooker Size: 5- or 6-qt.

Ingredients:

- 2-lb. beef top round roast, trimmed
- 3 cups water
- 1 cup light soy sauce
- 1 tsp. dried rosemary
- 1 tsp. dried thyme
- 1 tsp. garlic powder
- 1 bay leaf
- Three whole peppercorns rolls

Instructions:

1. Place roast in slow cooker. Add water, soy sauce, and seasonings.
2. Cover. Cook on Low 5—6 hours.
3. Remove meat from broth. Thinly slice or shred. Keep warm.
4. Strain broth and skim off fat. Pour broth into small cups for dipping.
5. Serve beef on rolls.

Barbecued Beef

(To serve 4-8)

Preparation Time: 20 minutes

Cooking Time: 3-4 hours

Ideal Slow-Cooker Size: 5- or 6-qt.

Ingredients:

- 1 medium onion, sliced into rings
- ¾ bottle barbecue sauce
- ½ 12 oz. bottle/can cream soda or root beer
- Leftover shredded beef
- Buns

Instructions:

1. Place all ingredients except the shredded beef and buns into the slow cooker.
2. Cook on Low for 3—4 hours.
3. Stir in the leftover beef and cook for 1 more hour.
4. Serve on your favorite kind of bun.

Week 9

This week's menu

Sunday: Minestra di Ceci

Monday: Turkey Fajitas

Tuesday: Turkey Fajita Soup

Wednesday: Sausage-Potato Slow-Cooker Dinner

Thursday: Swiss Steak

Friday: Rice and Beans-and Sausage

Saturday: Slow-Cooker Beef with Mushrooms

Minestra di Ceci

(To serve 4-8)

Preparation Time: 20 minutes

Cooking Time: 5-6 hours

Ideal Slow-Cooker Size: 5- or 6-qt.

Ingredients:

- 1 lb. dry garbanzo beans
- 1 sprig fresh rosemary
- 10 leaves fresh sage
- 2 Tbsp. salt
- 1-2 large cloves garlic, minced

- Olive oil
- 1 cup uncooked small pasta, your choice of shape, or uncooked Penne

Instructions:

1. Wash beans. Place in slow cooker. Cover with water. Stir in rosemary, sage, and salt. Soak 8 hours, or overnight.
2. Drain water. Remove herbs.
3. Refill slow cooker with beans and fresh water to i-inch above beans.
4. Cover. Cook on Low 5 hours.
5. Sauté garlic in the olive oil in a skillet until clear.
6. Puree half of garbanzo beans, along with several cups of broth from cooker, in the blender. Return puree to slow cooker.
7. Add garlic and oil.
8. Boil pasta in saucepan until al dente, about 5 minutes. Drain. Add to beans.
9. Cover. Cook on High for 30-60 minutes, or until pasta is tender and heated through, but not mushy.

Turkey Fajitas

(To serve 4-8)

Preparation Time: 20 minutes

Cooking Time: 3-4 hours

Ideal Slow-Cooker Size: 5- or 6-qt.

388

Ingredients:

- 3 lbs. turkey tenderloins
- 1 1¼ -oz. envelope taco seasoning mix
- 1 rib celery, chopped
- 1 medium onion, chopped
- 14½ -oz. can diced tomatoes and green chilies, undrained
- 1 cup shredded cheddar cheese
- Eight 7½ inch flour tortillas

Toppings:

- Lettuce
- Sour cream
- Sliced olives
- Chopped tomatoes

Instructions:

1. Cut turkey into 2½ -inch-long strips. Place in zip-top plastic bag.
2. Add taco seasoning to the bag. Seal and shake to coat meat.
3. Empty seasoned turkey into slow cooker. Add celery, onion, and tomatoes. Stir together gently.
4. Cover. Cook for around three to four hours on High 3-4 hours, or just until turkey is cooked through and tender.
5. Stir in cheese.
6. Warm the tortillas as per the package directions. Spoon turkey mixture evenly into center of each tortilla, and roll up.

7.   Serve with Toppings.

Turkey Fajita Soup

(To serve 4-8)

Preparation Time: 20 minutes

Cooking Time: 3-5 hours

Ideal Slow-Cooker Size: 5- or 6-qt.

Ingredients:

- 1 cup chopped red onion
- 1 red bell pepper, chopped
- 1 yellow bell pepper, chopped
- 1 orange bell pepper, chopped
- 1 cup mushrooms, chopped
- 1 tsp. olive oil
- 1 tsp. chili powder
- 1 tsp. sea salt
- 1 tsp. garlic powder
- 1 tsp. Onion powder
- 1/2 tsp. ground cumin
- ½ tsp. cayenne pepper
- 6 cups chicken broth
- Leftover turkey

Instructions:

1. Put all your ingredients into a slow cooker apart from the leftover turkey.
2. Cover and cook on Low for 3-4 hours.
3. Add in the leftover turkey and cook an additional 30-60 minutes, or until the turkey is heated through.

Sausage-Potato Slow-Cooker Dinner

(To serve 4-8)

Preparation Time: 20 minutes

Cooking Time: 7-9 hours

Ideal Slow-Cooker Size: 5- or 6-qt.

Ingredients:

- 1 cup water
- 1/2 tsp. cream of tartar
- Six medium-sized potatoes, thinly sliced, either peeled or not, divided
- Two lbs. Sausage links, any kind you like, divided
- 1 medium onion, chopped, divided
- ¼ cup flour, divided
- Salt, to taste
- Pepper, to taste
- 1½ cups grated cheddar cheese, divided
- 2 Tbsp. butter
- 10¾ -oz. can cream of mushroom soup

Instructions:

1. Mix water & cream of tartar in a good sized mixing bowl. Place potatoes in water as you slice them. When finished slicing, toss potatoes in water to keep them from turning brown. Drain off the water.

2. Layer half of potatoes, sausage, onion, flour, a sprinkling of salt and pepper, and half of cheddar cheese in slow cooker.

3. Repeat layers of potatoes, sausage, onion, flour, salt, and pepper until completely used.

4. Dot butter over the top. Pour soup over all.

5. Cover. Cook on Low 7-9 hours or on High 3-4 hours, or until potatoes and onions are tender.

6. Sprinkle reserved cheese over top just

Swiss steak

(To serve 4-10)

Preparation Time: 20 minutes

Cooking Time: 3-4 hours

Ideal Slow-Cooker Size: 5- or 6-qt.

Ingredients:

- 3-lb. round steak, cut into serving pieces
- 1 tsp. salt
- ½ tsp. pepper
- 1 large onion, sliced or 1 pkg. dry onion soup mix
- 16-oz. can tomatoes

Instructions:

1. Combine all ingredients in slow cooker.
2. Cover. Cook on Low 6—10 hours or on High 3-4 hours, just until meat is fork-tender.

Rice and Beans—and Sausage

(To serve 4-8)

Preparation Time: 20 minutes

Cooking Time: 5-9 hours

Ideal Slow-Cooker Size: 5- or 6-qt.

Ingredients:

- Three ribs celery, chopped
- 1 medium onion, chopped
- Two cloves garlic, minced
- ¼ cups tomato juice
- 2 16-oz. cans kidney beans, drained
- ¾ tsp. dried oregano
- ¾ tsp. dried thyme
- ¼ tsp. red pepper flakes
- ¼ tsp. pepper
- Leftover sausage

Instructions:

1. Combine all ingredients in slow cooker.
2. Cover. Cook on Low 3—4 hours.
3. Suggestion: Serve over rice. Garnish

Slow Cooker Beef with Mushrooms

(To serve 4-8)

Preparation Time: 20 minutes

Cooking Time: 2-3 hours

Ideal Slow-Cooker Size: 5- or 6-qt.

Ingredients:

- Two medium onions, thinly sliced
- ½ lb. Mushrooms, sliced, or 2 4-oz. Cans sliced mushrooms, drained
- Salt, to taste
- Pepper, to taste
- 1 Tbsp. Worcestershire sauce
- 1 Tbsp. Oil of your choice
- Paprika, to taste
- ½ cup beef stock
- Leftover steak
- Rice

Instructions:

1. Place all ingredients into the slow cooker.
2. Cover. Cook on Low 2-3 hours.
3. Cook rice. Serve beef over rice.

Week 10

This Week's Menu

Sunday: Savory chicken meal #1

Monday: A touch of Asia ribs

Tuesday: Savory chicken meal #2

Wednesday: Pork Thai stew

Thursday: Walking Tacos

Friday: Upside down pizza

Saturday: Beef Nachos

Recommended Side Dish: Chinese vegetables

Special Dessert: Pears in Ginger Sauce

Savory Chicken Meal #1

(To serve 4-8)

Preparation Time: 20 minutes

Cooking Time: 4-5 hours

Ideal Slow-Cooker Size: 5- or 6-qt

Ingredients:

- Four boneless, skinless chicken breast halves
- Four skinless chicken quarters

- 10¾ -oz. can cream of chicken Soup
- 1 Tbsp. water
- ¼ cup chopped sweet red peppers
- 1 Tbsp. Chopped fresh parsley, or 1 tsp. Dried parsley, optional
- 1 Tbsp. Lemon juice
- 1/2 tsp. paprika, optional

Instructions:

1. Layer chicken in slow cooker.
2. Combine remaining ingredients and pour over chicken. Make sure all pieces are covered with sauce.
3. Cover. Cook on High 4-5 hours.

A-Touch-of-Asia Ribs

(To serve 4-5)

Preparation Time: 20 minutes

Cooking Time: 4-8 hours

Ideal Slow-Cooker Size: 5- or 6-qt

Ingredients:

- 6 lbs. country-style pork ribs, cut into serving-size pieces
- ¼ cup teriyaki sauce
- ¼ cup cornstarch
- 27-oz. jar duck sauce
- 2 Tbsp. Minced garlic, optional

Instructions:

1.   Place the ribs at the bottom of the slow cooker.
2.   In a large-sized bowl, mix together the teriyaki sauce & cornstarch. Mix in the duck sauce, & garlic if you like.
3.   Pour the sauce over the ribs, making sure that each layer is well covered.
4.   Cover and cook for around eight hours on Low, or on High 4-5 hours.

Savory Chicken Meal #2

(To serve 4-8)

Preparation Time: 20 minutes

Cooking Time: 3-5 hours

Ideal Slow-Cooker Size: 5- or 6-qt

Ingredients:

- Leftover chicken and broth from Savory Chicken Meal #1
- 2 carrots
- 1 rib celery
- Two medium onions
- 2 Tbsp. flour or cornstarch
- ¼ cup cold water

Instructions:

1.   For a second Savory Chicken Meal, pick leftover chicken off the bone. Set aside.

2.   Return remaining broth to slow cooker and stir in thinly sliced carrots and celery, and onions cut up in chunks. Cook 3—4 hours on High.

3.   In a separate bowl, mix flour or cornstarch with cold water. When smooth, stir into hot broth.

4.   Stir in cut-up chicken. Heat 15—20 minutes, or until broth thickens and chicken is hot.

5.   Suggestion: Serve over rice or pasta.

Pork Thai Stew

(To serve 4-8)

Preparation Time: 20 minutes

Cooking Time: 3 hours

Ideal Slow-Cooker Size: 5- or 6-qt

Ingredients:

- Two cloves garlic, sliced
- 2 cups sliced red bell pepper
- ¼ cup rice vinegar
- ½ cup teriyaki sauce
- 1-2 tsp. red pepper flakes, according to your taste preference for the leftover rib meat
- ¼ -½ cup creamy peanut butter
- Rice, cooked
- Chopped peanuts

- Chopped green onions

Instructions:

1. Place garlic, red bell pepper, rice vinegar, teriyaki sauce, red pepper flakes, and leftover rib meat into the slow cooker.
2. Cook 2-2½ hours on Low.
3. Stir in peanut butter. Continue cooking for 30 more minutes, until heated through.
4. Serve over cooked rice.
5. Pass bowls of chopped peanuts and sliced green onions for each diner to add as they wish.

Walking Tacos

(To serve 4-8)

Preparation Time: 20 minutes

Cooking Time: 5-6 hours

Ideal Slow-Cooker Size: 5- or 6-qt

Ingredients:

- 2 tsp. garlic powder
- Two tsp. Onion powder
- 1 Tbsp. Ground cumin
- 2 Tbsp. Chili powder
- 1 tsp. salt
- 2 lbs. ground beef
- 1 small onion, minced

- 1 clove garlic, minced
- ½ tsp. dried oregano
- ½ tsp. red pepper flakes
- Individual-sized bags of Doritos, Fritos, or other corn chips of your choice

Toppings:

- Shredded lettuce
- Shredded cheese
- Diced tomatoes
- Diced onions
- Diced cucumbers
- Salsa

Instructions:

1. Place all of the spices in a bowl and mix it up.
2. Crumble the raw ground beef into your crock.
3. Sprinkle the seasoning mix onto the beef and stir it up.
4. Cook on High for 1 hour to brown the beef a bit. Stir it & break it up a bit. Then, cook it for around five to six hours on Low for 5—6 hours more.
5. To serve, give each person an individual-sized bag of Doritos, Fritos, or other corn chips of their choice. Each person can then open it, crush the chips by squeezing the bottom of the bag, then add beef and the toppings of their choice.

Upside-Down Pizza

(To serve 4-8)

Preparation Time: 20 minutes

Cooking Time: 4-6 hours

Ideal Slow-Cooker Size: 5- or 6-qt

Ingredients:

- 1 lb. ground beef
- 1 small onion, chopped
- ½ medium red or green bell pepper, chopped
- ½ tsp. dried basil
- ½ tsp. dried oregano
- 1 cup pizza or spaghetti sauce
- ¼ lb. Fresh mushrooms or 4-oz. Can chopped mushrooms, drained
- 1 cup grated mozzarella cheese
- Sprinkling of dried oregano
- Sprinkling of grated Parmesan cheese

Batter:

- 3 eggs
- 1½ cups milk
- 1½ Tbsp. oil of your choice
- ½ tsp. salt
- 1 tsp. baking soda
- 1¾ cups flour

Instructions:

1. Grease interior of slow-cooker crock.
2. If you have time, brown beef, onion, and pepper together in a skillet. Using a slotted spoon, lift beef and veggies out of drippings and place in a good-sized bowl. If you don't have time, place beef in the bowl and use a sturdy spoon to break it up into small clumps. Mix in onion and chopped pepper.
3. Spoon beef and vegetables into the crock.
4. Stir in herbs, sauce, and mushrooms.
5. Cover. Cook for around four hours on Low, or until hot in center.
6. Thirty minutes before the end of cooking time, prepare batter by beating eggs, milk, and oil together in good-sized mixing bowl.
7. Add salt, baking soda, and flour, stirring just until mixed.
8. Uncover crock. Top the beef and vegetables with grated mozzarella cheese.
9. Spoon batter over the top, spreading it out evenly. Do not stir.
10. Sprinkle with oregano and Parmesan cheese.
11. Cover. Cook on High 1 hour, or until the toothpick inserted in center of dough comes out clean.

Beef Nachos

(To serve 4-8)

Preparation Time: 20 minutes

Cooking Time: 45 minutes

Ideal Slow-Cooker Size: 5- or 6-qt

Ingredients:

- Leftover taco meat
- Tortilla chips
- 8 oz. shredded cheese, whatever kind you like
- ½ cup onions, chopped
- Additional Toppings:
- Shredded lettuce
- Salsa
- Chopped tomatoes
- Diced cucumbers
- Sour cream or Greek yogurt
- Green onions, diced guacamole

Instructions:

1. Preheat the oven to 400°F.
2. Spray your baking sheet with nonstick spray, then arrange as many chips as you wish across the baking sheet.
3. Top with the leftover taco meat, then evenly spread the oven across the chips. Cover all tortilla chips evenly with the shredded cheese.
4. Bake for 10-15 minutes or until cheese is melted.
5. Top with any additional toppings you wish.

Week 11

This week's menu

Sunday: Honey baked ham

Monday: Italian sausage, peppers, and potatoes

Tuesday: Verenike

Wednesday: Sausage town

Thursday: Black bean Ham soup

Friday: Salsa chicken

Saturday: Salsa chicken salad

Recommended Side Dish: Au Gratin green beans

Special Dessert: Cookie divine

Honey-Baked Ham

(To serve 4-8)

Preparation Time: 20 minutes

Cooking Time: 4-5 hours

Ideal Slow-Cooker Size: 5- or 6-qt

Ingredients:

- 5-lb. fully cooked ham
- ½ cup brown sugar
- ¼ cup dry sherry
- 3 Tbsp. honey
- 3 Tbsp. Dijon mustard
- ¼ tsp. coarsely ground black pepper
- ½ cup pineapple chunks
- ½ cup fresh cranberries

Instructions:

1. Grease interior of slow-cooker crock.
2. Utilizing a sharp knife, score the surface of the ham into diamond shapes, cutting about ¼ -inch deep. Place the ham in the crock.
3. Cover cooker. Cook on Low 3 hours.
4. While ham is cooking, blend together brown sugar, sherry, honey, mustard, and black pepper.
5. Brush ham with glaze. Cover and continue cooking.
6. After ham has cooked two more hours (for a total of 5 hours), brush again with glaze.
7. Using toothpicks, decorate ham with pineapple chunks and cranberries, spreading pieces over ham evenly.
8. Cover and cook on High another 15minutes.
9. When ham is heated through, remove from cooker with sturdy tongs and metal spatulas supporting. Slice meat.

10. Place slices on a deep platter, covering them with glaze.

11. Put any remaining glaze, and any pineapples and cranberries that have fallen off, in a bowl to pass around the table for diners to add more to their individual plates.

Italian sausage, peppers, and potatoes

(To serve 4-8)

Preparation Time: 20 minutes

Cooking Time: 4-6 hours

Ideal Slow-Cooker Size: 5- or 6-qt

Ingredients:

- 2 lbs. Sweet or hot Italian sausage. It should be cut on the diagonal into 1-inch lengths
- 1 lb. small red potatoes, each cut in half
- 1 large onion, cut into 12 wedges
- Two red/yellow bell peppers or 1 of each color, cut into strips

Instructions:

1. Grease interior of slow-cooker crock.
2. Put sausage, potatoes, and onion into the crock. Stir together well.
3. Gently stir in bell pepper strips.

4.   Cover. Cook for around four to six hours on Low, or on High 2—3 hours, or until sausage is cooked through and potatoes and onions are as tender as you like them.

Verenike (or Creamy Lasagna)

(To serve 4-8)

Preparation Time: 20 minutes

Cooking Time: 5-6 hours

Ideal Slow-Cooker Size: 5- or 6-qt

Ingredients:

- 12 oz. cottage cheese
- Two large eggs
- ½ tsp. salt
- ¼ tsp. pepper
- ½ cup sour cream
- 1 cup evaporated milk
- 1 cup leftover ham, cubed
- 4-5 uncooked lasagna noodles

Instructions:

1.   Combine all ingredients except noodles in a good-sized mixing bowl.
2.   Place half of creamy ham mixture in bottom of cooker.

3.   Stack in uncooked noodles. Break them to fit if you
        need to.

4.   Cover with remaining half of creamy ham sauce. Push
        noodles down so that they are fully submerged in the
        sauce.

5.   Cover. Cook on Low 5-6 hours, or until noodles are
        tender but not mushy.

Sausage Town

(To serve 4-8)

Preparation Time: 20 minutes

Cooking Time: 3-4 hours

Ideal Slow-Cooker Size: 5- or 6-qt.

Ingredients:

- 1 cup chopped onion
- ¾ cup dry lentils, rinsed well and picked clean
- ¾ cup shredded cheddar cheese
- Two cloves garlic, crushed
- ½ tsp. dried thyme
- ½ tsp. dried basil
- ½ tsp. dried oregano
- 1/8 tsp. dried sage
- ¼ tsp. salt
- Freshly ground black pepper, to taste
- Leftover sausage, cut into bite-sized pieces
- 4 14½-oz. cans chicken broth

- ¾ cup uncooked long-grain brown rice

Instructions:

1. Grease interior of slow-cooker crock.
2. Place onions, lentils, cheese, garlic, thyme, basil, oregano, sage, salt, black pepper, sausage, and chicken broth into the crock. Stir together well.
3. Cover. Cook on Low 6—7 hours.
4. Stir in uncooked rice.
5. Cover. Continue cooking on Low another 3 hours, or until both rice and lentils are as tender as you like them.
6. If the dish is juicier than you want, uncover during last 30 minutes of cooking and turn cooker to High.
7. Stir well and serve.

Black Bean Ham Soup

(To serve 4-8)

Preparation Time: 20 minutes

Cooking Time: 6-8 hours

Ideal Slow-Cooker Size: 5- or 6-qt

Ingredients:

- ½ tsp. chili powder
- ¼ tsp. hot pepper sauce
- 1 cup diced leftover ham
- 2 cups chopped carrots

- 1 cup chopped celery
- Two cloves garlic, minced
- 1 medium onion, chopped
- 2 15-OZ. cans black beans, undrained
- 2 14½ -oz. cans chicken or vegetable broth
- 15-oz. can crushed tomatoes
- 1½ tsp. dried basil
- ½ tsp. dried oregano
- ½ tsp. ground cumin

Instructions:

1. Combine all ingredients in slow cooker.
2. Cover and cook for around six to eight hours on Low or until vegetables are tender.
3. Tip: Serve with hot cooked rice.

Salsa Chicken

(To serve 4-8)

Preparation Time: 20 minutes

Cooking Time: 4-5 hours

Ideal Slow-Cooker Size: 5- or 6-qt

Ingredients:

- Eight boneless, skinless chicken thighs
- 1½ cups salsa, your choice of heat
- 2 Tbsp. Dry taco seasoning mix
- 1½ cups shredded cheddar cheese

- ¼ cup sour cream, optional

Instructions:

1. Grease interior of slow-cooker crock.
2. Lay the thighs in slow cooker. If you need to create a second layer, stagger the pieces so they don't completely overlap each other.
3. Spoon salsa over each thigh, making sure not to miss the ones on the first layer that are partly covered by pieces above.
4. Sprinkle taco seasoning mix over each thigh, again, making sure not to miss the ones on the first layer.
5. Cover. Cook for around on Low for 4 hours, or until instant-read meat thermometer registers 160—165°F when stuck into the meat.
6. Thirty minutes before the cooking time ends, scatter shredded cheese over each thigh, including those on the first layer that are partly covered.
7. Top each thigh with sour cream as you serve the chicken, if you wish.

Salsa Chicken Salad

(To serve 4-8)

Preparation Time: 20 minutes

Cooking Time: 1 hour

Ideal Slow-Cooker Size: 5- or 6-qt

Ingredients:

- Leftover chicken, chopped
- ¾ cup salsa
- ¾ cup sour cream
- 1 head of lettuce of your choice,
- Chopped (romaine would work great)

Additional Toppings:

- Crushed tortilla chips
- Diced avocado
- Chopped tomatoes

Instructions:

1. Warm the leftover chicken if you choose, or leave it cold.
2. Mix together the salsa and sour cream.
3. Place chopped lettuce in a bowl or dish, top with the desired amount of leftover chicken and pour some of the salsa-sour cream mixture over the top.
4. Add any of the additional toppings you wish.

Week 11

This week's menu

Sunday: Honey baked ham

Monday: Italian sausage, peppers, and potatoes

Tuesday: Verenike

Wednesday: Sausage town

Thursday: Black bean Ham soup

Friday: Salsa chicken

Saturday: Salsa chicken salad

Recommended Side Dish: Au Gratin green beans

Special Dessert: Cookie divine

Honey-Baked Ham

(To serve 4-8)

Preparation Time: 20 minutes

Cooking Time: 5-6 hours

Ideal Slow-Cooker Size: 5- or 6-qt

Ingredients:

- 5-lb. fully cooked ham
- ½ cup brown sugar

- ¼ cup dry sherry
- 3 Tbsp. honey
- 3 Tbsp. Dijon mustard
- ¼ tsp. coarsely ground black pepper
- ½ cup pineapple chunks
- ½ cup fresh cranberries

Instructions:

1. Grease interior of slow-cooker crock.
2. Utilizing a sharp knife, score the surface of the ham into diamond shapes, cutting about ¼ -inch deep. Place ham in the crock.
3. Cover cooker. Cook on Low 3 hours.
4. While ham is cooking, blend together brown sugar, sherry, honey, mustard, and black pepper.
5. Brush ham with glaze. Cover and continue cooking.
6. After ham has cooked two more hours (for a total of 5 hours), brush again with glaze.
7. Using toothpicks, decorate ham with pineapple chunks and cranberries, spreading pieces over ham evenly.
8. Cover and cook on High another 15minutes.
9. When ham is heated through, remove from cooker with sturdy tongs and metal spatulas supporting. Slice meat.
10. Place slices on a deep platter, covering them with glaze.
11. Put any remaining glaze, and any pineapples and cranberries that have fallen off, in a bowl to pass

around the table for diners to add more to their individual plates.

Italian sausage, peppers, and potatoes

(To serve 4-8)

Preparation Time: 20 minutes

Cooking Time: 4-6 hours

Ideal Slow-Cooker Size: 5- or 6-qt

Ingredients:

- 2 lbs. sweet/hot Italian sausage, cut on the diagonal into 1-inch lengths
- 1 lb. small red potatoes, each cut in half
- 1 large onion, cut into 12 wedges
- Two red/yellow bell peppers or 1 of each color, cut into strips

Instructions:

1. Grease interior of slow-cooker crock.
2. Put sausage, potatoes, and onion into the crock. Stir together well.
3. Gently stir in bell pepper strips.
4. Cover. Cook for around four to six hours on Low, or on High 2—3 hours, or until sausage is cooked through and potatoes and onions are as tender as you like them.

Verenike (or Creamy Lasagna)

(To serve 4-8)

Preparation Time: 20 minutes

Cooking Time: 5-6 hours

Ideal Slow-Cooker Size: 5- or 6-qt

Ingredients:

- 12 oz. cottage cheese
- Two large eggs
- ½ tsp. salt
- ¼ tsp. pepper
- ½ cup sour cream
- 1 cup evaporated milk
- 1 cup leftover ham, cubed
- 4-5 uncooked lasagna noodles

Instructions:

1. Combine all ingredients except noodles in a good-sized mixing bowl.
2. Place half of creamy ham mixture in bottom of cooker.
3. Stack in uncooked noodles. Break them to fit if you need to.
4. Cover with remaining half of creamy ham sauce. Push noodles down so that they are fully submerged in the sauce.
5. Cover. Cook on Low 5-6 hours, or until noodles are tender but not mushy.

Sausage Town

(To serve 4-8)

Preparation Time: 20 minutes

Cooking Time: 10 hours

Ideal Slow-Cooker Size: 5- or 6-qt

Ingredients:

- 1 cup chopped onion
- ¾ cup dry lentils, rinsed well and picked clean
- ¾ cup shredded cheddar cheese
- 2 cloves garlic, crushed
- ½ tsp. dried thyme
- ½ tsp. dried basil
- ½ tsp. dried oregano
- 1/8 tsp. dried sage
- ¼ tsp. salt
- Freshly ground black pepper, to taste
- Leftover sausage, cut into bite-sized pieces
- 4 14½-oz. cans chicken broth
- ¾ cup uncooked long-grain brown rice

Instructions:

1. Grease interior of slow-cooker crock.
2. Place onions, lentils, cheese, garlic, thyme, basil, oregano, sage, salt, black pepper, sausage, and chicken broth into the crock. Stir together well.

3.   Cover. Cook on Low 6—7 hours.

4.   Stir in uncooked rice.

5.   Cover. Continue cooking on Low another 3hours, or until both rice and lentils are as tender as you like them.

6.   If the dish is juicier than you want, uncover during last 30 minutes of cooking and turn cooker to High.

7.   Stir well and serve.

Black Bean Ham Soup

(To serve 4-8)

Preparation Time: 20 minutes

Cooking Time: 6-8 hours

Ideal Slow-Cooker Size: 5- or 6-qt

Ingredients:

- ½ tsp. chili powder
- ¼ tsp. hot pepper sauce
- 1 cup diced leftover ham
- 2 cups chopped carrots
- 1 cup chopped celery
- Two cloves garlic, minced
- 1 medium onion, chopped
- 2 15-OZ. cans black beans, undrained
- 2 14½ -oz. cans chicken or vegetable broth
- 15-oz. can crushed tomatoes
- 1½ tsp. dried basil

- ½ tsp. dried oregano
- ½ tsp. ground cumin

Instructions:

1. Combine all ingredients in slow cooker.
2. Cover and cook for around six to eight hours on Low or until vegetables are tender.
3. Tip: Serve with hot cooked rice.

Salsa Chicken

(To serve 4-8)

Preparation Time: 20 minutes

Cooking Time: 4-5 hours

Ideal Slow-Cooker Size: 5- or 6-qt

Ingredients:

- Eight boneless, skinless chicken thighs
- 1½ cups salsa, your choice of heat
- 2 Tbsp. Dry taco seasoning mix
- 1½ cups shredded cheddar cheese
- ¼ cup sour cream, optional

Instructions:

1. Grease interior of slow-cooker crock.
2. Lay the thighs in slow cooker. If you need to create a second layer, stagger the pieces so they don't completely overlap each other.

3. Spoon salsa over each thigh, making sure not to miss the ones on the first layer that are partly covered by pieces above.

4. Sprinkle taco seasoning mix over each thigh, again, making sure not to miss the ones on the first layer.

5. Cover. Cook on Low for 4 hours, or until instant-read meat thermometer registers 160—165°F when stuck into the meat.

6. Thirty minutes before the cooking time ends, scatter shredded cheese over each thigh, including those on the first layer that are partly covered.

7. Top each thigh with sour cream as you serve the chicken, if you wish.

Salsa Chicken Salad

(To serve 4-8)

Preparation Time: 20 minutes

Ingredients:

- Leftover chicken, chopped
- ¾ cup salsa
- ¾ cup sour cream
- 1 head of lettuce of your choice,
- Chopped (romaine would work great)
- Additional Toppings:
- Crushed tortilla chips
- Diced avocado
- Chopped tomatoes

Ingredients:

1. Warm the leftover chicken if you choose, or leave it cold.
2. Mix together the salsa and sour cream.
3. Place chopped lettuce in a bowl or dish, top with the desired amount of leftover chicken and pour some of the salsa-sour cream mixture over the top.
4. Add any of the additional toppings you wish.

Week 12

This week's menu

Sunday: Wine Tender roast

Monday: Santa Fe Stew

Tuesday: Cranberry-orange Turkey Breast

Wednesday: Fruited Turkey and yams

Thursday: 10-layer slow-cooker dish

Friday: Hamburger soup

Saturday: Company seafood pasta

Recommended Side Dish: Yummy spinach

Special Dessert: Festive Applesauce

Wine Tender Roast

(To serve 4-8)

Preparation Time: 20 minutes

Cooking Time: 6-9 hours

Ideal Slow-Cooker Size: 5- or 6-qt

Ingredients:

- 4—5-lb. beef chuck roast
- 1 cup thinly sliced onion

- 1 cup chopped apple, peeled, or unpeeled
- Six cloves garlic, chopped
- 1 1/2 cups red wine
- Salt and pepper, to taste

Instructions:

1. Grease interior of slow-cooker crock.
2. Put roast in slow cooker. Layer onion, apple, add garlic on top of roast.
3. Carefully pour wine over roast without disturbing its toppings.
4. Sprinkle with salt and pepper.
5. Cover. Cook on Low 6—8 hours, or until instant-read meat thermometer registers 145 degrees Fahrenheit when stuck into the center of roast.
6. Remove meat from the crock. Allow to stand for 10 minutes. Then slice or shred and serve.

Santa Fe Stew

(To serve 4-8)

Preparation Time: 20 minutes

Cooking Time: 4-5 hours

Ideal Slow-Cooker Size: 5- or 6-qt

Ingredients:

- Leftover roast meat, chopped
- 1 large onion, diced

- Two cloves garlic, minced
- 1½ cups water
- 1 Tbsp. Dried parsley flakes
- Two beef bouillon cubes
- 1 tsp. ground cumin
- ½ tsp. salt
- Three carrots, sliced
- 14½-oz. can diced tomatoes
- 14½-oz. Can green beans, drained, or 1 lb. Frozen green beans
- 14 ½ -oz. Can corn, drained, or 1-lb. Frozen corn
- 4-oz. can diced green chilies
- Three zucchini, diced, optional

Instructions:

1. Grease interior of slow-cooker crock.
2. Place all ingredients, except zucchini, into slow cooker.
3. Cover. Cook on Low 4—5 hours, or until meat is tender and vegetables are as tender as you like them.
4. One hour before the cooking time ends, stir in diced zucchini, if you want to include it.

Cranberry-Orange Turkey Breast

(To serve 4-8)

Preparation Time: 20 minutes

Cooking Time: 7-8 hours

Ideal Slow-Cooker Size: 5- or 6-qt

Ingredients:

- ½ cup orange marmalade
- 14-oz. can whole berry cranberry sauce
- Two tsp. Orange zest, grated
- 3-4-lb. turkey breast

Instructions:

1. Combine marmalade, cranberry sauce, and zest in a bowl.
2. Place turkey breast in slow cooker and pour half the orange-cranberry mixture over turkey.
3. Cover. Cook for around seven to eight hours on Low or on High 3¼ hours, until turkey juices run clear.
4. Add remaining half of orange-cranberry mixture for last half hour of cooking.
5. Remove turkey to warm platter and allow it to rest for 15 minutes before slicing.
6. Serve with orange-cranberry sauce.

Fruited Turkey and Yams

(To serve 4-8)

Preparation Time: 20 minutes

Cooking Time: 4-5 hours

Ideal Slow-Cooker Size: 5- or 6-qt

Ingredients:

- 1 large yarn, or sweet potato, cut crosswise into ½-inch-thick slices
- Leftover turkey, chopped
- ½ cup chopped mixed dried fruit
- 1 tsp. chopped garlic
- ½ tsp. salt
- ¼ tsp. pepper
- ½ cup orange juice
- 1/8 cup chopped fresh parsley

Instructions:

1. Place yarn slices in the slow cooker with leftover turkey on top.
2. Sprinkle with dried fruit, garlic, salt, and pepper.
3. Gently pour orange juice over the top, being careful not to disturb fruit and seasonings.
4. Cover. Cook for around four to five hours on Low for or until the potatoes are cooked through.
5. Sprinkle with parsley before serving.

10-Layer Slow-Cooker Dish

(To serve 4-8)

Preparation Time: 20 minutes

Cooking Time: 6 hours

Ideal Slow-Cooker Size: 5- or 6-qt

Ingredients:

- 2 lbs. ground beef, browned
- 3-4 medium potatoes, thinly sliced
- 1 medium onion, thinly sliced
- ½ tsp. salt
- ½ tsp. black pepper
- 15-oz. can corn, undrained
- 15-oz. can peas, undrained
- ¼ cup water
- 10¾-oz. can fat-free, low-sodium cream of mushroom soup

Instructions:

1. Brown ground beef in nonstick skillet. Set aside 1 lb. in the refrigerator for tomorrow's dinner. Then create the following layers in the slow cooker.
2. Layer 1: one-fourth of potatoes, mixed with one-half the onion, salt, and pepper.
3. Layer 2: half-can of corn.
4. Layer 3: one-fourth of potatoes.
5. Layer 4: half-can of peas.
6. Layer 5: one-fourth of potatoes, mixed with one-half the onions, salt, and pepper.
7. Layer 6: remaining corn.
8. Layer 7: remaining potatoes.
9. Layer 8: remaining peas and water.
10. Layer 9: ground beef.
11. Layer 10: soup.
12. Cover. Cook for around three to four hours on High or on Low 6 hours.

Hamburger Soup

(To serve 4-8)

Preparation Time: 20 minutes

Cooking Time: 6-7 hours

Ideal Slow-Cooker Size: 5- or 6-qt

Ingredients:

- Leftover ground beef
- 3 cups beef broth
- 14½-oz. can diced tomatoes
- 8-oz. Can tomato sauce oz. Tomato paste
- 1 cup chopped onion
- ½ cup chopped carrots
- ½ cup chopped celery
- ½ cup frozen corn
- 1 tsp. salt
- 1 tsp. dried basil
- ½ tsp. garlic powder
- ½ tsp. onion powder

Instructions:

1. Place all ingredients in the slow cooker.
2. Cover and cook for around six to seven hours on Low.

Company Seafood Pasta

(To serve 4-8)

Preparation Time: 20 minutes

Cooking Time: 2 hours

Ideal Slow-Cooker Size: 5- or 6-qt

Ingredients:

- 2 cups sour cream
- 3 cups shredded Monterey Jack cheese
- 2 Tb sp. butter, melted
- ½ lb. crabmeat or imitation flaked crabmeat
- 1/8 tsp. pepper
- ½ lb. bay scallops, lightly cooked
- 1 lb. medium shrimp, cooked and peeled

Instructions:

1. Mix sour cream, cheese, & butter in your slow cooker.
2. Stir in the remaining ingredients.
3. Cover. Cook for around one to two hours on Low.
4. Suggestion: Serve immediately over linguine. Garnish with fresh parsley.

Week 13

This week's menu

Sunday: Corned Beef with cabbage, carrots and red potatoes

Monday: Corned beef hash

Tuesday: Reuben in a crock

Wednesday: Lamb chops

Thursday: Lamb stew

Friday: Shepherd's pie

Saturday: Quick and easy spaghetti

Recommended Side Dish: Irish Soda Bread

Special Dessert: Harvey wall banger cake

Corned Beef together with Cabbage, Carrots, & Red Potatoes

(To serve 4-8)

Preparation Time: 20 minutes

Cooking Time: 9-10 hours

Ideal Slow-Cooker Size: 5- or 6-qt

Ingredients:

- 6-lb. low-sodium corned beef brisket
- 1 head of cabbage

- 3-4 large carrots
- 24 oz. baby red potatoes
- Salt, to taste
- Pepper, to taste
- Water

Instructions:

1. Put the brisket at your crock's bottom. It is going to come with a seasoning packet. Sprinkle the contents of that packet over your brisket.
2. Cover your brisket with water.
3. Place the veggies on and around your brisket.
4. Sprinkle your cabbage with salt and pepper to taste.
5. Cover and cook for around nine to ten hours on Low.

Corned Beef Hash

(To serve 4-8)

Preparation Time: 20 minutes

Cooking Time: 7-8 hours

Ideal Slow-Cooker Size: 5- or 6-qt

Ingredients:

- 1 lb. potatoes, peeled and diced
- 1½-2 cups diced leftover corned beef
- 1 cup diced onion
- ½ cup diced bell pepper (whatever color you like)
- 1 tsp. salt

- ½ tsp. pepper
- 2—3 cups chicken stock (just enough to cover your ingredients)

Instructions:

1. Place the potatoes, leftover corned beef, onion, bell pepper, salt, and pepper in your crock and stir.
2. Drain in the chicken stock, just until the mixture is just barely submerged.
3. Cook for around seven to eight hours on Low.
4. Tip: If there happens to be too much liquid left, leave the top off for a while and continue to cook, or add some gravy mix granules to thicken.

Reuben in a Crock

(To serve 4-8)

Preparation Time: 20 minutes

Cooking Time: 4 hours

Ideal Slow-Cooker Size: 5- or 6-qt

Ingredients:

- 1½ cups Thousand Island salad dressing
- 1 cup sour cream
- 1 Tbsp. Dried minced onion
- 12 slices dark rye bread, cubed, divided
- 1 lb. sauerkraut, drained
- 1½ cups leftover corned beef, cut thin

- 2 cups shredded Swiss cheese
- ½ stick (4 Tbsp.) butter, melted

Instructions:

1. Grease interior of slow-cooker crock.
2. In a bowl, mix together dressing, sour cream, and minced onion. Set aside.
3. Place half the bread cubes in the crock.
4. Top with sauerkraut, spread out evenly over bread.
5. Add a layer of corned beef, distributed evenly over sauerkraut.
6. Spread dressing mixture over corned beef.
7. Scatter shredded cheese over the top.
8. Top with remaining bread cubes.
9. Drizzle with melted butter.
10. Cover and cook for around three and a half hours on Low, or until mixture is heated through.
11. Remove the cover. Cook on Low 30 more minutes to allow moisture to escape.

Lamb Chops

(To serve 4-8)

Preparation Time: 20 minutes

Cooking Time: 4-6 hours

Ideal Slow-Cooker Size: 5- or 6-qt

Ingredients:

- 1 medium onion, sliced

- 1 tsp. dried oregano
- ½ tsp. dried thyme
- ½ tsp. garlic powder
- ¼ tsp. salt
- ½ tsp. pepper
- 4 lbs. loin lamb chops
- Two cloves garlic, minced
- ¼ cup water

Instructions:

1. Place onion in slow cooker.
2. In a small bowl, combine oregano, thyme, garlic powder, salt, and pepper. Rub over lamb chops. Place chops in slow cooker.
3. Top chops with garlic.
4. Pour water down alongside cooker, so as not to disturb rub and garlic on chops.
5. Cover. Cook for around four to six hours on Low, or until chops are tender but not dry.

Lamb Stew

(To serve 4-8)

Preparation Time: 20 minutes

Cooking Time: 7-8 hours

Ideal Slow-Cooker Size: 5- or 6-qt.

Ingredients:

- Two tsp. salt
- ¼ tsp. pepper
- ¼ cup flour
- 2 cups water
- ¾ cup red wine
- ¼ tsp. garlic powder
- Two tsp. Worcestershire sauce
- 6—8 medium carrots, sliced
- Four small onions, quartered
- Four ribs celery, sliced
- Three medium potatoes, diced
- Leftover lamb, chopped

Instructions:

1. Place salt, pepper, and flour into the slow cooker and briskly whisk in water and wine until smooth.
2. Add all remaining ingredients except the leftover lamb and stir until well mixed.
3. Cover. Cook on Low 7—8 hours, adding the lamb the last hour of cooking.

Shepherd's Pie

(To serve 4-8)

Preparation Time: 20 minutes

Cooking Time: 3-5 hours

Ideal Slow-Cooker Size: 5- or 6-qt

Ingredients:

- 1½ lbs. ground pork
- 1 Tbsp. Vinegar of your choice
- ¾ tsp. salt
- ¼ tsp. cayenne pepper
- 1 tsp. paprika
- ¼ tsp. dried oregano
- ¼ tsp. black pepper
- 1 tsp. chili powder
- 1 small onion, chopped
- 15-oz. can corn, drained

Topping:

- Three large potatoes, unpeeled
- ¼ cup fat-free milk
- 1 tsp. margarine
- ¼ tsp. salt
- Dash of pepper
- Shredded cheese, for garnish

Instructions:

1. Brown the pork in a pan. Put away half of this for tomorrow's recipe.
2. Combine remaining pork, vinegar, salt, hot pepper, paprika, oregano, pepper, chili powder, and onion and spread it in the bottom of the crock.
3. Spread corn over meat.

4.   Boil potatoes until soft. Mash with milk, butter, ¼ tsp. Salt, and dash of pepper. Spread over meat and corn.

5.   Cover. Cook on Low 3-4 hours. Sprinkle the top with cheese for a few minutes before you serve.

Quick and Easy Spaghetti

(To serve 4-8)

Preparation Time: 20 minutes

Cooking Time: 3-4 hours

Ideal Slow-Cooker Size: 3-qt

Ingredients:

- Remaining browned ground pork
- 1 medium onion, chopped
- ½ 26-oz. jar spaghetti sauce with mushrooms
- 10¾-oz. can tomato soup
- 14½-oz. can of stewed tomatoes
- 4-oz. can mushrooms, undrained
- ½ tsp. garlic powder
- ½ tsp. garlic salt
- ½ tsp. minced dried garlic
- ½ tsp. onion salt
- ½ tsp. Italian seasoning spaghetti

Instructions:

1. Combine all your ingredients in the slow cooker & Irish Soda Bread stir.
2. Cover. Cook for around three to four hours on Low.
3. Cook spaghetti according to package directions. Serve sauce over cooked pasta.

CONCLUSION

Pick the right vegetables

To get perfect nutritional nourishment from your slow-cooked meals, go for the heat friendly vegetables. These vegetables, among them, carrots, broccoli, tomatoes, kale and cabbage, release a high measure of antioxidants and vitamins, when cooked as opposed to their crude counterparts. Because slow-cooking warms and cooks your vegetables at a relatively low temperature, the cooking process ejects very little vitamins from your heat friendly vegetable meal than simmering or stewing. On the other hand, Vegetables like cucumber and spinach don't cook very well in slow cookers and may get less nutritious, or too soft.

Trap steam

The best way to guarantee that no supplements escape from your vegetables in the slow cooker is to trap the steam. When you put the water or stock into the cooker with your vegetables, twofold check to confirm the cover fits the pot as hard as could sensibly be normal. Check to confirm there are no parts or openings through which the steam may get away, to avoid being forced to remove the lid during the cooking process. As your vegetables cook, any expelled vitamins will be trapped in the juices so very little if any, will have been lost.

Eat the broth

Consume the broth alongside your vegetables to guarantee you're getting a meal that is as supplement rich as could sensibly be possible. When you remove your veggies from the slow cooker and strain out the water they were cooked in, you deny yourself and your family the nutritional benefits of vitamins like vitamin C, which adequately dissolve into cooking water. In the event that you require a slow-cooked supper with lots of veggies, take an attempt at making a soup or stew. Apart from giving an easy to-set up one pot supper, you will moreover guarantee that your family gets the entirety of the dietary benefits vegetables give. You can also hold the vitamin-stuffed cooking water for usage in a sauce or marinade, to run as an inseparable unit with your dinner, or as a soup base.

Use the lowest setting

Cook your vegetables on your slow cooker's most minimal setting to help keep vitamins, anti-oxidants and minerals bolted inside. On most slow cooking gadgets, the least setting will cook your nourishment at around 200 degrees Fahrenheit. Cooking a meal on the low setting takes a couple of hours longer, so you should prepare. Put together your ingredients in the slow cooker in the morning, for example, and return home from work to a completely cooked stew, soup or dish.

Made in the USA
San Bernardino, CA
29 September 2017